"Courageously and independently drawing on the ideas of a range of psychoanalytical and group analytical theorists and clinicians, this personal and contemporary text will be of value to colleagues and students in the mental health professions. Dr Sigmund Karterud is both a 'hermeneut' and a data driven scientist. His attempts to synthesise several perspectives and orientations are based on his appreciation of the restraints of the human body as well as the constraints of our societies and cultures. This contribution to NILGA illustrates the enduring importance of our diverse and multi-stranded intellectual foundations. We are also challenged to restore our identities as members of a profession which has not yet begun to realise its full potentials."

Earl Hopper, *PhD, Editor of the New International Library of Group Analysis (NILGA)*

"The author expands and revitalizes group analysis with perspectives from evolution, philosophy and psychology of the self, theories of emotions, mentalization and, above all, personality. An essential reading for people interested in the front-line of contemporary group analytic theory and practice."

Thor Kristian Island, *MD Founding director of IGA, Norway*

"For group psychotherapists of all schools, Sigmund Karterud presents a truly modern and integrative theory of group analysis as well as a treatment concept derived from it. Both should be incorporated into group-analytically modified treatment in psychiatric and psychosomatic clinics, day clinics and practices. By applying and testing them for practicability, further ideas and concepts should emerge that enrich and further develop the very lively landscape of psychodynamic group psychotherapies."

Prof. Dr. med. Ulrich Schultz-Venrath, *Professor of Psychosomatic Medicine and Psychotherapy at the Faculty of Health, University of Witten/Herdecke, chair of the German Institute of Group Analysis and Mentalizing in Groups (IGAM)*

Group Analysis

Group Analysis outlines how clinical group analysis can re-establish itself as a leading paradigm for group psychotherapy.

Sigmund Karterud explains how the focus of group analysis and its applications can be expanded by stronger emphasis on the philosophy and psychology of the self. The book is divided into four parts, with Part One reconsidering the historical roots of group analysis through its founder S. H. Foulkes and Part Two demonstrating how the fields of evolution, primary emotions, attachment, mentalizing, personality theory, and personality disorders can be integrated with group analysis. Part Three develops a philosophy of the self that includes a group self which accounts for the we-ness of groups, and Part Four illustrates how these concepts can inform the practice of group analysis through a series of clinical vignettes addressing the major challenges which face the clinician.

Group Analysis: A Modern Synthesis will be essential reading for all group psychotherapists in practice and in training. It will also appeal to students of group analytic psychotherapy.

Sigmund Karterud, MD, PhD, is a group analyst and professor of psychiatry, formerly at Oslo University, Norway. He has played a significant role in training, research, and organization of group analytic psychotherapy in Scandinavia. His other publications include books on self-psychology, personality, personality disorders, and mentalization-based treatment.

The New International Library of Group Analysis (NILGA)
Series Editor: Earl Hopper

Drawing on the seminal ideas of British, European and American group analysts, psychoanalysts, social psychologists and social scientists, the books in this series focus on the study of small and large groups, organisations and other social systems, and on the study of the transpersonal and transgenerational sociality of human nature. NILGA books will be required reading for the members of professional organisations in the field of group analysis, psychoanalysis, and related social sciences. They will be indispensable for the "formation" of students of psychotherapy, whether they are mainly interested in clinical work with patients or in consultancy to teams and organisational clients within the private and public sectors.

Sibling Relations and the Horizontal Axis in Theory and Practice
Contemporary Group Analysis, Psychoanalysis and Organization Consultancy
Edited by Smadar Ashuach and Avi Berman

From Crowd Psychology to the Dynamics of Large Groups
Historical, Theoretical and Practical Considerations
Carla Penna

A Psychotherapist Paints
Insights from the Border of Art and Psychotherapy
Morris Nitsun

Group Analysis throughout the Life Cycle
Foulkes Revisited from a Group Attachment and Developmental Perspective
Arturo Ezquerro and Maria Cañete

The Tripartite Matrix in the Developing Theory and Expanding Practice of Group Analysis
The Social Unconscious in Persons, Groups and Societies: Volume 4
Edited by Earl Hopper

Intersectionality and Group Analysis
Explorations of Power, Privilege and Position in Group Therapy
Edited by Suryia Nayak and Alasdair Forrest

Group Analysis
A Modern Synthesis
Sigmund Karterud

Group Analysis

A Modern Synthesis

Sigmund Karterud

Routledge
Taylor & Francis Group

LONDON AND NEW YORK

First published 2024
by Routledge
4 Park Square, Milton Park, Abingdon, Oxon OX14 4RN

and by Routledge
605 Third Avenue, New York, NY 10158

Routledge is an imprint of the Taylor & Francis Group, an informa business

© 2024 Sigmund Karterud

Designed cover image: Getty | peepo | Karterud, S. (2023). Gruppeanalyse og psykodynamisk gruppepsykoterapi. Oslo: Pax forlag.

British Library Cataloguing in Publication Data
A catalogue record for this book is available from the British Library

Library of Congress Cataloging-in-Publication Data
A catalog record has been requested for this book

ISBN: 978-1-032-69601-0 (hbk)
ISBN: 978-1-032-69594-5 (pbk)
ISBN: 978-1-032-69602-7 (ebk)

DOI: 10.4324/9781032696027

Typeset in Times New Roman
by Taylor & Francis Books

Contents

Foreword

This volume is based upon my (much larger) Norwegian textbook *Group Analysis and Psychodynamic Group Psychotherapy*, which was published in 1999 and later thoroughly revised in 2023. Parts of the content are translated, but the current volume is mainly a new text written for an international audience. It presents a brief account of the history of group analysis, its grounding in the theories and practice of the founding father S. H. Foulkes and the later developments after his death in 1976. Foulkes was also a psychoanalyst, rooted in ego psychology, "an analyst of a strictly Freudian persuasion" as he said, and one of his slogans for group analysis was "ego-training in action". The death of Foulkes coincided with the decline of ego psychology. It had no more to offer. Different schools of object relational theories came to dominate group analysis. However, history has shown that these theories failed to cope with the influx of an increasing number of patients with personality disorders into the mental health services of Western countries. Competing group therapies, e.g., cognitive behavioural groups, psychoeducational groups as companions to dialectical behavioural therapy, schema therapy and dynamic groups based on mentalization-based principles, entered the scene. It raised the question if group analysis was an appropriate approach for the mental health services, or if it was a kind of private practice group psychotherapy, suited for people with higher levels of personality functioning.

In this volume I argue that group analysis needs modernization. In particular, it needs the resources of modern theories of personality, evolution, attachment, mentalizing, self psychology, and hermeneutics. By these resources, "ego-training in action" acquires new meanings. Ego needs to be replaced by a concept of the self which is on terms both with philosophy and with the natural sciences. A hermeneutics of the self, in the sense of Paul Ricoeur (1992), might integrate the meaning-seeking endeavour of the reflective self with the energetic core self which harbours the emotions as defined by Jaak Panksepp (1998). This approach might even shed new light upon the group as such. Group analysts have paid much attention to the group-as-object (Nitsun, 1999). I propose that group analysts extend their perspective to the group self, i.e., the group-as-subject. The concept of the group self may also shed new light upon historical and societal group phenomena. I explore this avenue in a reflection about the group analytic group self.

In the last part of the book, with the resources I have mentioned, I proceed by outlining the clinical consequences for group analytic psychotherapy. I discuss the most important issues that confront the practicing group therapist and illustrate my points through 93 clinical vignettes. I end the clinical last part with an optimistic view that group analysis might become a flexible approach that includes "classical" group analysis as well as modified group analysis for patients with more severe personality problems.

For an English-speaking audience I will say something about my background: I am a professor of psychiatry from Oslo University, Norway and a former director of Department of Personality Psychiatry at Oslo University Hospital. My PhD thesis (Karterud, 1989a) was an empirical study of Wilfred Bion's theories of group dynamics. In collaboration with devoted colleagues from the Norwegian Psychiatric Organization, I organized the first group analytic block training course in Norway, led by Harold Behr and colleagues from Institute of Group Analysis (IGA), London, until the Norwegian IGA was founded in 1992. Thereafter I served as a training group analyst for IGA, Oslo until 2008. During these years I also studied self psychology in collaboration with Paul Ornstein and colleagues in US and founded the Norwegian Forum for Self Psychology. Malcolm Pines and Walt Stone helped building bridges between self psychology and group analysis (Karterud & Stone, 2003; Stone & Karterud, 2006).

My main professional task at Oslo University Hospital was to develop and validate group-based treatment programs for patients with personality disorders, mainly borderline patients. In 1992 I founded the Norwegian Network for treatment of personality disorders, which still exists as a clinical-research network for 20 different treatment units in the Norwegian mental health system (Pedersen et al., 2022). This Network has accumulated what presumably is the world largest database for the treatment of personality disorders, now consisting of approximately 14,000 cases. This database has been subjected to a host of empirical studies, among them studies of the validity of the various personality disorders (e.g., Johansen et al., 2004). These studies enabled us to reconceptualize the nature of personality as such (Karterud, 2017; Karterud & Kongerslev, 2019) and explicate the foundation of a Personality Psychiatry (Karterud, Wilberg & Urnes, 2010). Our TAM theory of personality defined the three major pillars of personality as Temperament, Attachment and Mentalization (self-consciousness). On the temperament side we received support from the collaboration with Jaak Panksepp and his neuroaffective-evolutionary work on primary emotions (Karterud et al., 2016), while dialogues with Anthony Bateman were helpful in constructing the mentalizing pole of personality.

In 2008 I reorganized the clinical services of the Department of Personality Psychiatry according to principles of mentalization-based treatment (MBT) and authored two manuals together with Bateman (Karterud & Bateman, 2010; Karterud & Bateman, 2011), followed by a manual for mentalization-based group therapy (MBT-G) (Karterud, 2015b). At the same time, I established, in collaboration with the Norwegian psychiatrist Finn Skårderud, the Norwegian Institute for Mentalizing. The Institute has arranged one year training courses in MBT-G and for the past 15 years, I have trained around 250 colleagues who have participated in challenging roleplays and displayed video-recordings of their groups from all over Norway (and some from Sweden and Denmark), containing around 1,300 patients altogether. Consequently, I have seen and studied a wide range of groups with different therapists, different compositions and in different settings, although the common denominators have been borderline dynamics and outpatient treatment. During the same time, I maintained my private practice with group analytic psychotherapy in a more classical sense. However, I realized that the boundaries between group analysis and MBT-G were not rigid. Some MBT groups could move in a more group analytic direction, while some analytic groups obviously could benefit from application of MBT-G principles.

The wide range of groups which is described above, has called for theoretical principles that are empirically grounded, conceptually coherent, and applicable to a wide range of psychopathological and group dynamic phenomena. The tradition of group analysis contains such principles. However, as I will try to demonstrate, they need to be extended and modernized. As will be apparent in the text that follows, I use the word "modern" in a Hegelian sense, meaning "closer to the truth". Some readers may disagree about that. That is as it should be. Truth is a complicated thing, which needs to be discussed continually. But first, my arguments should be read.

Part One

The evolution of group analysis

The legacy of S.H. Foulkes

Group analysis, which I will use synonym with group analytic psychotherapy, is the dominant kind of group psychotherapy in Europe. Formally, its theory and practice are managed by the organization EGATIN (European Group Analytic Training Institutions Network), which by 2022 consisted of 40 members, whereof 33 training programmes were considered "qualifying". According to the statutes of EGATIN, its member organizations should train therapists in *"Foulkesian group analysis"*. This explication is in a way remarkable. In comparison, it is not customary for psychoanalytic institutes to state that they train their candidates in "Freudian psychoanalysis". It is telling of the significance of S. H. Foulkes for the identity of group analysis. Accordingly, what could be more natural for a book on group analysis, to start with some reflections about the person and the work of S. H. Foulkes (1898–1976)?

I will not here recapitulate his biography. Details can be found in the writings of, for example, Schlapobersky (2016) and Barwick & Weegmann (2018). However, I will comment on some issues which seem significant for the evolution of group analysis. His German and Jewish origin is important. He recalls the impact Sigmund Freud had on him as a 22-year-old medical student in Heidelberg: *"This was in 1919, and ever since, Freud and his work have been the greatest influence in my professional life, and remains so at the present time. From then on, I knew exactly what it was that I wanted to be, namely, a psychoanalyst."* (Foulkes, 1968, p. 203). He followed this conviction, moved to Vienna in 1928 were he fulfilled his psychoanalytic training and befriended the upcoming generation of psychoanalytic candidates. He was loyal to Freud through his entire life, which witnessed dramatic professional controversies, like the battles with Wilhelm Reich, Sandor Ferenczi and Melanie Klein. His third wife, Elisabeth Foulkes (1990, p.12) wrote that *"He remained an active psychoanalyst of a strictly Freudian persuasion to the end"*. In self psychology terms, we would say that Freud became an idealized selfobject for him, something that probably became even more important

DOI: 110.4324/9781032696027-1

when he had to establish a new private and professional home in England. He fled from Nazi Germany in 1933.

Other important influences which coined his theory of group analysis, came from his psychiatric training at Frankfurt Neurological Institute during the years 1925–28. The Institute was led by the charismatic Kurt Goldstein, who was a prominent figure in European neurology and gestalt psychology. Foulkes concepts of the individual and the group in a fluctuating figure-ground relationship as well as the individual conceived as a nodal point in the communicative network, the matrix, of the group, were inspired by the teachings of Goldstein.

Finally, we need to mention the inspiration of the Frankfurt school of sociology and philosophy, led by prominent critical intellectuals such as Karl Mannheim and Max Horkheimer, followed by figures such as Theodor Adorno, Herbert Marcuse and from our time, Jürgen Habermas and Axel Honneth. During the years 1930–33 Foulkes was head of the Frankfurt Psychoanalytic Institute which was in the same building as the Institute of sociology and the Institute for social research. They did not only share the same location, but also ideas in mutual seminars. Foulkes' closest friend and colleague from these days was the sociologist Norbert Elias, who later joined him in London.

To sum up: Foulkes' thinking was inspired 1) by Freuds theories about the inner world of the psyche and how to conduct clinical psychoanalysis; 2) by Goldstein's ideas about the brain and its influence upon the mind; and 3) by the Frankfurt school and its theories about how social dynamics, and in particular power relations, came to influence the mind of the individual. Could these broad theories work together and inspire clinical practice?

Yes, they could. Foulkes started his first therapeutic group, at the age of 42, in the small English town of Exeter, during the winter of 1940. He stayed in Exeter, out of war-time London, for two or three years. During this period, he treated around 50 individuals in groups. Some of them, together with the psychologist Eve Lewis as co-therapist. Most patients also received individual sessions concomitant with the group therapy. His first paper on group analysis was published in 1944: *"Group analysis: studies in the treatment of groups on psycho-analytical lines"* (Foulkes & Lewis, 1944).

During the years 1943–45 Foulkes served as military psychiatrist at Northfield Military Neurosis Centre, not far from Birmingham. Northfield has since then become a legendary site for group analysts. It became a melting pot of new ideas and practices of how to conduct psychotherapy in larger social settings where different individual and group dynamic processes interacted. The site gathered prominent psychiatrists like Wilfred Bion, Tom Main, Pat de Maré, Harold Bridger, and others, and the concept of "the therapeutic community" was born (Main, 1946).

When Foulkes returned to London, he worked at several psychiatric hospitals, for most of the time at Maudsley Hospital, until he retired in 1963. He combined his psychiatric services with private psychoanalytic and group analytic practice. In addition, he wrote numerous articles on group analysis, four books on the topic, conducted supervisory and training groups, initiated Group Analytic Society (GAS) in 1952 and Institute of Group Analysis (IGA) in 1972, maintained a broad international correspondence and founded the journal Group Analysis.

The principles he outlined for group analysis in his first paper (Foulkes & Lewis, 1944) were surprisingly "modern" except for his conduct of conjoint group and individual psychotherapy and separating men and women in different groups. The groups contained around eight members, and the weekly sessions lasted for an hour and a half. He observed that the group members where more engaged in their mutual relations than in relation to the therapist(s). In a technical jargon: the patient-therapist transference seemed to become diluted. This allowed the therapist to be somewhat withdrawn. His/her main task was to facilitate communication. Already in this very first paper on group analysis, he compared the therapist role to "a conductor directing an orchestra". He highlighted what we today would label "common factors" in group psychotherapy, that the group 1) often reacted as a whole; 2) counteracted personal isolation and promoted a social situation where the individual could express him/herself freely, feeling him/herself understood and display understanding and empathy to others; 3) facilitated a kind of mirroring process whereby own personal problems were revealed while engaging in others; 4) facilitated access to unconscious material; and 5) facilitated a kind of learning from the experiences of other group members.

Reflecting upon his experiences at Northfield, Foulkes (1946a, b, c) would emphasize even more the significance of the group-as-a-whole. As I will discuss in depth later, this concept is quite problematic since it can obscure the very phenomenon of which one is speaking. There is a risk of investing the group with its own will-power, as in the concept of a "group mind". Reflecting upon Northfield, Foulkes (1946a) wrote *"The group meetings became more group-oriented, more like a treatment of the group than in the group"*. The essence of group analysis has later been expressed as *"treatment of the individual, in the group, by the group"*. At Northfield, the task of the ambitious psychiatrists was to create a therapeutic community which realized Tom Main's slogans (1977) *"the hospital as doctor"* through *"a culture of enquiry"*. The idea was that prosocial forces of the individual were stimulated and liberated and neurotic strategies likely to be abandoned, when individuals were more or less forced to co-operate with peers in a benign environment which facilitated reflections upon their experiences. If the group functioned well, the individual was likely to be integrated in prosocial collective efforts. The main task then, for the group leader/therapist/conductor was to assist the group-as-a-whole in its endeavour to co-operate constructively. This ideal raises an interesting and important question: How do the group know that it is *"working constructively"*? Or better: How do the group members know that *they* are working constructively? This question is basically a variant of the question "how do I know myself"? The answer, with reference to philosophy and psychology of the self (Hegel, 1807/2019; Ricoeur, 1992; Fonagy et al., 2002), is by being "minded", and recognized and validated by the (representatives) of the society to which you belong. Within the social fabric of a therapeutic community, the group, as a designated entity, will receive confirmatory (or critical) commentaries from others which will validate its (narrative) identity. These acts will confirm both the "sameness" of the group, with which it can be identified, and the "we-ness" of the group: Sameness when we are talking about Group A which belongs to Wing B in the hospital and which meets three times a week, and we-ness when we are talking about the subjective processes of belonging to this particular group and the group's significance for the identity of the individual.

Although Foulkes never explicated the dialectics of sameness and we-ness of the group, he stimulated theoretical and clinical explorations of what it meant to be an individual and a group (and a society). That is what makes European group analysis more profound and interesting than its American counterpart of psychodynamic group psychotherapy which has been more pragmatic, more concerned with "does it work?" We are facing a delicate balance here. Group analysis risks neglecting obvious pragmatic concerns (do the patients get better?) and get lost in unproductive metapsychological speculations. Therefore, we should *"take the group seriously"*, to quote the group analyst Farhad Dalal (1998). My response to this call will be to turn to a hermeneutics of the group which will be explored in Part 3 of this book. Such an investigation will explore the concept of group identity as hinted to above, as a dialectics of sameness and we-ness. I suggest that Foulkes overlooked the significance of external confirmation and validation when he spoke about groups at the Northfield Military Neuroses Centre. As for groups in outpatient settings, and in particular private practice, which advocate the ideal of a stranger group where members do not meet outside the group, the crucial element of external recognition is missing. How do the group then know when it is working constructively? This question challenges the role of the group analyst. To state it bluntly: Should he tell the group? Foulkes instinct was to be reluctant. A psychoanalyst is trained not to "gratify" the needs and wishes of the patient. As we will see later, this attitude might be constructive for more "neurotic" patients but carry some risks when it comes to severe personality disorders.

In his first textbook, *Introduction to Group Analytic Psychotherapy* (Foulkes, 1948), expanded and explicated his theory and practice of group analysis. Here I will comment upon some few but crucial issues. The first is the relationship to Freud and psychoanalysis. Foulkes' dilemma was how to balance his own need to keep Freud as an idealized parent imago and remain a respected member of the British Psychoanalytic Society, with his needs to explore new mental territories where the current psychoanalytic concepts were of limited help, to say it mildly. This dilemma has later been labelled the conservative versus the radical Foulkes (Dalal, 1998). The conservative Foulkes tried to be loyal to the paradigm of ego psychology, while the radical Foulkes hoped to construct a theory that could embrace the individual, the group, and the society. The mission was impossible and left lacunas in the theory of group analysis. Ego psychology was what later was labelled a one-person-psychology. Adequate concepts were not yet available for Foulkes.

We need to empathize here with Foulkes. He developed a theory of groups that was basically optimistic in a theoretical landscape that emphasized man's innate destructive tendencies, harbouring a death instinct. When Foulkes was challenged at this point, he would, in allegiance with Freud, admit to the theory of a death instinct, but his group analytic theory and practice clearly rested on a theory of innate prosocial forces in man which constituted a core of man's essence and were vital for group formation. He reiterated that man *"was social to the core of his being"*. However, he needed some concepts that could be compatible with ego psychology and found those in the American psychoanalyst Erik Homburger Erikson who coined the term ego-identity. Erikson had maintained that one's ego-identity contained a search for being *"a successful variant of a group identity"* which was important for one's experience of similarity and continuity in *"one's meaning for others"*. Foulkes embraced the expression *"ego-identity in the light of the historical circumstances that dominated the childhood environment"* (Foulkes, 1948, p. 13). This ego-identity was based upon historical experiences with others and would maintain social (group) life. As we shall see, later conceptualizations will situate the social need even closer to the core of human existence.

Maybe this problem with localizing prosociality was the ultimate reason for Foulkes to situate the group almost outside the individual, as if prosociality was a force that came from *"the group itself"*. It is here (Foulkes, 1948, p. 14) he formulates what has later become a kind of credo in group analysis, that the group literary *"permeates"* the individual and that the individual is a *"nodal point in the network"* that constitutes the group (and society). In these formulations, Foulkes relies on concepts from his years in Frankfurt with gestalt psychology and we are struck by the mechanistic flavor: The "individual" is a "permeated" "nodal point" in a "network" that is a "group". Later he would add that "transpersonal forces" pass through the "individual" in the "group". The advantage of this objectifying and mechanistic view on groups is that it emphasizes *"forces"* that impact on group dynamics, forces which cannot be located to the individual in isolation. Any theory of group dynamics that neglect such forces tend to be naïve and idealistic. However, what seems more difficult with this conceptualization is to grasp the nature of the pro-sociality of this group. Where does it come from? One must ask if this pro-sociality ultimately rest on an aspect of the being of groups which is not covered by Foulkes' theory. I have earlier hinted at the we-ness of groups. This we-ness rests on a basic need of the self, not of the ego (!), which has to do with the *"wish to live together"* and that *"man needs friends"* (Ricoeur, 1992). The we-ness attest to a kind of identity that in fact is even more apparent in groups than for the individual, a kind of identity that cannot be reduced to the "forces" that penetrate groups. *It concerns loyalty.* Without loyal members that stand up for the group, the group will cease to exist. More about that later.

Even if he could not account properly for the pro-sociality of group life, Foulkes acted as if it was a reality. From this conviction emanated his slogans for group analysis: *Serve the group. Follow the group. Trust the group. Listen to the group. Don't push the group.* And from there emanated his technical recommendations that the main task of the group analyst was not to inter-pret, as in individual psychoanalysis, the content and process of the group, but to *analyze* the group, which basically meant to comment on and liberate the process of communication in the group. According to Foulkes, this pro-cess took place in the *matrix* of the group. The matrix became another crucial concept in his group-analytic theory. The matrix was conceived as the (mostly) unconscious web that held the group together by a dynamic flow of (transpersonal) forces. In this respect, the individual was a nodal point in the matrix. According to Foulkes, healing processes took place when repressed or disavowed parts of the individual were captured, so to speak, by the commu-nicational process of the group and got symbolized in a way that allowed verbal designation and reflection. That is the meaning of his slogan *"group analysis is ego-training in action"*. In my opinion, these words depict the essence of group analysis. It is something radically different than making the unconscious conscious by way of the expert psychoanalyst. However, what does actually "ego-training in action" mean today, in an era when the ego is dead? That will be a topic for later discussions.

A last part of Foulkes' legacy must be mentioned, also that belonging to his optimistic views on the nature of groups. In his 1948 textbook, he (p. 30) formulates a "Basic Law of Group Dynamics":

> *"The deepest reason why these patients, assuming for simplicity's sake Psycho-Neurotics, can reinforce each other's normal reactions and wear down and correct each other's neurotic reactions, is that collectively they constitute the very Norm, from which, individually, they deviate. That is not really surprising, once it is understood. The community, of which they are a miniature edition, itself determines what is normal, socially accepted behavior. It happens like this: each individual is to a large extent a part of the Group, to which he belongs. This collective aspect permeates him all through – as we said before – to his core. To a smaller extent, he deviates from the abstract Model, the Standard, of this "Norm", he is a variant of it. Just this deviation makes him into an Individual, unique, which he is again all through, even to the finger prints. One could picture him, crudely,*

as being submerged in a common pool, but sticking his head out of it. Now each such Therapeutic Group, like any other Group, has much more in common than it knows at first. It is struck by its differences, which provoke curiosity, hostility and fear. As it proceeds, it finds more and more of individuality and community. The sound part of Individuality, of character, is firmly rooted in the Group and wholly approved by it. The Group, therefore, respects and supports the emergence and free development of individuality ..."

Obviously, therapeutic groups will contain resistances and defences, and it is a main task of the group analyst to assist the group in dealing with that. However, gradually the prosocial forces of the group will prevail and support the growth of the individual. Much can be said about the quotation above and we will proceed with the discussion if these views are flawed idealizations of the individual and the group. Let me just point out the personification of the "Group" which is invested with intentions and desires of its own, as well as the notion of the "Individual" whose identity is limited to that of sameness, "unique ... even to the finger prints". I.e., the selfhood of the individual has disappeared, as well as the we-ness of the group has expanded to a grand hyperbole. That will also be a topic for further discussion.

In the preceding paragraphs, I have condensed some essential features of Foulkes theory of group analysis and his basic recommendations for the practicing group analyst. After his death there surfaced a discussion if group analysis had to adopt a more "realistic" view on the nature of man and groups. Did Foulkes neglect man's (innate) destructivity? In the following I will approach this question by the route of Foulkes' main opponent during the 1950s and 1960s: Wilfred Bion.

The challenge of W. R. Bion and the anti-group

It may sound like an exaggeration to label Bion as Foulkes' main opponent. After all, Bion left the group scene in the early 1950s, although his famous book *"Experiences in groups"* was published in 1961. They shared a common interest in groups, group dynamics and therapeutic communities since the days at Northfield. However, Bion's interest seems to have been more on a theoretical level than providing new therapeutic innovations to the public. After Northfield, Bion worked for the Tavistock clinic (and later Tavistock Institute of Human Relations) and conducted outpatient groups for a short period (1947–52). He left a "Tavistock way of doing group psychotherapy" that was opposed to group analysis as well as a lasting theoretical contribution through his publication of *Experiences in groups.*

Bion was struck by the *problem of co-operation* in the therapeutic groups where he was assigned the role of a "leader". He observed that group participants often displayed great problems in rational co-operation around tasks in the group, but that they often co-operated quite well when the group as a whole seemed to be affected by some commonly shared assumptions. Rational co-operation seemed difficult, while co-operation based upon some shared assumptions seemed easy, as if it had not to be learned at all. It came "natural" so to speak. As we have seen, also Foulkes were occupied by these forces which "penetrated the individuals to their inner core". However, Bion went a step further and wanted to uncover their very nature. In order to do that he adopted a kind of scientific distance to the groups where he was assigned "leadership". Firstly, he adopted a kind of phenomenological stance where he observed and ordered his observations. Next, he told the group (and the readers) what he observed. Then he described the fears involved in the dynamics of the group and the dilemmas the group were facing. Sometimes he described the ultimate fears which the group seemed to flee from.

It is my clear impression that what group therapists favour the most, is the phenomenological part. It is Bion's descriptions of so-called *"basic assumption" group phenomena.* Bion maintained that there was a dynamic interplay in all kinds of groups, not only therapeutic groups, between a rational level which he denoted "the work group" and an irrational or affective level that he denoted "basic assumption groups". The basic assumption (BA) groups could be figured either as 1) a fight/flight group; 2) a dependency group; or 3) a so-called "pairing" group. His descriptions of these modalities were illuminating and intellectually brilliant. Most group therapists smile and nod and recognize own group experiences when they read Bion's descriptions of the angry group that demands a scapegoat, or the dependency group where people find themselves anxious and helpless and in search for an omnipotent leader, or the pairing-group which is light-hearted, flirtatious, and optimistic with respect to the future. People have seemingly no problems with co-operating within such group modalities. It comes natural to them. However, there are differences between individuals which basic assumption they "favour" so to speak, when frustrated. In order to emphasize their involuntary nature, Bion labelled these inclinations as the "valence" of the individual. The main task of the therapist should be to interpret the current basic assumption in order to assist the group in maintaining a rational group discourse.

However, there is a paradox here when it comes to therapeutic groups. Since the task of such groups is to explore unconscious mental life, the pursuit of this task will in itself activate basic assumptions, in contrast to, for example, a task group who works with an external mechanical problem. Bion explained this destiny by resorting to Kleinian theory. He maintained that in the mind of the participants, the (image of) group would approximate the internal mother and mother's body, and that to approach it/her implied activation of *"an extremely early primal scene"* (Bion, 1961, p. 164) loaded with envy and hatred and psychotic anxieties as in the paranoid-schizoid position. The ultimate fear in, for example, the fight flight group, according to Bion, is the fear of the destructiveness of one's own envy and hatred, that it should viciously attack the internal object who in revenge would attack and destroy the self. Therefore, the whole dynamics had to be externalized and the individuals in a group would unconsciously co-operate in finding an external object that could be attacked and by that contain one's own destructive impulses. Thus, the individuals co-operate, unconsciously, by the mechanism of collective projective identification.

There is a fairly wide agreement, supported by the study of Malan and colleagues (1976), that group psychotherapy according to Bion's principles is no good idea. People in need of psychotherapy need something else than being caught up by a group therapist that interprets their behaviour in terms of hatred and envy towards him/her. In clinical circles, the approach was minimalized after a public report on scandalous conditions at Paddington Day Hospital in London, which were conducted according to principles advocated by Bion's companion Henry Ezriel (Baron, 1987).

However, Bion's phenomenology and theoretical explanation have survived to a surprisingly extent. My impression is that many colleagues have accepted a soft version of the theory of projective identification. This means that they do not take Bion seriously. The soft version implies that projective identification is a projective maneuver in order to get rid of anger and envy (or other unwanted or despised aspects of self). However, Bion was as Kleinian as it is possible to be. He believed in an innate destructiveness, an inborn splitting with hate and envy that literally attacked the breast which the infant would find already occupied with part-object penises, etc. In our times, true believers of Kleinian theory have shrinked considerably. The theory resides on a discourse which is beyond scientific ideals of validation or refutation. It's a theory for believers.

But what about the phenomenology? My own research during the 1980s is probably the most thorough empirical study of Bion's BA theory (Karterud, 1989a). I observed and rated 75 group therapy sessions at three different therapeutic communities. I rated 28,950 verbal statements from 91 patients and 53 staff members for their emotional content (fight, flight, dependency, pairing, and neutral) according to Group Emotionality Rating System (Karterud & Foss, 1989) and analyzed the group dynamics qualitatively according to Group Focal Conflict Theory (Whitaker & Lieberman, 1964; Karterud, 1988b). By these methods, I could identify typical basic assumption sequences and study them in detail, sentence by sentence, through graphs and statistics as well as by interpretations. Furthermore, I could explore Bion's valence theory and how group culture phenomena were related to the content and manner of therapist's interventions.

What did I find? Basic assumption sequences flourished in these groups. They could be identified, and the phenomenology was similar to what Bion had described. However, I could also observe significant nuances (Karterud, 1989b). Firstly, fight and flight did not always accompany each other. I could observe flight groups without much aggression, and fight groups without much fear. Furthermore, I could observe pairing groups with much sexuality and pairing groups with little sexuality but more grandiosity. I observed what I labeled as "pseudogroups", which had to be separated from dependency groups (Karterud, 1989c). Concerning valence, I could demonstrate that borderline patients had a higher valence for BA fight-flight than other patients (Karterud, 1988a). In addition, BA phenomena were clearly related to poor therapist performances: Messy boundary conditions, unclear tasks and roles and insulting behaviour here-and-now (Karterud, 1988c). In other words, BA phenomena seemed to have multiple causes, a mixture of personality characteristics, levels of personality functioning, unclarity about tasks and goals, and therapeutic insults as well as self-object failures. One should remember that this was prior to the era of "rupture-repair" in psychotherapy (Safran et al., 2001). Overall, the results indicated that BA phenomena were more related to poor treatment conditions that did not take into account the level of personality functioning, than psychotic anxiety being activated by approaching the internal imago of a bad breast filled with triumphant penises (Karterud, 1989d).

To sum up, when we deconstruct Bion's theory we find a partly valid description of important group phenomena but invalid explanations that overemphasize Kleinian speculations at the cost of relevant interpersonal transactions. Just as important is Bion's flawed theory of affects (or more precisely – emotions) that underpinned the theory. It was a theory of innate aggression (Thanatos) and sexualized love (Libido – Eros). Bion constructed his basic assumption theory upon these affects. Today, this theory is outdated. Today we would rather say that Bion approximated a general "law" concerning the relationship between cognition (rationality) and emotions. Cognition needs to be informed by emotions, but too high emotional activation impedes cognition (Fonagy et al., 2002). In current language we speak about the risk for "mentalizing breakdown" and mentalizing proper being replaced by psychic equivalence thinking (which Bion and Klein conceptualized as belonging to the paranoid-schizoid position). According to a modern theory of emotions, we would therefore reformulate Bion's BA theory in the following way:

Rational co-operation in groups might be undermined by too high activation of any of the following primary emotions (italics here to comply with the writing style of Panksepp): SEEKING, FEAR, RAGE, SEXUAL LUST, SEPARATION ANXIETY, CARE, and PLAY. These emotions may come in rather pure modes, or they may be mixed with one another. The typical fight/flight-group is dominated by RAGE. Think of a Hell's Angels group. The typical dependency group is dominated by a mixture of SEPARATION ANXIETY, FEAR, and CARE. Think of a group of insecure but true believers lead by their patron. The typical pairing group is a mixture of SEXUAL LUST, SEEKING, and PLAY. Think of a group in the entertainment industry. In addition, there are pure sex-groups as in groups set up for group sex. There are pure play groups, as in training for stand-up comedians, and there are pure seeking groups as in groups for devoted explorers. And many more ... These groups must control their basic emotional groundings in order not to be overwhelmed by the emotionality therein and consequently suffer collective mentalizing deficits.

Let us now move to the decades after Foulkes' death. Morris Nitsun became the spokesperson for group analysts who felt that Foulkes had underestimated destructive forces in groups. In 1991 Nitsun published an article in Group Analysis on "the antigroup", later expanded to a book (Nitsun 1999). In the history of group analysis, this was an important development by highlighting some real shortcomings in Foulkes' theory and practice. Yes, Foulkes had idealized (therapeutic) groups and neglected destructive forces which had left some confusing lacunas in theory, training, and practice. Moreover, the difficulties in realizing this state of affairs, seemed to be connected to a collective idealization of Foulkes within group analytic circles (Karterud, 1992b). Nitsun coined the term "anti-group" for forces in and around therapeutic groups that raised mistrust, hostility, and anger towards the very project of group analysis, as expressed from patients who resented being referred to group therapy, a low esteem in public opinion, disrespect from colleagues and institutions, harsh attacks from frustrated patients, etc.

Nitsun voiced a real concern. How could this concern be explained? He argued that by ignoring the reality of man's destructiveness, this very destructiveness would be insufficiently dealt with and as a consequence it would turn its head, so to speak, towards the group in retaliatory attacks. Nitsun traced this neglect to Foulkes's rather bleak adherence to Freud's theory of a death instinct, the Thanatos. He then went to a great length in "rehabilitating" object relational theories in general and Bion's group dynamic theory in particular, a course which Foulkes had rejected. In my opinion, his "diagnosis" was correct, but his theoretical cure was erroneous. A deficient theory (Foulkes') does not become more valid by adding a flawed theory (Bion's). To the contrary. In the preceding paragraphs I have explained the errors in Bion's theory. Nitsun neglected these arguments and proceeded as if Bion (and Klein) represented valuable corrections to a somewhat naïve Foulkes. A highly problematic consequence of this line of thought was Nitsun's conception of the group as object, which can be understood as an extension of (individual) object-relation theory to the realms of groups:

> "As a guiding principle, I start from the conception of the group as object. This formulation is implicit in the views of numerous writers. In Bion's work (1961), for example, the notion of a group entity, established through the operation of the basic assumptions, in essence describes a group object. ... In the group as object, properties of the group stimulate

the perceptions and projections of the membership, combining to establish the group as a form of container in which both recognized and disowned psychic phenomena are vested and in which shared object relationship systems reside. Once established, the group as object, an entity in its own right, invites its own form of object relationships with the group membership, in a way which powerfully influences further development. In the case of the anti-group, the group as object becomes a fragile, dangerous, or aversive container, and it is the evolution of this process which forms the subject of this and the subsequent chapters."

(Nitsun, 1996, p.107)

The problems with this conceptualization are manifold. It is claimed that the group (object) is "an entity in its own right". This is close to speaking about a "group mind" which exist independent of the mind of the participants. We (and group members) become confused. For example, where is this object located? In the matrix? And where is that? A softer version will say that the group as object is not an object that can be located in time and space. It is a mental object. But even mental objects need to be located somewhere. The obvious answer is that it is located in the mind of the participants. But if so, how do we know that the group image of one member is equal to the internal group of another? That they share the same group image (instead of different group images)? When asked questions as these, Nitsun would probably respond with reference to Bion, for example, that the participants share some common basic assumptions and that these assumptions are what unites them. One assumption would be that what all of them is preoccupied with is to combat a common enemy (as in a BA fight-flight). If so, this enemy would be the group object. It would even be invested with malicious intentions. But how do we know if this actually is the case, in the minds of the participants? The fact is that people are highly different with respect to how they perceive and imagine the same group (Bakali et al., 2010). Some reports an experience of high group cohesion, while others may report low. Sometimes the group members react in symphony, other times they do not agree. Groups are highly volatile. Emotions and opinions come and go. Trying to simplify this diversity into a simple object-relational scheme where all members participate, is a risky business. The group analyst risks a position of repeating well-worn clichés of the group (object) appearing to be poisonous, devouring, neglecting, revengeful etc. What is being lost in such global characterizations, is the particularity and individuality of the person in the group. What exactly went on in the group when member X said ... and member Y responded with ... while member Z nodded, and member W frowned? When examined more closely, it seems apparent that *the* group object does not exist other than in the mind of the therapist. The other group members most probably have other (internal) group imagoes. If he is lucky, his/her imago will sometimes approximate some of the other's imago.

Sadly, individual differences have been a neglected topic in group analysis (and in psychodynamic group psychotherapy). Individual characteristics are the obvious number one variable at risk for antigroup processes. Nitsun is aware of this connection when he advocates that the group analyst should be careful in selecting patients for analytic groups. In a chapter on "to what extent is the anti-group preventable" (Nitsun, 1996, p. 153–173), he discusses individual differences with respect to group-object relations and warn against candidates with "powerful underlying disturbances in the group-object relation". When it comes to factual group dynamics, however, he maintains that these differences coalesce. Nitsun regrets that so far it is difficult to assess group-object qualities but advocates the therapist to do as best as he/she can. He has little positive to say about other modes of assessment, including "simplistic personality classification" (!). He mentions shortly three categories of people whom one should assess more carefully: "Highly aggressive individuals", "isolated, schizoid individuals" and "patients with severe early trauma". Altogether, in a book with 318 pages, he mentions the term borderline two times!

If Nitsun's book had been presented to a publisher today with its original content, it would not probably have been published in its present form because of this arrogant and antiscientific attitude. However, in 1996 the zeitgeist was different. Sadly, for Nitsun and the group analytic community, time has not been on Nitsun's side. The concept of group-object relations has not caught any interest among researchers. There is no valid study on the subject. However, what Nitsun dismisses as "simplistic personality classification" has expanded to a huge literature with researchers from all over the world who engage in explorations of personality and personality disorders (Karterud, Wilberg, & Urnes, 2010/2017). In his text, Nitsun does not even mention the concept of personality disorders. Regrettable, since it later has been demonstrated that level of personality functioning is the most important variable for the outcome of group-analytic psychotherapy (Lorentzen et al., 2014).

In retrospect it is important to reflect upon this neglect of the topic of personality disorders. It says something about the isolation of the group-analytic community in London during the 1990s. Even while Nitsun and many other group-analytic colleagues worked within the National Health Services (NHS) who presented them with abundant cases of difficult to treat personality disorders, they did not engage properly in the intense international discussions of how to understand and what to do with these patients. The 1990s were the decade when group analysis started to lose terrain in comparison to arising rivals like mentalization-based treatment (MBT) (Bateman & Fonagy, 1999), dialectic behavioural treatment (DBT) and schema therapy. This process accelerated during the first decades of the 21st century. If Nitsun had read the critical studies on Bion (Karterud, 1988a, 1989b, 1989c, 1989d), taken Bowlby's theory of attachment more seriously

(Bowlby, 1988), read Fonagy et al. (2002) on self development and engaged himself in how to conceptualize personality disorders (DSM-IV in 1994), things might have been different. What characterizes the contributions above is an empirical approach to mental states in that hypotheses about mental states and structures can be tested empirically. For example, basic assumptions can be measured and their phenomenology and assumed etiology can be investigated. The same is true for attachment patterns, reflective functioning, self-development, and personality structures. However, the group analytic community have tended to avoid such empirical approaches (with some few exceptions, see Blackmore et al., 2012). Instead, one has favoured metapsychological speculations about concepts such as "group objects".

Concerning how to prevent anti-group processes, Nitsun should be acclaimed for his attempts to provide the group analyst with a larger technical repertoire than what Foulkes recommended:

> *"One of the strongest and most important considerations in the text is the necessity for the conductor to be more active in relation to the anti-group than is usually the case in group-analytic psychotherapy. This begins with the fundamental importance given by group analysts to establish as firm and holding an environment as possible in which the group can develop."*
>
> (Nitsun, 1996, p. 282)

It extends to *"a variety of interventions … as ways of dealing with the anti-group, such as strengthening the linking function; maintaining a group perspective; and positive connotation, indicating that there are means of taking greater control in potentially disruptive group situations"* (ibid, p. 282).

The problem with these suggestions is that they are somewhat disconnected and lack a coherent theoretical foundation. In the last part of this book, I will outline a valid alternative.

In the footsteps of Malcolm Pines and Dennis Brown

S. H. Foulkes was a highly social and networking man. Besides inviting several patients to the same consulting room, he engaged in groups with colleagues, initiated the Group Analytic Society (1952), thereafter, Institute for Group Analysis (1971) and founded the GAIPAC (Group Analysis. International Panel and Communication) (1967). GAIPAC was the forerunner of the journal Group Analysis (1982). Through GAIPAC, Foulkes maintained a broad network of colleagues all over the world who discussed themes related to group analysis. However, in his writing style he seldom referred to other group therapeutic approaches or controversies or developments in the realm of psychoanalysis. Consequently, after his death there were considerable lacunas to be filled and bridges to be built to relate group analysis to neighbouring fields. As already mentioned, Morris Nitsun tried to connect with

Bion and the Kleinian object relational school. Personally, I am more at ease with the route of Dennis Brown, and in particular Malcolm Pines. Both opened for self psychological perspectives, although they hesitated with a fuller integration.

In 1994 Dennis Brown and Louis Zinkin published a collection of essays with a bridging purpose, "The Psyche and the Social World". The collection contained the essay *"Self development through subjective interaction. A fresh look at 'ego training in action'"* by Dennis Brown. These thoughts were obviously in the air, but it was a bold step of Brown to condense them in a text. At that time, it was obvious that ego psychology had fulfilled its historical role in the development of psychoanalysis. It had no more to give. Its resources were depleted and the ego-psychological way of doing psychoanalysis were experienced as increasingly alienating. When in psychotherapy, modern people expected to meet a person, not an interpretation-machine.

So, if the ego was dead, how could it be reawakened? In other words, how could the theories and practice of the ego-psychologist S. H. Foulkes be reformulated and modernized? The first tiny, but crucial step was merely linguistic. Replacing the word ego by the word self. But what did that imply? What were the crucial differences between the concepts of the ego and the self? Brown only scratched the surface of this formidable theoretical question. He focused more on the clinical challenges which were highlighted by the concept of *intersubjectivity*. The ego was an agency in the apparatus of the mind. The self carried the vulnerabilities of the person who was in the midst of intersubjective processes in his social field. The self is a vulnerable self. It is in need of respect and recognition and of emotional atunement from significant people around. Among people, there is a constant "negotiation" going on in their intersubjective fields. Mental health is to a large degree contingent upon the individual's competence in navigating intersubjectively. From a modern perspective, it is obvious that this mode of reasoning gives much more sense to Foulkes' clinical descriptions than his own ego-psychological (self-)understanding. In other words, Foulkes was ahead of his time intuitively, in much of his clinical practice and clinical reasoning, but his theoretical conceptualization of what he was experiencing and doing was limited by his ego-psychological position. Brown does not go so far as to say that group analysis should find a new home in self psychology, but he opens the road to self psychology in the more classical sense, as in the work of Heinz Kohut (1971, 1977), and to its intersubjectivity offshoots as in the work of Stolorow and Atwood (1992). Brown's co-editor, Luis Zinkin, however, is a bit concerned about this move. He fears for the identity of psychoanalysis and group analysis. He is concerned of:

> *"... so radical a revision of Freud that many would not recognise the theory as psychoanalytic. A revision in this direction is at present being undertaken in self psychology following Kohut, where intersubjectivity is*

indeed coming to the fore. But should it be taken to the point where drive theory is altogether abandoned?"

(Brown & Zinkin, 1994, p. 234)

Today we would say, yes, of course. Because the drive theory is a flawed theory. It should be replaced be a valid theory of emotions. However, at that time this controversy was experienced as threatening the very identity of psychoanalysis.

Nevertheless, in his conclusion, Brown writes (1994, p. 98):

> *"In summary, it is proposed that the process of self development in group analysis is circular and spiral: the experiences of being empathised with, and failed enough – as in early infancy – sets in motion the three stages enumerated in the beginning of this chapter: fuller discovery of our inner world, which allows us to discern the difference between old internal object relationships and new ones, and in a step towards maturity to learn to attune ourselves to other people's experience as well as our own. On the way to more mature, intimate and reciprocal relationships with others, we mitigate the effects of earlier empathic failure and ossification of internal object relationships. I call this self development through subjective interaction, and I believe its attainment during group analysis is a test of how well the group is functioning."*

During the 1990s Pines emerged as a leading figure of group analysis. He was everywhere; in GAS and IGA, in London, at seminars, conferences, workshops all over the world, as president for the International Association of Group Psychotherapy (IAGP) and as editor of the journal Group Analysis. Earl Hopper (1998, p. 11) writes:

> *"Although S. H. Foulkes, his training analyst and mentor and the founder of group analysis, had more than one child, it is widely acknowledged that Malcom Pines is his eldest son. It is virtually impossible for the eldest son of a founding father to be acknowledged as a 'father' in his own right, but Malcolm personifies the institutionalization of group analysis."*

In the same text, Hopper (p.11) acclaims Pines for his intellectual broadmindedness and writes that:

> *"Malcolm has searched for a school of psychoanalysis that he felt was compatible with group analysis. As an alternative to classical Freudian psychoanalysis and British object relations thinking, he eventually found self-psychology, again tempered by his own interpretation of it."*

However, also Hopper is concerned with the seemingly abolishment of the drives:

> *"I would suggest that, like many others who have found intellectual nour-ishment in self-psychology, Malcolm's work is marred by his apparent neglect of the forces of destruction and perversion, ..."*
>
> (ibid, p. 13)

If one consults Pines' writing, however, Hopper's characterization seems somewhat exaggerated. There is hardly any group analyst that have written more extensively on borderline conditions, both as a kind of personality disorder and as a challenge in group analysis. And borderline personality disorder is the condition above all which harbours destructiveness, both directed outwards as violence, and inwards as self-hatred and self-destruction. Pines discusses borderline conditions through multiple theoretical lenses and only gradually he comes to favour self psychological perspectives. We should also add here that borderline was not Kohut's favourite condition. The prototype for his theoretical and technical elaborations was narcissistic personality disorder, gradually expanded to narcissism in general and subsequently to the vicissitudes of the vulnerable self.

Pines adopted the viewpoints I outlined earlier in this chapter on the differences between ego and self. The philosophy and psychology of the self appealed also to his broadminded intellectual interests (Pines, 1996a). Not at least he was inspired by Kohut's (1976) concept of *the group self*. However, let us take the encounter between group analysis and self psychology and Pines' role in it a bit more chronologically.

Initially, group analysis and self-psychology were two approaches quite distant from each other, geographically as well as professionally. Self-psychology concerned itself with individual psychoanalysis in Chicago, and Kohut was as sceptical about group psychotherapy as most psychoanalysts (Arensberg, 1998). Group analysis was located in London. The first time we encounter a reference to Kohut is in GAIPAC's columns in 1972. Pines had given the keynote address to the Second European Symposium in Group Analysis in London the same year. The lecture was reproduced in GAIPAC (Pines 1972). Pines discusses here the relationship between psychoanalysis and group analysis and argues that group analysis, inspired by its particular practice, had been more open to the concept of the self than psychoanalysis: *"The word 'self' was taboo for many years in psychoanalysis"* (Pines, 1972, p. 89). He argued that group analysis was more relaxed with talking about self and others, self-development, self-differentiation, self-representation, self-annihilation, etc:

> *"However, over the past couple of years, there has been a developmental leap in psychoanalytic conceptualization that brings it in line with or even*

past group analytical thinking, and perhaps we should also go a step fur-
ther to keep up with this development. What I am referring to is the work
of Heinz Kohut, ..., who is still little known in this country, and who has
recently published a book entitled The analysis of the self."

(Pines, 1972, p. 89)

Pines then provides an extensive account of the ideas in this book. Among
other things, he writes:

"We must learn to accept the existence of narcissistic forces. I think we
have always done this in group-analytic psychotherapy, but intuitively and
unconsciously. If we think through the fundamental aspects of group-ana-
lytic psychotherapy, what is curative and healing, it is not least through the
way in which the group can represent a reservoir of narcissism for its par-
ticipants. I think about how the matrix and the relationships within the
group give back, not a reduction in narcissism, but opportunities for a more
mature ability to accept, take back, and integrate into the self, fragmented
and denied primitive narcissistic feelings."

(ibid., p. 90)

Pines was early on the spot, just a year after Kohut had published *The Ana-*
lysis of the Self (Kohut 1971). However, the group-analytic community was
seemingly not ripe for such a step as Pines proposed. Hopper wrote in a
commentary that *"the discussion that followed Dr. Pines' lecture was, in my*
opinion, disappointing" (Hopper 1972, p. 94). The colleagues were not ready
to follow Pines in such a theoretical discussion and preferred to spend their
time finding out more about their relationship with each other (!). When
reading Hopper's frustration, I recognize a smile in myself. When group
therapists meet, it is mostly the "here and now" that takes precedence: Who
am I, and who are you, and how do we feel together, rather than "boring"
and "alienating" theoretical discussions. In such contexts, it is important what
the "leader" does. Foulkes was very much present at the 1972 meeting. How
did he position himself? Did he accept the challenge and enter a discussion
with Pines? Unfortunately, the minutes say nothing about this. But none of
what Foulkes wrote in those years indicates that he perceived that something
called self psychology was developing, and that this was relevant to group
analysis.

   Pines' initiative in 1972 apparently fell flat. It would be several years before
self-psychology reappeared in GAIPAC's columns. In 1976 the Swiss group
pioneer Raymond Battegay published a note about narcissism and groups
with reference to Kohut (Battegay 1976). In 1978, Pines elaborated on his self
psychological viewpoints in a wide-ranging article on psychoanalysis and
group analysis (Pines 1978). He returned to the same theme in 1979 (Pines
1979). At this time, an interest in self psychology among Italian group

analysts was expressed by Paparo (1981). In 1981 the IGA, London, on the initiative of Pines, Fabrizio Napolitani, and Franco Paparo, organized a separate workshop on "self-psychology and group analysis". During the 1980s the frequency of articles and comments on group analysis and self psychology increased. Besides Pines, the key actors were Paparo (1984), Gerald Wooster and Jason Maratos (1986), as well as the American pioneers Irene Harwood (1986, 1992) and Walt Stone (1992, 1996). Furthermore, as already mentioned, the connection between group analysis and self psychology was a central concern in the writing of Dennis Brown (1994). In 1996 *Group Analysis* published a special issue on self-psychology and group analysis (Maratos, 1996). In 1998 Pines and Irene Harwood edited the book *Self Experiences in Group. Intersubjective and Self Psychological Pathways to Human Understanding*. This was the first book of its kind on self psychology and group psychotherapy. The book built an explicit transatlantic link between American self psychology (Harwood, 1998a, 1998b; Arensberg, 1998; Bacal, 1998) and European group analysis (Pines, 1996b; Paparo & Nebbioso, 1998; Karterud, 1998). In 1998 IGA organized a ten-week course in self psychology where the lectures (Pines and colleagues) were followed by experiential groups with the aim of "exploring the expression of self in the group".

For some reason or other, the flirtation between group analysis and self psychology declined during the following decades. The engagement did not result in a lasting marriage. How come?

The lasting contributions of self psychology and some limitations

There are multiple reasons for the failure of self psychology to become integrated with group analysis. One is the general intellectual and professional "climate". Self psychology never took root in the UK. The tradition of object relations was too strong, and some would say that self psychology was superfluous since Donald Winnicott in essence had expressed some similar views. However, as Paul Ornstein (1991) has emphasized, self psychology is not just another object relation theory. Could it be that self psychological viewpoints were integrated in a more "silent" way into a kind of broader version of group analysis? However, if one scrutinizes modern textbook-like outlines of group analysis, as in Schlapobersky (2016) and Barwick & Weegmann (2018), one finds that self psychology occupies a marginal position. It is referred to in a polite way, but not really integrated. A third reason might be that Pines and colleagues failed in fulfilling the task of a more profound integration because of limitations in the theories of self psychology and group analysis that were poorly understood.

Self psychology originated as an American phenomenon. The heydays lasted longer in the US and the tradition became institutionalized through the International Association for Psychoanalytic Self Psychology. However, also here the contributions on self psychology and group psychotherapy gradually declined. The pioneers remained Arensberg (1998), Bacal (1998), Paparo (1984), Harwood (1998a), Pines (1978), Segalla (2021), Karterud (1998), Livingston (1998), and above all Walter Stone (2009). Stone was important also as a co-author (with Scott Rutan) of the influential textbook Psychodynamic Group Psychotherapy which has appeared in numerous editions since the 1980s (Rutan, Stone & Shay, 2014), and as president of the American Group Psychotherapy Association. The main contribution from these authors was 1) to explain Kohut's theory, and particularly the concept of selfobject needs, to a wider audience; 2) to explain the relevance for group psychotherapy; and 3) provide a range of convincing clinical vignettes that demonstrated the importance of the approach. The theory of the vulnerability of the self, the vicissitudes of self fragmentation, the rupture of the therapeutic bond/alliance and the need for repair in the group situation, remain lasting contributions to the canon of group psychotherapy. However, the literature became a bit repetitive around these issues. It was as if these authors fulfilled a historical task, culminating in the global acceptance of the "rupture and repair" dynamics of the therapeutic relationship (Safran et al., 2001).

In my opinion, (a revised) self psychology has more to offer than the themes mentioned above. However, the self psychology movement has been a bit stuck in an idealization of Heinz Kohut. After all, Kohut did not leave a legacy of a "complete" theory and practice. To the contrary, he made a mistake when he insisted that the sole theoretical grounding of psychoanalysis was by way of empathy and (a phenomenological) hermeneutics. The natural sciences were discarded. Thus, his theory of the self remained incomplete. For example, he failed to compensate for the ambivalent rejection of the drives. Consequently, self psychology has lacked a valid theory of emotions. If we add a general scepticism towards traditional research and traditional diagnostics, self psychology was reluctant to enter the world of "evidence-based psychotherapies". Consequently, it remained in a marginal position that did not appeal enough to young psychotherapists. In Scandinavia at least, younger generations prefer approaches like Emotion-focused psychotherapy and Intensive short-term dynamic psychotherapy which can refer to numerous studies that prove their efficacy. And when it comes to more serious psychopathology, self psychology lost terrain to DBT, MBT, Transference-focused psychotherapy and Schema therapy.

However, most important was the failure to develop the concept of the group self which Kohut indicated in 1976. Stone (2006) and Pines (1996b) did some efforts that left no traces. As I will explain in Part 3, one must approach the concept of the group self in a far more radical way (Karterud, 1998). To reach at the core of what a group is all about, one must go beyond psychology.

The limitations which I have described, does not mean that the psychology of the self is dead, suffering the same destiny as the ego half a century ago. However, parts of the theory should be reformulated, and it must find its place in a broader theory of personality and what it means to be a person and a member of groups and societies. This task requires a detour both with respect to empirical sciences and to a philosophy of the self. From there we can return to group analysis.

Part Two

Neglected areas

In Part One I have discussed the theoretical and clinical legacy of S. H. Foulkes, the broadening of group analysis after his death and in particular the tension between different perspectives on the nature of man and groups. In Part Two I will change the tone, so to speak, and turn to developments in areas that should be relevant for group analysis but which, for various reasons, have been neglected. The developments I have in mind indeed have relevance for the nature of man, but they derive from sources that are more empirical than the more traditional metapsychological discourse of group analysis. It concerns the nature of personality and its disorders.

The challenges from personality disorders, particularly in borderline patients

During the 1990s it became increasingly clear that a large part of patients being referred to mental health outpatient departments harboured not only burdensome symptom disorders but serious personality problems as well. How should these personality problems be conceptualized? As already mentioned, Malcolm Pines engaged himself in this discussion at an early stage. In 1984 he published the article "Group analytic Psychotherapy and the Borderline Patient". He (reprinted in Pines, 1990, p. 94) highlighted what we today would denote as mentalizing deficits:

> *"The borderline patient has not developed certain higher-level structures and functions of the mind. One of these functions that is essential for psychic growth is what Schaffer (1968) has called 'reflective self-representation', by means of which we know we are thinkers of our own thoughts (Bach 1980)."*
> *"If this capacity for reflective self-representation is suspended or unavailable, the thinker vanishes but the thought remains. The thought is now a thing, an event, a concrete external reality, for there is no thinker to know it for what it is."*

DOI: 10.4324/9781032696027-2

"We can also relate the psychic experience of the borderline patient to a failure in symbolic functioning."

"It is not possible to treat a group made up entirely of borderline patients. A group must have the capacity to operate at higher levels of functioning lacking in borderline patients, but available to the neurotic, to the normal person and to the therapist. A group of borderline patients will scarcely represent the norm of society from which each is a deviant, which for Foulkes (1948) was the basic law of group dynamics. Foulkes seemed to be thinking not so much of a group of psychotics or borderline patients as of a group composed of neurotic personalities. It is perfectly possible, using our model, to include in a group one or two persons functioning at a much more primitive level than others, for the capacity of the group to maintain higher-level functioning would be well establishes and, indeed, there are considerable advantages for the group as a whole if there are persons in it who are determined to bring the group into contact with the powerful and primitive forces of the psyche. A growing amount of written evidence, however, shows the attempt to run completely borderline groups is doomed to disaster".

His last prediction was wrong! Modern evidence prove that it is possible (Bateman & Fonagy, 2001; Kvarstein et al., 2015; Schultz-Venrath & Felsberger, 2016), although with resources that were not available at the time when Pines wrote his article. Pines is ahead of his time when he in this article describes what we today will label psychic equivalent thinking which occupy a central position in modern conceptualizations of borderline pathology (Fonagy et al., 2002). However, he neglects the topic of emotions and thus fails to see the relationship between emotional arousal and psychic equivalence thinking. He, like many others, also talks as if he knows what borderline "is". The reality is that what most professionals thought about "borderline patients" in 1984 was based upon dubious theories and insufficient empirical knowledge. Nevertheless, Pines was a pioneer when it comes to personality disorders and group analysis, although he overlooked other personality types than borderline and narcissistic. However, this engagement did not enjoy much support. If we jump to the modern group-analytic textbook by Schlapobersky (2016), the words borderline and personality disorders have disappeared from group-analytic discourse. The words are not even found in the index!

So, what is personality disorders in general and borderline PD in particular? Personality disorders were first conceptualized in a criteria-based way by DSM-III in 1980. However, it was the revision with DSM-IV in 1994 that spurred more intense scientific and clinical interest. Research was intensified concurrent with the revision processes that lead to DSM-5 in 2013 and ICD-11 in 2017. Personality disorders were found to affect around 12–14 % of the population of Western countries. The evidence for discrete categories were weak, since the overlap between, for example, the DSM-IV categories were substantial. Accordingly, "borderline personality disorder" is a heterogenous construct, not a distinct "disorder". In a study from my department, we argued that there were 264 ways of being borderline by way of borderline criteria combinations alone (Johansen et al., 2004). In addition, come variations like borderline with additional avoidant, dependent, histrionic, narcissistic, paranoid or schizotypal traits as well as different symptom constellations. The variation is large. The heredity was also found to be substantial. Genetic factors accounted for around 30–50 % of the variance among identical twins. Heredity was found to be related to differences in emotional reactivity (Montag et al., 2016), including temperament components such as social dominance (versus submission), conscientiousness and effortful control (Posner & Rothbart, 2000). Crucial environmental factors were additive experiences of childhood neglect, maltreatment, violence, and abuse (Hughes et al., 2017) which produced insecure or disorganized attachment patterns, emotional and identity confusion as well as poor mentalizing and intersubjective competencies. Young people with this mental luggage have poor chances for navigating safely during the turbulent social world of adolescence. The risk for derailment of their expected personality development is high and most often their symptoms and interpersonal dysfunction find their debut in adolescence. Furthermore, research clearly indicated that personality traits and features are dimensional. In short, one can be more or less borderline. Thus, there is a severity dimension. DSM-5 defined that as *level of personality functioning*. It is a valid and reliable construct (Christensen et al., 2020) and defined by four components. It measures on 0–4 points scale the person's capacity for: 1) Identity; 2) Self directedness; 3) Empathy; and 4) Intimacy/closeness. In addition to the level of personality functioning, DSM-5 defines a set of personality traits which will supply the person in question with a personality profile (for example, being more or less introverted, antagonistic, etc.). This substantial progress is what impels me to criticize Nitsun for his derogatory remarks about "simplistic personality classification".

There is no doubt that group analysts need the kind of knowledge and skills which I have sketched in the paragraph above. They need it for assessment purposes and for their capacity to reflect upon the dynamics of the group: What personalities is the group composed of and how do they interact? But group analysis also needs it for more socio-political reasons, like being able to communicate with the surrounding health agencies.

However, group analysts might say that the kind of knowledge and skills which I refer to above, has only marginal relevance for the conduct of group analytic psychotherapy. It is mostly descriptive knowledge, not dynamic. To a certain degree they are right. International classification systems are careful not to be experienced as proponents of any particular "school". They should be "neutral" and "objective". What the classification systems so far has turned away from, is the following crucial question: What does the personality look like, which the personality disorders are disordered from? In a series of books and articles, I and my co-workers have tried to answer this question. Unfortunately, most of these texts are written in Norwegian. The most relevant articles for an English-speaking audience are Karterud, Folmo & Kongerslev, 2019; Karterud & Kongerslev, 2019; Karterud & Kongerslev, 2021. In the next chapter I will summarize what is most relevant for a group-analytic audience.

Group analysis needs the resources of a modern theory of personality

In the publications mentioned above, we argue that the major components of personality are 1) Temperament (which mainly consists of primary emotions); 2) Attachment pattern; and 3) Mentalizing competencies. These components (TAM) have an evolutionary history which is important for a proper understanding of the ontogenesis of the individual and the group (Karterud, 2010). But most importantly, these components are intertwined by virtue of the self.

Let us start with the self. It is not a thing. It's a relation. Moreover, to cite the Danish philosopher Søren Kierkegaard, it's a relation that relates to itself. Above all, what the reflective self relates to, is the core self. Thus, the reflective self is, or rather should be, in dialogue with the core self. However, this dialogue may be disrupted. The person may deny, fear, hate or despise aspects of the core self, which then turns to something alien, something the person wants to get rid of, more than conduct a dialogue with. Consequently, the alien parts of the core self turn into symptoms. Psychotherapy is to (re-) establish a dialogue with the alien parts and thereby transform them. Foulkes describes very well in his books and articles why and how such transforming dialogues can be cultivated in therapeutic groups.

So, what is this core self? It has some similarities with Freud's "id", but overall, it is a totally different conceptualization. The core self is a conceptualization by neuroscientists like Antonio Damasio (2000) and Jaak Panksepp (Northoff & Panksepp, 2008). It links to the development of consciousness which most probably occurred around 500 million years ago. By then, the brains of the most advanced creatures were large enough to contain neuronal networks which could produce maps of the surrounding world, and, most importantly, maps of the internal state of the organism. Co-ordinates in these maps were sensory impressions of sight, hearing, smell and touch whereby the outer world could be sensed, and interoceptive impressions of the spatial position of the body, its homeostatic state (e.g. thirst and hunger) and, above all, its emotional state. The global "broadcasting" of all this information occurred in what we today will label "working memory" (Carruthers, 2015). From there some sort of "rational decision" was undertaken as to what to do in a given moment of time. This "rational decision" in the mind of higher-level animals, is of course not based upon any kind of self-consciousness and self-reflection. It is "rational" from the point of view of the creature. We could likewise use the word purposeful. What goes on in their mind, is possibly some kind of evaluating mental images. However, the main point is that higher level animals are not stimulus-response-robots. They possess a capability of evaluating the state of the world relative to the state of their own organism and take purposeful action thereof. That is what we label the core self.

Throughout evolution, owing to larger and more sophisticated brains, the core self also becomes more sophisticated. The most significant development occurs with the dawn of mammals (Panksepp & Biven, 2012). This evolutionary step gives birth to the prosocial emotions of LOVE/care, SEPARATION DISTRESS, and PLAY/joy, which become new motivations for the core self. By the advent of mammals, family group formations also enter the stage.

Foulkes tried to anchor his theory in evolutionary reasoning, but he seldom went further than to say that man was social to its inner core. In the 1964 volume with James Anthony, he goes a bit further. He discusses what happens when a *"number of isolated individuals are brought together"*:

> *"In this struggle we can observe bewilderment, suspicion, fear, and impulses to withdraw, and yet, in the face of these, an overwhelming strong impulse, amounting to an absolute and irresistible need, to make contact and to re-establish the old and deeply rooted modes of group behavior. We think indeed that as soon as the group takes hold and the formerly isolated individuals have felt again the compelling currents of ancient tribal feeling, it permeates them to the very core and that all their subsequent interactions are inescapably embedded in this common matrix."*
>
> (Foulkes and Anthony, 1957, p. 235)

As modern research has proved, "ancient tribal feeling" is not *one* feeling but a complex set of feelings which constitutes a sense of *belonging*, whereof the most important is a feeling of being loved and being cared for and being relieved of one's separation distress, as well as a loving and caring feeling towards other members of the family and the group. For Foulkes and many subsequent group analysts, it was a pity that their version of psychoanalysis was not built upon the foundation for mammal life, which is pro-sociality, but emphasized an erroneous inborn destructiveness.

As pointed out earlier, modern neuroaffective science has identified seven primary emotions which constitute motivational forces in the core self (Panksepp, 1998). We are driven by SEEKING, FEAR, RAGE, SEXUAL LUST, SEPARATION ANXIETY, LOVE, and PLAY. These emotions are universal for mammals. For humans we must add the social emotions of shame, guilt, envy, jealousy, greed, etc. A great lesson from Freud is that emotions demand what he labelled "discharge". They are literally *forces*. He attributes that to their drive character. Today we will say that emotions strive for "discharge" because they come with inborn action programmes. When we are frightened, we will hide or run, when enraged, we will attack, when left alone we will cry, etc. Animals are poor actors; they display what they feel. Humans become socialized and learn to hide their feelings. They may be so good at it that they not only hide their feelings for other people, but also for themselves. They may develop what Lee McCullough labelled "affect phobia". What they fear is seemingly condemnation from fellow beings, but essentially, they fear the expression of what is inside themselves. A major task of group therapy is to alleviate these fears. However, we anticipate our story. We still need some more evolution.

The primary emotions among mammals pave the way for social bonding in families and groups. Our label for humans is attachment. Also, the attachment pioneer John Bowlby (1988) was a Londoner. Initially he was quite controversial in psychoanalytic circles. That may be the reason why he left so little stamp on group analysis. He lived in London, held some seminars at the Institute of Group Analysis, London in the 1980s and had a good spokesperson in Mario Marrone (1994). As for self psychology, attachment perspectives are present in group analytic literature, but do not occupy any central position (Schlapobersky, 2016; Barwick & Wegman, 2018). However, empirical research has proved that attachment pattern is a decisive factor when predicting the life course of the individual. Disorganized attachment in early childhood even predicts psychopathology in early adulthood (Lyons-Ruth et al., 2013).

In his seminal books, Bowlby characterized attachment as a drive. May be it thereby was easier to "sell" the theory to psychoanalysts. Later attachment authorities describe attachment as a "system" (Fonagy et al., 2000). A jargon in the literature on mentalizing is "activation of the attachment system". However, both drives and systems are unwarranted labels. The phenomenon of attachment is clearly a result of the primary emotions that come with the mammals. It is the lost offspring which utters distress calls, owing to SEPARATION ANXIETY, and FEAR, being responded to by the mother/parent who intervenes, owing to the LOVE/concern system and rescues the infant, comfort the infant, and downregulates its emotional arousal, whereby the infant reactivates SEEKING and undertake a new tour to the world in order to PLAY. By such "circles of security", there will be constructed a trustworthy inner object with a good enough "working model of the mind" (Bowlby) in the mind of the infant.

Attachment does not come as discrete categories, which the attachment literature indicates, as either secure or insecure, as overinvolved, distanced, or disorganized, but as dimensional phenomena. We are all more or less secure/insecure and the attachment pattern of most of us may become more secure in some areas of our relating to persons close to us. Thus, assisting the person to become more secure with respect to attachment will be an important goal in most psychotherapies. In therapeutic groups, attachment patterns will reproduce themselves. Group participants will display their typical way of dealing with their personal distress in the way of relating to the group and its members. Therefore, it is important for group analysts to know the prototypical patterns, the theory behind them, typical responses to them and how to challenge them in an appropriate way. This theme will be dealt with in more detail in the last part of the book.

A (strange) consciousness of the world comes with birth. Mentalizing is a slow process whereby relations to the world acquire meaning. Self-consciousness is an outcome of this process, which take years. Mentalizing is the "spiritualization" of nature. It builds upon primary emotions and attachment. Primary emotions are the "hard" natural part of the core self and contingent upon genes which accounts for 30–50 % of the variation among identical twins (Montag et al., 2016). To a large degree they are "fixed" although individuals differ with respect to their threshold for emotional activation as well as the intensity of their reactions. These differences manifest themselves as different personality types. For example, borderline patients have low thresholds for RAGE and SEPARATION ANXIETY, and the intensity of their emotional responses is high, often overwhelming. Schizoid patients come with a very high threshold for CARE. Literally – they don't care. Narcissistic patients come with a low threshold for social dominance and a denial of SEPARATION ANXIETY ("America first!" And – "I did not lose that election"), etc. However, attachment patterns are not genetically bound in the same way. If we say that primary emotions are nature, attachment can be said to be culture. Secure attachment presupposes being cared for. Maltreated animals become as insecure as maltreated human children. Mentalizing, however, is civilization. Thus, the TAM model (Karterud & Kongerslev, 2019) integrates NATURE – CULTURE – CIVILIZATION.

In order for mentalizing to occur in the first place, you need being mentalized (Fonagy et al., 2002). One's SEEKING towards the word, one's homeostatic affects (hunger, thirst, tiredness) and one's emotional reactions need to be assigned meanings according to the prevailing zeitgeist (norms and discourse) in one's local community. We are now approaching the bedrock of a theory of groups, which will be expanded in later parts of the book. The first milestone concerns the fundamental difference between a social group of animals and a group of humans. The animal group is based upon culture, upon a bonded family and herd, but it is not civilized in the meaning of being "spiritualized". The word "spiritualized" here, is with reference to the German philosopher Georg Wilhelm Hegel. I will return to Hegel later but let me just emphasize that spiritualized means that the human group is invested with spirit in the sense of meanings, values, norms, roles and a history that can be narrated. Being born into a human group means being born into a spiritual world that is already there. A more modern way of expressing this, without the religious connotations of the word spirit, is to say that the human group is minded. On the other hand, the word minded may be an underestimation of the significance of the enormous text-corpus that civilization has created, and which operates in the background of the individual mind, mediated by the zeitgeist. Each human newcomer is instantaneously inscribed with meanings that relate to the family, groups, society and civilization at large. How does this come about during evolution?

The story that follows is profoundly inspired by the research and theories of the German psychologist Michael Tomasello, former director of the Max Planck Institute for evolutionary anthropology in Leipzig. The theory postulates an evolution (among pre-humans) of a capacity for joined and later collective intentionality that paves the way for co-operation among humans and thereby evolution of language and the formation of minded groups ("spiritualized") who will ascribe its mindset into the mind of the new-born who thereby will develop a consciousness about itself. This is another, more modern and empirically grounded version of Foulkes' thesis that the individual is born out of the matrix of the group. But let us take it somewhat more detailed.

Based upon a range of empirical studies, experts on primate cognition conclude that, for example, chimpanzees perform a kind of mental operations that should be accepted as cognition (Tomasello, 2014, 2019). They seem to possess mental images that are processed with respect to goal attainment. What qualifies this kind of processing for the label "cognition" is that it contains the following elements: 1) schematic cognitive representations; 2) the ability to make causal and intentional inferences from these cognitive representations; and 3) monitoring oneself during the decision-making process. The entire process concerns the ability to reach thoughtful behavioural decisions which goes beyond the ability to perform "off-line" simulations of potential perceptual experiences. Furthermore, primates communicate with gestures and sounds.

However, what chimpanzees seem to lack, according to Tomasello (2014), is *shared intentionality*, which goes beyond the capacity for shared attention, i. e., attending to the same object. Shared intentionality lies at the heart of the extensive collaboration which characterizes subjects of the *Homo sapiens* species. It evolved probably around 2 million years ago (Homo erectus) as a selection of capabilities that favoured collaborative foraging. Shared intentionality is a crucial step in the evolution of *Homo sapiens*. It implies the advent of a "we" and later of collectivity. In shared intentionality, we are the agent. When we do things together, joined by shared intentionality, we have come to terms by a mutual agreement where I know that you know (and vice versa) that the nature of our project is basically co-operative, from planning through execution to sharing of outcome. Such kinds of projects presuppose the capacity for intersubjective (and thereby self-) monitoring, for example, the need to know when we have agreed upon something, if we have agreed upon the same project and where you are and where I am in relation to you (intentionally and emotionally) during the execution.

When group theorists speak about man "being social to the core of his/her existence", they mostly refer to phenomena that belong to the faculty of shared intentionality, for example, related to emotional attunement and implicit mentalizing. One cannot help being affected by other subjects and one cannot help interpreting others (and consequently monitor oneself). These abilities belong to the fabric of the human self.

Shared intentionality presupposes communication (vocalization and gestural signs), but not verbal language. Verbal language evolves, according to Tomasello (2014), in concert with (group) cultural practices that depends upon *collective intentionality*. Collective intentionality concerns matter of interest for the group as a whole, not only for two (or few) persons collaborating around foraging. Verbal language evolves as a tool for handling communal and political (group) affairs. Language is the common agreed upon and culturally sanctioned signs, metaphors and inference rules that come to represent the "common ground" of the group. Since language rules are culturally sanctioned, and not being the invention of any particular subject, verbal utterances may acquire the appearance of "objectivity". Inferences made according to the group's standards for rationality makes it possible to assert "how things really are". In Tomasello's words (p. 108, 2014):

> *"And so, with modern human such things as intentional states, logical operations, and background assumptions could be expressed explicitly in a relatively abstract and normatively governed set of collectively known linguistic conventions. Because of the conventional and normative nature of language, new processes of reflection now took place not just as when apes monitor their own uncertainty in making a decision, and not as when early humans monitor recipient comprehension, but rather as an "objectively" and normatively thinking communicator evaluating his own linguistic conceptualization as if it were coming from some other "objectively" and normatively thinking person. The outcome is that modern humans engage not just in individual self-monitoring or second-personal social evaluation but, rather, in fully normative self-reflection."*

Fully normative self-reflection is another word for explicit mentalization. When did it enter the historical scene? Estimates are obviously highly speculative, but genetic data (FOXP2 gene) suggest that brain structures that are essential for language can be traced back to around 300,000–200,000 BCE) (Coop et al., 2008). However, language in the pragmatic sense of Tomasello (and Wittgenstein) developed slowly, in concert with developments in group cultures. There are reasons to believe that as a result of general development and evolution, migration and climate change, complexities of group living took a new turn in around 35,000 BCE among *Homo sapiens* settlements (the Gravettian culture) in the Caucasian area (Finlayson, 2009). These developments in language and cognition might be the seeds of the Indo-European language. The next event that took language and cognition to new levels and sophistication were the invention of *written language* which took place around 5,000 years BCE in the Middle East region of Euphrates and Tigris that hosted the agricultural revolution.

When does the *individual* acquire the ability for explicit mentalization? It is a gradual process culminating with the "cognitive revolution" between the ages of four and six years old. With the capacity for explicit mentalization, i. e., being aware of different mental perspectives on the same phenomenon and by that being able to consider oneself from the perspective of another (the group), core self phenomena can be thought about in an "objective" way. By that, self-consciousness becomes "anchored", no longer being only fleeting and constantly changing mental states. The faculty of imagination is an extension of this capacity for offline self-reflection. Through imagination the subject can consider multiple future scenarios in the light of the past and present and choose the most appropriate path.

We are thus reminded that self-consciousness is not an on-off phenomenon. The self acquires consciousness about itself through a series of "steps". On the road to self-consciousness, the self must transcend its embeddedness in self-absorbed desire. It is the encounter with other minds that slowly push the self towards a realization of social reality inhabited by different selves and minds, with their own agendas and their own perspectives on the world, including different opinions about the person in question. The person eventually finds him/her-self embedded in an intersubjective field where recognition of mutual dependence requires a transcendence of self-absorbed desire. In a more technical jargon – we witness the process of abandoning psychic equivalent thinking, where the person insists on defining the world according to his/her thoughts and desires about the world, and acquires the capacity of representational thinking which scales down ones grandiose claims about the world, to more modest realizations of one's own fallibility and dependency of others (points of view).

The Romanian philosopher Radu Bogdan (2013) makes a strong case for additional incentives that motivate the individual in its ontogenesis in the midst of the group matrix. He maintains that human children begin their life in a kind of *sociocultural captivity* and that they cannot help but trying to find out the rules and meaning of their sociocultural surround in order to master it and becoming informed members of it. The greatest challenge is to come to an understanding of the sociocultural as a matrix of mental states and mental processes. To do so they activate their innate capacity for intuitive psychology (implicit mentalizing) and mental rehearsal. By pretend play they engage in sociocultural learning of adult roles and games (mother–child, doctor –patient, fighting in wars, etc.):

> *"Children cannot help but imitate adults (they are imitation machines), and once stimulated, cannot inhibit the action schemes inspired by the adult behaviors, especially in novel sociocultural contexts."*

> (Bogdan 2013, p. 119)

However, more complex group dynamics call for sociopolitical strategizing. By the advent of explicit mentalizing and self-consciousness proper, after the age of five, most children become mentally and neurobiological ready for a larger world and will adapt to the pressures of juvenile sociopolitics. That requires an ability for strategizing, which means to:

> "… mentally figuring out and metamentally rehearsing offline how to handle the thoughts, attitudes, utterances, and actions of others, and in response, one's own. Differently said, strategizing is metamentally rehearsing offline how to reach one's goals by means of the mental states and actions of oneself, either altruistically, co-operatively, or with ulterior selfish motives. It is primarily the mental states of others and oneself used projectively as means to ends that define strategizing, and in turn foreshadow Imagining.
>
> Examples of strategizing, so construed, include: rehearsing what to say and what to do, thinking how others think of you; planning how to relate to others and how to react to their reactions; deliberate and planned lying or obfuscation; gossip, including self-involving gossip; elaborate stories or communicative exchanges mixing reports of one's mental states with those of others; justifying publicly one's motives, reasoning, and actions; autobiographical recitations; fantasizing about what one could do in the future in relations to others; self-evaluation and criticism as well as self-advertising; defending one's opinions; interpersonal diplomacy; and many other exploits along the same lines."
>
> (Bogdan 2013, p. 176)

By not adapting, or adapting poorly, to this world of juvenile and later adult sociopolitics, one's capacities for explicit mentalization will stay behind. The capacity for social co-operation will suffer and consequently the trust in the "objective" evaluation of self and others. There is a link to Foulkes here, to his so-called basic law of group dynamics. A therapeutic group may approximate a discourse where the prosocial norms of civilization prevail, where the individual will find him-/herself adequately mirrored and thereby engage him-/herself in a renewed attempt to develop the capacity for explicit mentalizing and trustful co-operation.

In Part Two, I have discussed modern conceptualizations of personality disorders and the major components of personality. The perspectives have been empirically and evolutionary. However, group analysis also needs a philosophical foundation. That will be the topic of Part Three.

Part Three

A philosophy of the individual and the group self

Group analysis is full of *implicit* philosophical and epistemological assumptions (Karterud, 2000). Foulkes took few initiatives to discuss these assumptions. Had he done so, it would probably, as with Henry Guntrip, have led him in opposition to Freud. It was essential for Foulkes to avoid such opposition. The post-Foulkes generation has shown a somewhat greater philosophical interest. Malcolm Pines (1991, 1998) has through a series of articles discussed the historical and philosophical assumptions of group analysis. Hans Cohn is the one who has argued most strongly for a phenomenological-existentialist basis for group analysis (Cohn 1993, 1996, 1997). Cohn argued that such a position was implicated in Foulkes' thinking. He referred to Foulkes' radical understanding of the individual-group relationship, his radical understanding of the mind as something other than intrapsychic processes located to the brain, the matrix concept, the understanding of mental disorders as dysfunctional states in a social network, etc. The totality of Foulkes' thinking testified, according to Cohn, to an intuitive understanding of the *intersubjective existence* of man, as expressed by philosophers within the phenomenological-existential tradition, like Edmund Husserl, Martin Heidegger, and Maurice Merleau-Ponty. This tradition was, among other things, a reaction to the dualism found in Rene Descartes who conceptualized man as an isolated thinking being. Man in Husserl's universe cannot be understood detached from his "*Lebenswelt*". Heidegger characterized human beings as "being-there" ("*Dasein*"), as "thrown into the world" and Merleau-Ponty argued that subjectivity was based upon intersubjectivity. In Merleau-Ponty, intersubjectivity was a prerequisite for subjectivity in the same way as the group was a prerequisite for the individual in Foulkes' thinking. Cohn therefore argued that *"though Foulkes never referred to any particular philosophical school, I believe that he should be considered an early representative of a phenomenological-existential approach to psychotherapy"* (Cohn 1996, p. 301).

Personally, I largely agree with Cohn's assertion of similarities between Foulkes' theory and practice and what Cohn labels the phenomenological-

DOI: 10.4324/9781032696027-3

existential philosophical tradition. It resonates with the reasons for my own fascination with group analysis. But I wouldn't go so far as to characterize Foulkes as a *representative* of this philosophical tradition. Ever since Freud and Breuer started the talking cure, there has been a mismatch between the practice of psychoanalysis and its theoretical and philosophical self-understanding. This tension amounted during the era of ego psychology, until it was replaced by the "relational turn" during the 1990s. Already from the start of psychoanalysis, a hermeneutic-intersubjective discipline was practiced to a certain degree, but the theory was infiltrated by modes of thought belonging to the natural sciences. Foulkes' group-analytical (as opposed to his individual psychological) conceptual apparatus was more compatible with a hermeneutic-intersubjective discourse. However, Foulkes never reflected over these issues in his texts. He did not explicitly attach himself to the phenomenological-existential tradition and did not make use of the *resources* this tradition could offer. Therefore, it is sought to denote Foulkes a representative of this tradition. On the contrary, it is important to highlight the gap between group analysis and phenomenological-existential tradition. This void refers to a *developmental deficiency* in the group-analytic group self that is important to fill in. Thereby, a healthier inner balance will be created. As it stands, group analysis in this area conflicts with itself.

Group analysis is a distinctly Western cultural project. It unites ancient Greek and modern Western ideals. It unites Socrates' ideal of "know thyself" and Jürgen Habermas' ideal of "dominion-free communication." In group analysis, modern man has an unprecedented arena where he can slowly, but surely, week after week, year after year, learn to know himself within what is the prerequisite for our culture, a distinctly human way of minding communal living. If we leave the Western cultural circle, the cultural assumptions of group analysis become particularly clear. Colleagues who have tried to establish group-analytical groups in countries and cultures characterized by religious fundamentalism, extreme women's oppression, dictatorship and warlike conditions can tell of a wall of suspicion and widespread sabotage. These experiences make it clear that group analysis presupposes a cultural level where human rights are fairly well integrated into society.

The theory and practice of group analysis are thus closely linked to social development. It was only after World War II that social and historical assumptions enabled group analysis. Illustrative in this respect, Foulkes' first groups were gender homogeneous. It was radical enough to offer group treatment, and he did not take the chance of further provoking the public by treating women and men in the same group!

It is, in my opinion, no coincidence that the birth of group analysis coincided with the defeat of Nazism and fascism and the subsequent declaration of human rights (in 1948). The Declaration of Human Rights was an expression of the (temporary?) victory of humanism and democracy over totalitarianism. It is the same values and the same historical tradition that form the basis for group analysis. Group analysis is based on the principle of free and open communication between people, and it presupposes freedom to think, express oneself and organize without fear of societal reprisals.

At one level, this is about the boundary conditions for group analysis. But it runs deeper than that. It also concerns the zeitgeist out of which group analysis was born. In this respect we are in dept to the German philosopher G. W. F. Hegel (1770–1831). Hegel is known for his thinking on dialectics, the phenomenology of spirit, and philosophy of law. The most important to our purpose is his theory of *recognition* ("Anerkennung") (Hegel, 1807/2019; Honneth, 2021). Hegel opposed the thesis of contemporary philosophers that the formation of society was a consequence of man's self-preservation urge, i. e., his pursuit of power and wealth. More fundamental than this, Hegel says, is man's pursuit of *self-creation*. Man is not a self born out of nature. The self is something that comes into being. And it does not come into being through itself, but by virtue of the other. It is the *other's recognition that initiates and confirms the self*. If man can be said to have some kind of natural being, a consciousness comparable to that of animals, it is like an immediate experience of the world dominated by what Hegel labelled as "desire" (which we today would label primary emotions). Through the recognition by the other, an awareness of oneself is established accompanied by an awareness of the other's likewise need for recognition. This realization calls for a "negation" of one's desire in the service of mutual considerations. Furthermore, recognition provides an anchorage beyond the immediate experience of the world, from which it is possible to judge oneself. According to Hegel, recognition is the prerequisite for self-awareness and (self)reflection.

Thus, the Hegelian self is both desire and intersubjective considerate, bound to a series of dialectics, between immediate experience and self-awareness/self-reflection, between (selfish) desire and mutuality. Psychologically, recognition manifests itself as *self-esteem*. Society is an arena for (regulated) struggle for power and wealth, but above that a struggle for *recognition*, for honour, (self)respect, dignity, and reputation. And it is the recognition that ultimately legitimizes power and wealth. I may have goods and gold in my possession, but it is not *my property* until it is recognized by another authority. Similarly, with identity and self-esteem. My identity is linked to a name I have been (appreciatively) given by others, and an enrolment in a social community (born of x in year y, belonging to genus z and the people w), and self-esteem is the product of a series of socially appreciative experiences. Hegel also emphasizes that recognition is not given once and for all. Since recognition is a social phenomenon, it is fleeting. One will therefore seek to make recognition permanent through *institutionalization*. The rule of law is the highest form of institution, and legislation will ensure property rights. Personal recognition is also sought institutionalized. This is most clearly expressed in the rules and rituals of diplomacy and royal houses for social ranking. In the social arena, the struggle for personal recognition appears side by side with the struggle for power and wealth. This link to Hegel when it comes to a philosophy of the self, is important, although such a philosophy was not his major concern. Hegel's concern was the phenomenology of the spirit, which is about how our civilization can reflect about itself. It's about collective self-reflection. However, he was a pioneer in demonstrating how this collective self-reflection which we construe as spirituality is dependent on a kind of self-consciousness that owes its nature to mutual recognition.

Nearly 150 years passed before the thought-figure about the birth of the self through the other took root in practical psychology. It is a fundamental thesis of Kohut's self-psychology and embodied in the most important concept of self-psychology, that of *selfobjects*. Selfobjects, or *selfobject functions* so as not to reify the phenomenon, are those aspects of the other that serve to develop the self (in the child and in psychotherapy) and maintain the coherence and vitality of the self (in the adult). Recognition is labelled mirroring by Kohut, and the mirroring other is called a mirroring self-object. Kohut also maintains that "man needs self-objects from the cradle to the grave". It's not a need we outgrow when we become adults and "independent." Self-objects are like oxygen in the air. We take it for granted when it's there and perish if it ends. Just as the lungs "expect" the air to contain oxygen, this is how the child, according to Kohut, expects the social environment to contain self-objects. The child is programmed to expect development-promoting social responses.

Heinz Kohut developed his ideas based upon psychoanalytic experiences. Daniel Stern based his book *The interpersonal world of the human infant* (1985) on infant research. This book represented an epochal transcendence of developmental ego-psychology which reached its peak with *The Psychological Birth of the Human Infant* (Mahler et al., 1975). Here the idea of an *original symbiotic unity* between mother and child was still being pursued. This symbiosis was portrayed as a psychological egg from which the child was later, at the age of around three months, hatched. Stern rejected the theory of an original symbiosis and argued (inspired by Kohut, among others) that infant research had to be based on *the method of empathy*. This means that researcher should strive to understand the world through the child's eyes. *From the outset*, according to Stern, there was an interaction between child and caregiver that was crucial for the establishment of *self-structures*. The formation of the self through the recognition of the other starts at the moment of birth. In this sense, the self is thoroughly social. But it's *not unconditionally* social. It is *genetically predisposed* to a wide variety of cognitive, affective and social functions.

The theory of mentalizing took this tradition of thinking a step further by demonstrating that it is fundamental for the child to be *empathically thought about*, and thereby related to. The mind, and the self, is created through another mind, through "minding minds", and "behind" this two-some interaction does the culture operate with words, concepts and forms of understanding that thinking (minding) caregivers make use of. There is a dialectic here of improvised and spontaneous interaction through phenomena such as "proto-conversation", where parent and babies play with each other, and thinking/mentalizing in the parent about the framework itself and what happens during the proto-conversation. This is convincingly documented in so-called Still-Face experiments (Tronick & Weinberg, 1997). Proto-conversation is training in intersubjective interaction and consolidation of the core self. This process is not a kind of "internalization" as psychoanalysts like to express it. The basic fabric of the self is shaped through social interaction.

The hermeneutic tradition

The goal of group analysis is to promote self-development and self-understanding in the group participants. I deliberately use the term self-understanding and not insight. In psychoanalysis, one has traditionally talked about insight. This gives associations of looking into something, into a container, a closet or a (psychic) apparatus. When the fog of repression lifts, one sees more clearly one's own psychic landscape. Self-understanding gives other associations. Understanding is something else than seeing. Understanding is the domain of hermeneutics. To understand is to interpret. Understanding oneself does not necessarily imply understanding something "inside oneself". The self is not a psychic apparatus, nor is it reducible to either something organic or intrapsychic. Understanding oneself implies understanding oneself in the world.

Hermeneutics was basically a doctrine of interpretation. Its origins can be traced back to disputes over the "correct" interpretation of the Bible and legal documents. From there, hermeneutics evolved into a doctrine of the interpretation of texts in general. The "correct" interpretation of a text was linked to an understanding of the author's intentions. What has the author really meant by his writing? In the early 1800s interest expanded to the question of how to understand/interpret another human being at all. Understanding another human being was now linked to the concept of *empathy* (Friedrich Schleiermacher). Although in this German tradition of philosophy one spoke not of empathy, but of *Einfühlung*. Einfühlung is not a purely intellectual achievement. It is an attempt to *live with* in a holistic experience of the world. Again, we note that philosophy anticipated psychology by an estimated 150 years.

The next step was a turn to *the context*. To understand another human being is to understand it from his/her assumptions and in a certain context. For example, what *ideas* did the Vikings have about man and the world, and what *communicative codes* did they operate within? Hermeneutics was now intimately linked to *the understanding of history* (Wilhelm Dilthey). Norbert

Elias was a typical representative of this tradition. He set out to survey the history of European *mentality*. With Heidegger (1927), hermeneutics became a *philosophy*. Heidegger emphasized that interpretation was not an accidental characteristic of man. Interpretation was a necessary part of man's *conditions of being*. In a modern version: "Man is a self-interpreting animal" (Taylor, 1989). Hans Georg Gadamer continued to work on the questions of hermeneutics as philosophy, as understanding of history and as methodology. Hermeneutics has a methodological aspect, but cannot *be reduced* to a method, Gadamer (1960) argued. In a sense, he rehabilitated *the concept of tradition* and gave the concept of *prejudice* a positive denomination. We always understand from prejudices that are grounded in certain traditions. In our being, we are historically *situated*. We cannot completely situate ourselves outside the traditions of which our own self-understanding is an inherent part. But we can reflect on this relationship (tradition – self-understanding) and thereby change it. Gadamer emphasized that history worked through us in this way ("Wirkungsgeschichte"). Foulkes would have liked this concept. In his words – the group works through us. Although, Foulkes was more occupied by *forces* than meanings and conceptual schemes.

Habermas (1968) criticized Gadamer for legitimizing conservatism through his affirmation of tradition and downplaying of the oppressive aspect of (traditional) ideologies. According to Habermas, one should have a far more active, critical, and revealing relationship with prejudices and traditions (ideologies). Hermeneutics should be *critical*; it must be aware of the power struggles in history and society and engage in man's projects of liberation against the attempts of ideologies to *deceive him/her*. Habermas saw psychoanalysis as an important tool in such a process of liberation, precisely by virtue of its critical perspective. Psychoanalysis sought to look *behind the phenomena*. Symptoms are surface manifestations, and if one is captured by the rhetoric of the symptoms, one misses out on underlying communication-distorting mechanisms. It's the communication-disorder that matters. To reach it requires a *depth hermeneutics* that is open to unconscious communication-distorting mechanisms. Pointedly, one can speak of a *hermeneutics of suspicion*. Psychoanalysis, however, has the problem, said Habermas, that it has a distorted conception of itself *qua* science. It understands itself as a natural science and not as a hermeneutic discipline and therefore suffers from a "scientific self-misunderstanding" (Habermas, 1968).

The counterargument from psychoanalytic point of view, shared, for example, by Kohut, was that the scientific position of psychoanalysis would rather be weakened since hermeneutics was about *understanding meaning*. Hermeneutics is suitable for understanding intentions and motives, but *not for explaining causal relationships*. After all, mental disorders are about man being *driven* by irrational *forces*. In this debate, analysts referred to the early hermeneutics' distinction between *understanding and explanation* (Dilthey). The natural sciences sought explanations of causal relationships, while hermeneutics sought an understanding of meaningful relations. It should be admitted that psychoanalysts had a point here, owing to weaknesses in the early conceptualizations of what hermeneutics was all about.

Understanding and explanation. The group as text.

The French philosopher Paul Ricoeur posed this contradiction between understanding and explanation as his entrance to a new way of defining hermeneutics. The problem resided in the conceptual system of Dilthey, Ricoeur argued. However, there is no basis for claiming such a radical distinction between understanding and explanation. Understanding and explanation are in a dialectical (interdependent) relationship to each other. Ricoeur justified this claim through a new analysis of the original object of hermeneutics, which were texts. For those who wish to go to the sources, consult two key articles by Ricoeur from the early 1970s: *"What is a text? Explanation and understanding"* and *"The model of the text: meaningful action considered as a text"* (reprinted in Ricoeur, 1981). Ricoeur argues here that Dilthey was on a wrong track when he expressed that the ultimate goal of hermeneutics was *"to understand the author better than he has understood himself."* In his argument, Ricoeur emphasized the radical differences between oral dialogue and written text. Written text implies an *objectification,* and this object (text) lives its life independently of the author. Hermeneutics is basically a doctrine of interpretation related to this (meaningful) object. Faced with a written text, it becomes clear that the object has been separated from the author's dominion. Words and sentences, not to mention whole texts, are *ambiguous.* In contrast to the dialogical situation, the author cannot clarify with additional words, intonations, or body language what he "really" meant. The interpretation of the text must relate exclusively to the meaning that is articulated in writing. Meaning and the intention of the author are once and for all separated from each other.

It is this objectification that, according to Ricoeur, allows the human sciences to be called sciences. Objectification of the text implies:

1   that its meaning is fixed;
2   that it is separated from the intentions of the author;
3   that it does not refer to an immediate conversation situation (local surroundings), but to a general lifeworld with potential relevance to "everyone"; and
4   that it caters to a universal readership.

Moreover, the text is bound by the language and the laws of language. It is also bound by its own genre (poetry, drama, legal text, etc.). The text likewise has its individuality as a specifically organized whole. Furthermore, the reader's position vis-à-vis the text is different than that of a local interlocutor. The reader must relate to the text in the above objectified sense and find his own approach. But regardless of the approach, the reader is forced to follow a *hermeneutic circle*, i.e., an understanding and explanatory process in which the whole is seen in the light of the parts, and the parts in the light of the whole, where parts and wholeness change until one stop at a sufficiently achieved understanding. In this hermeneutic circle process, according to Ricoeur, both explanation and understanding are applied. Yes, in extreme cases one can apply an almost purely explanatory perspective by analyzing the text linguistically or by analyzing its narrative (narrative) structure. When one explains the text, it is not with concepts *borrowed from the natural sciences*, but with concepts and explanatory principles from the human sciences itself. Thus, the objection that the human sciences, if they are to call themselves sciences, must be so on the premises of the natural sciences lapses.

Interpretations of texts therefore have a greater degree of objectivity than can be attributed to a more immediate understanding of the author's intentions. But interpretations are not true in the same way that a mathematical proof is true. Interpretations are *valid* in the sense that some interpretations are stronger argumentatively than others. Validation is not verification. The degree of truth of an interpretation is closer to probability calculation. A text is not open to any interpretation. During the interpretation process, the reader generates educated guesses that he seeks to substantiate through a form of evidence similar to the evidence a judge uses in his attempt to establish facts in a trial. Is the defendant guilty or innocent? What speaks for, and what speaks against?

Some readers may now feel we have moved far away from group analysis. What is the relevance? The group analyst incessantly interprets a highly complicated ongoing human drama and is expected to intervene constructively in crucial phases. What resources do we have at our disposal to determine whether an interpretive intervention is good or bad? One criterion is whether depth and surface are brought into contact. Does Ricoeur make any contribution to such problems?

Yes, this is a crucial point for Ricoeur. With reference to linguistics and research on myths and narrative structures, he emphasizes that the text has an *in-depth semantics*. There is an inner logic in the relationship between elements of language and the elements of a story. A fairy tale can be explained as a (universal) plot that unfolds between a limited number of actors and deals with, or refers to, a limited number of existential dilemmas. It could be, for example, the evil stepmother who, full of envy, seeks to destroy the beautiful and good stepdaughter's future, and who deceives the kind (but naïve) king, but who is outsmarted by the bold prince.

In the interpretation of texts, according to Ricoeur, one oscillates between understanding the "superficial" meaning of the text and explanations based on the structure of the text. The relevance to group analysis will now hopefully become clearer. In the group analytical situation, the group analyst strives to understand the meaning of the ongoing group conversation *while* seeking an explanation on a deeper (structural) level. I understand the meaning of the dialogue between patients X and Y in the group when they talk about experiences with authoritarian leaders in the workplace. At the same time, I think they're talking about it *because*, as a therapist, I've recently added a new member to the group, something which X and Y have disliked. The meaning on the surface refers to an *outside* world problem for X and Y, i. e., a problem in their local world. But on a deeper level, it is not about a (local) outside world problem, but about a general existential problem that refers to a general world: How to deal with one's own powerlessness and anger in relation to dominant authorities on which one also depends?

It is this general world to which the text refers when it is freed from the intentions of the author. To interpret a *text is to interpret it as a reference to this general (spiritual) world, rather than understanding the author's intentions.* We should note the concept of *spiritual world.* Ricoeur here refers to Hegel who spoke of history as a *spiritual history* ("Geschichte des Geistes"). Throughout history, the spirit develops and comes to awareness of itself. In everyday speech, we even talk about the zeitgeist. That the spirit comes to awareness of itself can be benevolently laid out so that culture is increasingly able to reflect on itself *qua* culture. We conceive of cultural *actors* (writers, historians of ideas, philosophers, psychoanalysts, etc.) who undertake culturally acts of self-understanding on behalf of civilization. Hegel, however, spoke of an *absolute spirit* reflecting on itself, something Ricoeur rejected. We will return to this issue in our discussion of *the group self.* The main point in this context is the distinction between the local world and the spiritual world and that this has a parallel in the group-analytical situation to which the distinction between the local world to which the group conversation superficially refers, and the deeper and general existential dilemmas to which the speech also refers, and to which philosophy, literature and art are concerned. Ricoeur expresses the dilemma or tension between the outside world and the spiritual world in an unusually sharp way for him:

> *"Textual interpretation as a model shows that understanding has nothing to do with an immediate comprehension of a foreign psychic life or with an emotional identification with a mental intention. Understanding is communicated entirely through the totality of explanatory procedures that anticipate and accompany understanding."*
>
> (Ricoeur 1981a, p. 220)

Some of the same is expressed in the following quote:

> *"What would we know about love and hate and about moral feelings, and even what we call the self, if this had not acquired linguistic expression and been articulated through literature?"*
>
> (Ricoeur 1981a, p. 143)

Are we now making too fast a leap from text to group? In a sense. We have skipped Ricoeur's analysis of human actions understood as text. A text, according to Ricoeur, is a limited field for possible interpretations. Actions, like a text, are ambiguous. But this ambiguity, too, is limited. Given a certain situation, not all interpretations of an action are equally valid: I wave my hand, and that can mean goodbye, hello, waving a cab, and the like. The context limits the possibilities for interpretation. In light of the context, the action takes on its meaning, and the meaning refers back to my *intent.* Yes, the purpose was to stop a cab. Alternatively, my waving with my hand had actually no meaning. It was due simply to an intense pain in the shoulder. I couldn't help it. I was driven to it. We would then say that *the cause of* the cranking lay in the shoulder pain. Human actions thus find themselves between the extremes of being intended or cause driven. Even more complicated, purpose and cause will often be woven into each other. Here, too, there is no absolute distinction between understanding and explanation. When we say, "he was driven to it by jealousy", it implies *both* an understanding of meaning *and* a causal explanation.

Much of human interaction takes place by virtue of immediate understanding of meaning. When everything goes smoothly, we don't struggle to understand each other. That's what we today call implicit, or automatic mentalization. But if I am faced with a complicated problem in myself or others, the interpretation procedure, according to Ricoeur, takes place in the same way as with a textual interpretation. How can I understand myself? What drives me to do this? What are my motives? First, I must create a distance to myself. I must turn the action into a gestalt, into a figure against a background. Through *distancing* and *objectivization,* I create an object that corresponds to the text as an object, and which I make the subject of an interpretive procedure. Which understanding of meaning and which causal explanations are most likely? What speaks for one, and what speaks for the other? Text interpretation is the very paradigm of the social sciences, Ricoeur argues.

Objectification and distancing are important elements in group analysis. Through the special form of conversation that I call *the discourse of self-understanding*, gestalts are constantly formed that are offered at different distances for exploration in the group.

Example: *In one group, a patient struggled with his relationship with his schizophrenic brother who calls him six to seven times a day and wants comments and advice about his (delusional) beliefs. Our patient is his brother's best support, and he makes a heroic effort to shield his brother from their invading and unstable mother. But it takes a hard toll, and it affects his own newly started family. Then another patient says: It's like you're out in deep water struggling to get ashore. You swim for life, but on your back, you have your brother clinging on. You want to save both, but is it possible? This gestalt created a distance that in this case was optimal. Our patient recognized himself and could reflect upon important aspects of himself in light of these metaphors. The group could now speak of a long-term twin relationship (Kohut) between the two brothers in which the distinction between the two could be blurred, and in which our patient nearly lost himself in desperate attempts to help in his brother's struggle for survival.*

Now let's go back a bit in Ricoeur's arguments. We remember that he contrasted the dialogue with the written text. In a dialogical situation, ambiguity can be clarified by examining the context, nonverbal communication and asking the interlocutor to clarify ambiguities. That way we can better understand the intention of the interlocutor. And is this not the essence of psychotherapy, to immerse oneself in the other person's imaginary world and understand the other's intentions? Is this not what we understand by empathy, and is this not precisely what Kohut and other psychologists have defined as the methodological basis of psychotherapy? Does Ricoeur believe that textual analysis is also paradigmatic for the kind of understanding that occurs in psychotherapy? If so, do not the principles of distancing and objectification represent a setback to old-fashioned psychoanalytic practice?

At this point we should specify Ricoeur' conceptualization of a *hermeneutics of detour*. It is the detour that ensures the human sciences their scientificity. And this was Dilthey's great project: to give the human sciences a philosophical and methodological foundation that was as robust as the natural sciences' grounding in positivism. But such an anchoring cannot be based on "Einfühlung", according to Ricoeur. The notion of knowledge of the other through an intuitive and immediate immersion is a legacy of romanticism. When Ricoeur becomes polemical, it is to emphasize this point: *Science* cannot be built on this foundation. Knowledge of the human being must be based on the *traces* he leaves behind, in embedded texts, art objects, buildings, cultures, social patterns, written case histories, recorded group analytic sessions, and the like. And the interpretation of these traces must be based upon already established knowledge within the human sciences. Or to put it with Ricoeur: "It takes the detour of the world."

What then about the conversation between two people, does it not have as a prerequisite an ability for intuitive and immediate understanding of the other? To that, Ricoeur would respond that what we associate with the ability to intuitively and immediately understand the other is due to the internalization of the same cultural values and norms. The world is taken into us. Today we would add that there are also biological components. We react with our mirror neurons and certain affect expressions seem universal. Across cultures, people immediately seem to understand, for example, facial expressions and postures that are characterized by grief, as the same thing. Certain signs, or signals to the world, therefore, seem to be so fundamentally significant that they are safeguarded by a genetic code. On the receiving end, we must also assume that there is a genetically coined interpretive apparatus.

Today, we understand such phenomena in light of the theory of primary emotions. Immediate and intuitive understanding of the other is, therefore, a component of the process of comprehension that is otherwise characterized by internalized values and norms alongside an actively reflective component that exercises the activity that we usually call judgement.

Now, psychotherapy is not just any conversation between people. It is far from a free and unrestrained dialogue. Psychotherapy is a distinctly rule-based discourse tradition. When Ricoeur contrasts the oral dialogue with the written text, I would argue that psychotherapy as dialogue leans far towards the side of the text. In the dialogue that occurs in a chance meeting between people, anything can happen. In the psychotherapeutic dialogue, it is important to put a written textual tradition into practice. The psychotherapist lends himself to this tradition. In principle, therefore, psychotherapists are interchangeable. They are communicators. To a large extent, it is the psychotherapeutic tradition that speaks through them, albeit acquired by them. We are talking about a craft that has a scientific basis. It is acquired in different ways, most often as a combination of self-treatment, long-term theoretical studies, and a master-apprentice-learning relationship. The apprentice presents his own psychotherapeutic work as an objectified text to his supervisor, and together master and apprentice examine this text or narrative. Together, they examine the text considering what are recognized as "standards of excellence" in the field, in the same way that an architecture professor evaluates the drawings of an architecture student. The psychotherapy student is assumed to learn about the legalities that regulate the psychotherapeutic dialogue, in the same way that the architecture student is assumed to learn and synthesize building principles and aesthetics. Empathic ability is one of many prerequisites for a fruitful psychotherapeutic dialogue. However, the psychotherapeutic understanding of the other as a complex person in the world with a contradictory relationship with himself is mainly conveyed via "a detour of the world", i.e., via psychotherapeutic and philosophical/cultural texts.

The above interpretation of the psychotherapist as a mediator of tradition does not contradict the psychotherapist as a unique person in an existential encounter with another. The general and the particular are dialectically related to each other. The therapist is not a programmed machine that speaks. But he/she cannot be reduced to an unconditional fellow human being. The therapist is both a technical expert and a fellow human being, in the same way that the patient suffers from something that is *both* general (can be understood and handled through previously acquired theory and technique), and something that is unique to him (particular). In this place in our text, however, it is imperative to emphasize the *objectivity* of the process of interpretation. Later, we'll look at the subjective elements of the interpretational process.

The group-analytical culture is suitable for illuminating the dialectic between the objective and the subjective, the general and the particular. I largely agree with Foulkes who argued that the group analyst's most important task is to help create and maintain the group analytical culture. Such a group culture cannot *be reduced* to authentic, close, and warm encounters between people. An analytic group culture is a manifestation of the special form of discourse that characterizes group analysis proper. A good analytic group culture signals that the group analyst has managed to compose a good group and brought it up to a sophisticated level. He has managed to put the group-analytic discourse into practice, which means that he has managed to realize the group analytic textual tradition. He has dealt with a wide range of problems that are of an objective and general nature. He has thus laid the *foundation* for the particularity of the individual members of the group to unfold and be understood. His work can be compared with a theater director more than a conductor of an orchestra. A director who does not understand the text, and who does not know his craft, can destroy the spirit of, for example, Henrik Ibsen, and frustrate both the actors and the audience. A master director, on the other hand, can fill the theater space with an intensely vivid drama that shakes everyone present.

The objectifiability to which the text refers is about structures that, for human beings, are about identity. How should we understand this?

The self is not identical to itself

The previous chapter dealt with the fact that the subject cannot intuitively understand him/herself by virtue of him/herself, any more than it can intuitively understand the other. Self-understanding requires a detour about the world and the other. The self is not the same as "I". The difference is clearly expressed in a sentence like "I don't understand myself". Our task as group analysts is to help people understand themselves *better*. The benefit we may have from delving into the concept of the self is that we are better able to oscillate between an understanding of the self as a *general category (the hermeneutics of the self)* and the individual concrete self as designed in *a particular person (self- and personality psychology)*.

The concept of self is closely related to the concept of *identity*. By and large, I am myself today in the same way I was yesterday. I'm the same. If I *don't* experience it that way, you'd say I have a problem, an identity problem. One of the main points of Ricoeur (1992) in the volume *"Oneself as Another"* is that the self has a *two-dimensional form* of identity: identity in the sense of "*sameness*" (as *idem* identity, of the Latin word *idem* which translates as "the same") and identity as "*self-hood*" (as *ipse identity*, of the Latin word *ipse* which translates as "self").

This two-dimensional form of identity emerges through an analysis of the relationship between *time and identity*. At first glance, it may seem as if the time perspective is only linked to identity understood as same-ness (*idem*). Same-ness can be understood as *numerical identity*, as when a thing appears several times. We recognize the thing as the same when it reappears. We recognize the car that drove out of the garage in the morning as the same one that comes back in the afternoon. Furthermore, we have *qualitative identity* in the sense of extreme equality so that two things are practically interchangeable. We say that another has the same car as us despite the fact that it is not the same in the sense of numerical identity. Owing to the passage of time, we may come into doubt about numerical versus qualitative identity. That car I saw on the street, was it mine or was it someone else's? When I am asked as a witness in a trial to identify the perpetrator, I may have doubts: He looks similar in appearance (qualitatively), but is he really the same as I saw that night (numerically)? Moreover, we have *uninterrupted continuity*. Although I have changed, I will say that I am the same now as I was sixty years ago. I was and still am Sigmund Karterud. What happened at the age of 10 happened to *me* and not someone else. Similarly, we would say that it is the same tree even though now that the years have passed, it has become twice as tall. It's also the same boat even though we replaced half of the tables last year. These examples of uninterrupted continuity refer to a *structure* that remains permanent through time even though the "content" may change. Regarding personal identity, we can say that I am identical to myself, I am myself, in the sense that I am the same in terms of numerical identity, qualitative identity and uninterrupted identity. This refers to the *same-ness of the self*.

The question now is: Does the self's "self-hood" imply a form of permanence in time that cannot be reduced to the substrate (structure) that underlies same-ness? If I turn the question "who am I?" inward, in answer to this question I find two factors that refer to permanence in time: my *personality and keeping my word*. According to Ricoeur, over time, the permanence of personality refers to an overlap of *idem* and *ipse*, while keeping promises refers only to ipseity (self-hood). Identity such as *ipse* and *idem* therefore refers to two different dimensions. One cannot be reduced to the other. And here comes an important point at Ricoeur: It is *narrative identity* that binds together and mediates between the two dimensions of the self.

Let's first discuss the concept of personality. In what way does this imply an overlap of *idem* and *ipse*? By personality, Ricoeur understands a set of *lasting dispositions* through which a person is recognized as the same. Faced with a person who has undergone a sudden personality change, as in the case of a breakdown, we can say: I do not recognize him. He's not the same. Or: He's not himself. Character traits are something that is embodied (sedimented) in the personality, and that refers to a story. Acquired identifications refer to *how the other enters the composition of the same (idem)*:

"To a large extent, in fact, the identity of a person or of a community is made up of these identifications with values, norms, ideals, models and heroes, in which the person or the community recognizes itself. Recognizing oneself **in** *helps to recognize oneself* **by**. *The identification with heroic figures clearly displays the otherness assumed as one's own, but this is already latent in the identification with values which make us place a 'cause' above our own survival. An element of loyalty is thus incorporated into character and makes it turn toward fidelity, hence toward maintaining the self. Here, the two poles of identity accord with one another."*

(Ricoeur 1992, p. 121)

As Ricoeur conceives it, personality represents the "how" aspect of the question "who". Who am I? I can answer this by talking about how I am. I may be frugal, conscientious, sociable, etc. If I answer a personality test, such as the NEO-PIR, the expert can tell how I am in the language of the five-factor model, i.e., with regard to neuroticism, extroversion, openness to experiences, agreeableness and conscientiousness. But answering the question with "how" does not give a complete answer to *who* I am.

According to Ricoeur, there is another model of permanence in time as for personality, where *idem* and *ipse do not* overlap, in which the self-hood (*ipse*) is separate from its same-ness (permanent character traits). *It's keeping what you promise in fidelity* to what you've once said. *"You can trust me. In spite of the passing of time, I will keep my promise. I'll come tomorrow. When it is mobilized, you will find me in the line of soldiers."* Or *"I'm here at the appointed time for the next therapy session."* Keeping promises refers to a *self-constancy* that is essentially different from the permanence of personality traits. The permanence of personality traits is more like the robustness that characterizes a substance. Personality traits reveal themselves unconsciously. They are not the product of any willing act. While self-constancy has more to do with the kind of permanence that characterizes a friendship.

In the concept of personality, *idem* emerges and tends to cover up *ipse*. At the same time, this can obscure the relationship with ethics and morality. But ethics and morality are not something that is imposed on the subject from the outside. It springs from the constitution of the self. Ethics and morality cannot be reduced to psychology. Psychology, ethics, and morality must go hand in hand. If one wants a "pure" psychology, it is an obvious choice to put "selfhood" in parentheses and concentrate on "sameness", for example by focusing on automatic thoughts (invariant forms) that cognitive therapy deals with. As we shall come back to, this is not an option for group analysis. On the contrary, it is important to exemplify the ethical and moral aspects of group analysis and offer a form of therapy that challenges both *idem* and *ipse* and the balance between them.

According to Ricoeur, it is *narrative* identity that anchors the identity inherent in *ipse* and *idem*. Or put in simpler words: Self-understanding takes the form of a (tellable) story that includes my personality (*idem*) and my notions of a good life (*ipse*). In self-understanding, history returns to the enduring dispositions embodied in me. We know this movement well from psychotherapy: "*Yes, now I understand why I am so careful. My father had a huge need for control, and it became a hell of a time if everything didn't go on his terms.*" In psychotherapy, we hear and (re)construct long and complicated stories (narratives) that can eventually be summarized in seemingly simple sentences like the one above. Likewise, the story gives form and content to my notions of a good life. My self-constancy is related to values I am loyal to. In a narrative form, these values are concretized to human actors and situations: "*I don't want to be so careful anymore. It inhibits me and stops me from realizing essential aspects of myself. I want to be more like Irene in the group. I admire her integrity as evidenced by the story of her family tragedy. But then I must commit more to these aspects of myself. In the past, I've wobbled so badly*" (bad self-constancy).

According to Ricoeur, we take stories and narrative structures as we find them in fiction as models for our own self-understanding. A similar view was claimed by Harold Bloom in connection with the debate on *The Western Canon* (Bloom 1994) and which provoked the psychotherapeutic public, when he argued that Shakespeare was more important to western culture's self-understanding than Freud. Ricoeur claims that literature can be thought of as a vast laboratory for experimentation with different character designs and different self-constancy under different temporal and societal conditions. My life brought to light as a narrative gives me (and you) a narrative unity of life where I can also inscribe my life project. But how far can one stretch this connection between literature and the fate of fictional characters, with the life lived? Literature is written by an author. Unfortunately, I am not the (one) author of my life. On the contrary, it can often be the case that I live my life as a supporting character in a plot where others determine the premises. I'm entangled in other(s) stories. Furthermore, it is too easy to say that my life is *a* narrative. My life can be told through a variety of narratives, multiple plots with different characters, and none of them are exhaustive to my life as a whole.

That's true enough, but: "*By narrating a life of which I am not the author as to existence, I make myself its co-author as to its meaning*" (Ricoeur 1992, p. 162).

And: "*It is precisely because of the elusive character of real life that we need the help of fiction to organize life retrospectively ...*" (ibid., p. 162).

Ricoeur concludes that literary narratives and life stories lend to each other. They are in their constructions interdependent.

The American philosopher Alasdair MacIntyre (1981, p. 215) expresses the narrative perspective in the following way:

> "*Man is essentially a storytelling animal, in his activities, his practices and his fictions. ... If you deprive your children of the stories, you leave them*

without manuscripts, like anxious stutterers in both word and deed. There-
fore, there is no way to give us an understanding of society, including our
own, except through the stock of stories that constitute its original dra-
matic resources. Mythology, in its original meaning, is at the heart of
things. Both Vico and Joyce were right. And, of course, so has the moral
tradition of heroic society to its successors in the Middle Ages, where tell-
ing stories played a major role in teaching us the virtues".

MacIntyre's pursuit of 'teaching us the virtues' brings us to ethics.

The intention of ethics, according to Ricoeur, is this: *it aims at the good life*
together with and for others in just institutions. We note that the definition has
three components: 1) the good life; 2) with and for others; and 3) just
institutions:

> *"In terms of content, the good life, for each of us, is the network of ideals*
> *and dreams of achievements by which we evaluate life when deciding whe-*
> *ther life is fulfilled or not."*
>
> (Ricoeur, 1992, p. 179)

We find a clear parallel in Kohut's self-psychology. Kohut claimed that mid-
life crises, often as depression with a strong suicidal tendency, should mainly
be seen as a crisis in the self where one is confronted with one's betrayal of
living up to the good life in this sense. The tragedy is that I have squandered
my chances and that it now seems too late to turn back. It should be
emphasized, however, that the good life according to Ricoeur is no narcissistic self-realization. On the contrary, one of his main motives is to demonstrate
that the self is *not* "narcissistic". The other is inscribed in the self, and the
nature of the self is such that it cannot unfold without the presence and
assistance of the other.

The primary need of the self is not sexual or aggressive discharge, but
friendship. Ricoeur relies here on a philosophical tradition from Aristotle, but
also has a reference to Kohut (1992, p. 332). When Ricoeur joins Aristotle's
statement "man need friends," it is reminiscent of Kohut's statement that "the
self needs self-objects." Ricoeur expresses this by saying that others have a
mediating role in the process by which the self's potentials reach realization.
Or to put it another way: the self is a set of possibilities. They can only be
realized through the participation of others, preferably caring individuals who
want me well, i.e., "friends". Self-object function is a one-way traffic, something the other performs for me (although it is my interpretation of the
other's performance that counts). However, friendship is reciprocity. In
friendship, we are self-objects for each other. Friendship is based on solicitude. Taking care of others is taking care of oneself. *One takes care of the*
other as oneself and oneself as another. Self-esteem arises in the reflexive

encounter with myself where I see myself in the light of the demands of the good life, the care of others and just institutions.

We have now arrived at the last point in Ricoeur's definition of the ethical goal: fair institutions. By institutions, Ricoeur understands coexistence as it takes shape within a historical society – people, nation, region, group – as a structure that cannot be reduced to interpersonal relationships. This relationship can often seem forced and sustained by power and tyranny, but deep down, according to Ricoeur, it is founded on a *desire to live together because of friendship*. Cohabitation in institutions brings *the third* to the fore, i.e., the one who is more of a citizen than a friend in an intimate sense. Institutions bring *everyone* ("each") on the field. In cohabitation, we are linked together in a community of destiny that is the destiny of the institution (the group). I cannot reach everyone with care, but with justice and equality. Ricoeur quotes Rawls (1971, p. 3):

> *"Justice is the first virtue of social institutions, as truth is of systems of thought."*

When it comes to equality, there is not necessarily mathematical equality. Aristotle discussed proportional equality in which the person's efforts counted.

Equality, Ricoeur says (1992, p. 202), *"is to life in institutions what solicitudes is to interpersonal relations. Solicitude portrays to the self another who is a face ... Equality portrays to the self another who is an each".*

For our purposes, we are at the end of the review of the hermeneutics of the self. However, we have not finished our discussion of the self and morality. There is also a pragmatics here, i.e., that the realization of the ethical goal presupposes certain *norms*. Norms are concretized and value-based rules of living together. We will return to this topic in a later discussion of group norms.

The hermeneutics of the self and the psychology of the self

Ricoeur's main points were the following: The self has a two-dimensional constitution characterized by *idem*-identity ("sameness") and *ipse*-identity ("selfhood"). Self-constancy in the *idem* sense is that my personality traits today are essentially the same as yesterday, while self-constancy in the *ipse* sense is that today I keep the promise that I made yesterday. Furthermore, I have a narrative identity that connects *idem* and *ipse*. Stories make my character traits (*idem*) understandable as embodied experiences with others. Self-understanding as story(s) about myself needs detours about others and the world, i.e., what I understand myself *in light of*. Through such self-understanding, I can get hold of my life project that is aimed at the future, and that challenges my *ipse* identity (being true to myself). The self is not something that can only be attributed to me in the first person singular, but also to you, he, she, and everyone. The self is not self-sufficient. It needs others ("friends") to move from opportunities to realization (of properties and projects). Being true to others is therefore inseparably linked to fidelity to oneself. Against this background of idem, ipse, life project and inter-wovenness with others, the following ethical goals can be formulated: to aim for the good life with and for others in just institutions.

This overarching understanding makes good sense to Foulkes' implicit understanding of self and others that underlie group analysis. When we later add to this understanding the concept of the group self, the pieces fall further into place. However, the hermeneutics of the self in Ricoeur's sense is a *philosophy* of the self and not a psychology of the self. The latter is a discipline that integrates philosophy with empirical knowledge. The psychology of the self is in great dept to the pioneering work of Kohut. He formulated his theory about 50 years ago. What is still relevant? In the following, I will challenge Kohut from two angles. The one is hermeneutics, the other is empirical and concerns the emotional motivational forces of the core self.

Several analysts before Kohut had written about the self but conceived as part of the *content of a psychic apparatus* (as self-representations). Kohut is the one within the psychoanalytic tradition who places the self at the *centre* of theoretical and clinical explorations. Starting with Kohut, the self became an *overarching* theoretical and clinical concept. Historically, this change occurred in the early 1970s (Kohut 1971, 1977).

According to Kohut, this change was grounded on the fundamental sig-nificance of *empathy*. Already in a lecture in 1957 (published in 1959), Kohut argued that empathy is a methodological prerequisite for psycho-analysis. This article and the views he expresses here, he keeps returning to until his death in 1981 (Kohut's last lecture, given four days before he died, bore the title *On empathy*). This article and Kohut's later elaboration of the topic of empathy are supported by all modern strands of self psychology. If we examine the empathy article carefully, we find that Kohut expresses views that largely coincide with Dilthey's, and which Ricoeur has made great efforts to refute.

Kohut starts his article as follows:

> "*Man and animals examine their surroundings with the aid of the sensory organs; they listen, smell, watch, and touch; they form cohesive impressions of their surroundings, remember these impressions, compare them, and develop expectations on the basis of past impressions. Man's investigations become ever more consistent and systematic, the scope of the sensory organs is increased through instrumentation (elescope, microscope), the observed facts are integrated into larger units (theories) with the aid of conceptual of thought bridges (which, themselves cannot be observed);*

and, thus, gradually, by imperceptible steps, evolves the scientific investigation of the external world.

The inner world cannot be observed with the aid of our sensory organs. Our thoughts, whishes, feelings, and fantasies cannot be seen, smelled, heard, or touched. They have no existence in physical space, and yet they are real, and we can observe them as they occur in time: through introspection in ourselves, and through empathy (vicarious introspection) in others."

(Kohut 1959, p. 205)

We note that empathy is understood along the lines of introspection. Introspection is usually connected to the idea of an immediate and direct access to one's inner self. There's virtually nothing *between* me and myself when I look inward to study myself. Empathy understood as vicarious introspection feeds the same thought figure. Through empathy, I immerse myself in the other person's world, and through introspection in my experience as a fellow living (vicariate) I gain access to the other person's experiential world.

It's a similar mode of thought by Dilthey that Ricoeur characterized as a legacy of romanticism. As we recall, Ricoeur argued that man's understanding of others (and thus himself) is linked to the interpretation of the meaningful signs (language signs, gestures, actions, cultural products) in which life expresses itself. Understanding, therefore, takes a *detour*, it is not direct and immediate. When I understand myself through introspection, it is, as we have previously laid out, through an objectification of an (intrapsychic) phenomenon and distancing that together are necessary components of self-reflection. At this point it is necessary to address a topic that we did not touch on in the previous comments of text analysis. What we left out is the element of text analysis that *makes the text meaningful to me*, and which is a necessary addition to objectification and distancing. A written text address *anyone* (who can read). When I read it, I repeal everyone in the sense that I *personally* acquire the text. *Acquirer* is for Ricoeur a key concept ("appropriation", "Aneignung"). When I acquire the text, it implies that the interpretations take on a *subjective* character. The human sciences never quite escape such a subjective stamp, but as we have previously seen, this colouration is balanced by an anchoring in objective textual interpretation. Personal, subjective meaning is a dialectical moment in the hermeneutic circle. It involves saying goodbye to pretensions of absolute truth.

Ricoeur: " When it comes to absolute knowledge and hermeneutics, one must make a choice."

(1981c, p. 193)

If we now put the objective text comprehension in parentheses, can the subjective element, appropriation, shed light on the empathy problem? What does it mean to acquire a text? According to Ricoeur, *it is opening up to the world the text conveys.* The text is about *something.* It refers to a (imaginary) world. Through this text, this world speaks to me. It concerns me in the sense that it concerns my life. And it concerns me across historical eras. I can read Homer's Iliad in a textually critical (literary scientific) way, but if I remain *untouched* by the text, my interpretations become sterile. When I immerse myself in the text, I *immerse myself* in a world where I become involved in stories that describe human destinies and existential dilemmas. I can live with it in an intense way, the lyrics can concern me enormously, and I can cry deeply over tragedies that befall characters that I care about.

Let me illustrate with a personal example. I recently read the book *The Postman and Pablo Neruda* by A. Skármeta (filmed in 1997 under the same title). The story of this poor fisherman's son who, as a postman grasps the importance of metaphor, and who becomes the confidant of the poet Pablo Neruda, is (to me) deeply moving. If we now equate empathy and "Einfühlung", the question is this: Do I immerse myself differently in the postman (as a literary figure) than in the living patients I have? I will answer no. Empathy is not a question of immediate access (possibly via introspection) to the mental life of one (concrete) other. *Empathy is opening oneself to the content, the story, the existential dilemmas, the emotions in what the other is talking about, whether the other is expressing him/herself in speech or through writing. Empathy is acquiring this content, i.e., being touched by it in the sense that it also concerns me.* The art of psychotherapy consists of allowing oneself to be touched in this way, but not carried away. It is to engage in a hermeneutic circle in which empathy is included as a dialectical moment in a reflective move that, incidentally, makes use of my entire arsenal of clinical experience and theoretical knowledge (explanatory principles) about the self and the pathologies of the self.

The most important difference between my relationship with the postman and my patients is that I have the opportunity in practice to provide CARE to the patients. When we use the adverbial form and talk about empathic, that I act empathic towards my patients, there is empathy in the above sense of appropriation and compassion *combined with care.* The caring becomes linked to *acting.* Listening, as an act in itself, can be perceived as caring and sooner or later I, in the role of a therapist, will respond by *speech acts.* The term speech acts refers to Austin's (1962) and Searle (1969) speech act theories ("how to do things with words"). When we say something, we often want to do something at the same time. For example, when saying "I promise", I am simultaneously performing an act (making the promise) as I pronounce the sentence. Psychotherapy is full of speech acts, from therapists as well as patients. *Speech acts characterized by care and influenced by appropriation and compassion, are what we characterize as empathic.*

Kohut went to great lengths to argue that empathy itself had a curative effect. Today, we'll say yes, it is confirmed by empirical research as an important, although "unspecific" ingredient of psychotherapy (Wampole & Imel, 2015). And in particular, if empathy is accompanied by *a corrective emotional experience*. However, from the perspective of the psychology of the self, today we will emphasize even stronger the "cognitive" element of empathy, i.e., that of being thought about by another (in an empathic way), i.e., of "being minded" in the sense of Peter Fonagy and colleagues (2002). Being minded implies being understood by words, concepts, and narratives that our culture has produced (the detour of the world). We are talking about highly complex mental operations. The controversial part of it concerns our theories of what is the nature of man's motivational forces. Kohut held the view that the nature of these forces should be understood from within the theory and practice of psychoanalysis, with empathy as the foundational method. However, this position sediments the separation of understanding from explanation, the humanities versus the natural sciences, which we have explored in previous chapters.

The losers in this plot, are the *forces* of the mind. Kohut vividly portrayed the despair of not being properly understood and responded to, but he did not *explain* where this despair came from. It is at this juncture that a modernized theory of self psychology should interpolate the empirical knowledge of primary emotions. After all, Freud was right in his assertion that there is something in the brain/mind that urges for discharge. However, this is not the drives of Thanatos and Eros. The case is that primary emotions come with an innate programme for actions. They are not only feelings. Thus, inhibited emotions contain inhibited actions, which generates FEAR in their own right. Leigh McCullough and colleagues (2008) were right. There develops an "affect fobia". We are not so much afraid of phenomena in the outer world, as we are of own disavowed emotions becoming known to others as well as to ourselves. From the beginning, primary emotions and attachment needs are there to be understood as obscure texts with obscure claims within us that must be interpreted (and contained) by others to become manageable. There will always be unmentalized emotional experiences that can linger in us as aching wounds that sooner or later can flare up as what we call symptoms. Unmentalized emotions will remain as something alien in us, something that arouses discomfort, something we want to get rid of. In the core self, in my same-ness, there is something that the reflective self, like *ipse*, does not understand or will not accept, which therefore cannot become part of a (conciliatory) narrative about myself (Karterud, 2022). And the more alien I am to myself, the more alien I will be to similar emotional experiences in others. *Psychotherapy is about opening up an (empathic) dialogue with "the stranger" in oneself and with what is perceived as alien in others.* Group analysis is a great medium for this. The group offers unexpected but demanding opportunities. There will be a permanent temptation to let the alien remain an alien, deny it, ostracize it, locate it in others, etc.

Kohut (1971) developed a theory where the self had some basic needs, so-called *self-object needs*, that had to be satisfied to a reasonable degree for the self to develop properly. He spoke of the tripolar self, of 1) basic needs for mirroring; of 2) need for closeness to an idealized other; and of 3) the need for someone who is equal to oneself ("twin," "alter ego"). Especially mirroring and idealizing needs, but also twinship needs, are something we see abundantly in therapeutic groups. Nevertheless, the theory of the tripolar self has limited explanatory power. Today, we would say that the self's basic needs must be supplemented with the ability to own its own emotions, to be taken care of, and to be helped to develop the ability to think about themselves and others (mentalization).

What Kohut called mirroring is primarily about the primary emotion SEEKING. Mirroring is an affirmation of the desire to explore the world. An affirmative other who responds to "look what I found," "isn't this great," "look what I can do" provides an experience of ME and of myself as an ACTOR; it is recognition in the deepest sense of the word. I/ME become recognized as a (little) person that counts in the world. Many patients are deficiently mirrored. In psychotherapy, this need will be reawakened. In Kohut's terminology, then, we are talking about *mirroring self-object transference*. In group analysis, this is expressed in abundance, as evidenced by numerous vignettes in the last part of the book.

The self comes with a readiness for FEAR and FEAR can be overwhelming. That's why we have attachment figures that help to install mechanisms for fear alleviation. The self needs to be calmed down and comforted.

The self also comes with a sometimes crippling SEPARATION ANXIETY and has a strong need to be included in the herd again.

The self needs to develop the innate CARE ability that enables one to care for and love others.

Kohut has placed love and the regulation of fear and separation anxiety under the umbrella of idealizing self-object needs. They are brought to life in psychotherapy as *idealizing self-object transference*. We need someone who can heal our wounds and sorrows, who we can look up to and admire and who we feel close to.

The self comes with a readiness for RAGE to defend itself and fight for own survival needs and desired mating. The person needs to learn to civilize his/her anger. In worst case it turns into narcissistic rage, envy, violence, revenge, and destruction.

The self comes with a readiness for SEXUAL LUST. When this explodes during puberty, one needs good mentalizing abilities to be able to handle it in constructive ways through the jungle of pubertal politics.

And the self comes with the need to PLAY with like-minded others. PLAY civilizes RAGE by, for example, rough and tumble play. Among *Homo sapiens* it is most crucial for the ability to play with words and concepts as a transition from psychic equivalence to representational thinking (Fonagy et al., 2002). Kohut labelled this as alter ego self-object function.

Very condensed, then, modern form self psychology can be conceptualized like the following, when informed by hermeneutics, primary emotions, attachment and mentalization:

1 The self is an overarching concept. It is not a content of a psychic apparatus (for example, the sum total of self-representations).
2 The self is centre for experiences of continuity in time and space, of initiative, of ownership to thoughts and feelings, included feelings of connectedness to humanity.
3 The self is not identical to itself; it is a relation.
4 The core process of the self is a dialectic interplay between the core self and the self-reflective self whereby the core self (nature) and experiences of the world become mentalized.
5 The "engine" of the self is the emotional driving forces that expresses itself through the core self.
6 These emotional driving forces must be mentalized for the person to be able to relate to himself and thus master life in a self-reflective (spiritualized, and minded/minding) society. This need for being mentalized becomes a driving force in itself.
7 The self needs caring (empathic) and meaning-making others (a wide range of nourishing self-object functions) to develop optimally. The self needs above all to be *recognized* within an attachment relationship.
8 The term self-object refers to phenomena in the external world that contribute to the development, maintenance, and repair of the self. A self-object can be a (significant) person, a tradition of ideas (e.g., Christianity), a group (e.g., the girlfriend club), a pet or a (significant) thing (e.g., the image of a loved one). The term self-object does not refer to the person (or thing) itself, but to the aspect of that person that is significant to the person in question. One therefore speaks of self-object functions.
9 The most important difference between an object and a self-object is that an object is something I direct my interest towards, whereas a self-object is something I expect something from.
10 Metaphorically, one might say with Kohut that the nascent self has a genetically determined "expectation" that self-objects exist, like the "expectation" of the lungs that the air is full of oxygen.
11 Self-object needs are not something that disappears at a mature age. Man has self-object needs from the cradle to the grave. However, the quality of these needs will change. Infantile self-object needs are compelling while mature needs are to be endured. Throughout life, "man needs friends".
12 Self-object needs arise from the semi-stable nature of the self. Man needs support to exist in a mentalized (spiritual) world. Kohut limited himself

to three main modes: *mirroring self-object needs* which are needs to be seen, recognized (Hegel!), valued, encouraged, appreciated, praised, and the like. *Idealizing self-object needs* that are needs to feel cared for, being held, being part of, and protected by an idealized other (attachment). *Alter ego (twin-ship) self-object needs* that are needs to feel affirmed by the experience of equality with another being in thinking, judgement, behaviour, and emotional life.

13 In addition, the self needs help to mentalize fear, anger and sexuality and the more social emotions like shame and guilt.

14 When development has taken place optimally, the motivational forces of the self will be attuned to and support each other. The self is coherent, robust, harmonious (tuned), energetic and vital. This person has well-defined aspirations, and these ambitions are well integrated with ideals that respect the basic needs of others and themselves. The person has adequate skills and abilities to realize his/her ambitions and to enjoy the results. And, above all, the person has capacity for intimacy and an ability to acquire, hold on to and develop a nurturing self-object environment. These abilities are well described as the highest level of personality functioning in DSM-5 (2013).

15 When development has gone badly, the self suffers structural deficits. There develop defensive and compensatory self-structures to protect the self and, if possible, compensate for it's lack. The faulty developed self has archaic self-object needs (e.g., extreme needs for persistent mirroring or extreme needs to deal with overwhelming separation anxiety) and a self-structure characterized by inner conflicts, disharmony, poor coherence, vulnerability to fragmentation, pressure from unmentalized emotional experiences, and alternation of vitality and energy. This structural weakness of the self, combined with defensive self-structures leads to interpersonal problems which in turn will undermine the fulfillment of the person's general self-object needs. The person has difficulties in realizing his/her own projects and has a reduced ability to acquire, maintain and develop a nurturing self-object environment and at the same time difficulties with relating to these deficits (impaired mentalization ability). The capacity for co-operation with others and for intimacy will suffer. These deficiencies are of a dimensional nature, and they are well described in the level of personality functioning scale of DSM-5 (2013).

16 In psychotherapy, the past will be reproduced through basically two different types of transferences. One is the *repetitive dimension of transference*, where previous defensive and compensatory patterns appear vis-à-vis the therapist (e.g., the therapist is met with great scepticism). The second type is *self-object transference*. Self-object transference means that archaic self-object needs are brought to life and manifest themselves towards the therapist. Through archaic self-object need reactivation, the self tries to resume the developmental process that was stopped in

childhood and adolescence. The key to deeper personality change goes through dealing with such archaic self-object needs.

17   Since stalled development is ultimately about primary self-object failures that are deeply buried in the self's "history book," the activation of archaic self-object needs are accompanied by a *fear of retraumatization*. Such fear manifests itself as resistance to self-object transferences. The fear is also fuelled by a deep shame at harbouring deep-seated infantile needs.

18   Intense self-object needs directed at the therapist may be experienced by the therapist as frightening by virtue of their demanding character and can easily activate defensive countertransference reactions. Intense idealization, for example, may activate the therapist's own grandiose self, which may well contain archaic remnants of desires for greatness and exhibitionism. Hearing that you are outstanding and "certainly the best therapist in the country" is not always easy to endure and can easily give birth to so-called "reality confrontation".

19   Intense self-object needs and signaling potentially intense reactions (e.g., suicide intentions) in the event of new disappointments can make therapists go to great lengths. Archaic self-object needs have something absolutist about them which even the best therapist will fail to live up to. *Within the psychotherapeutic situation, self-object failures are inevitable.* It is inevitable that the therapist offers a limited number of hours a week, takes vacations, goes to congresses and meetings, occasionally is sick, sometimes being poorly aware, forgets things, misunderstands, makes bad interpretations and reacts with countertransference. As long as self-object failures are of moderate magnitude and not outright violations that the therapist insists on the justification of, such failures are among the most important elements of the therapeutic process. Through exploring what meaning therapeutic failures acquire for the patient, how they are understood, what they remind of past experiences, what defensive or compensatory mechanisms they activate (withdrawal, indifference, revenge, arrogance, increased symptom levels, etc.) and what it takes for a trusting dialogue to resume (forgiveness!), significant pieces of therapeutic work are done. Self-understanding increases in several directions: what needs one has in relation to other people, one's vulnerability, one's emotional reactions and defensive self-delimitations, and one's own responsibility to do something different and not only repeat old dysfunctional patterns, but to resume an interrupted dialogue. The accusation that self psychology "places all the blame on the parents" is thus misleading. The patient is responsible for maintaining destructive patterns of interaction in his/her adult life. *But for this responsibility to become real, it must be experienced in a situation where there also is a real choice.* It is the therapist's responsibility to bring the patient to such situations of awareness. Patterns need to be objectified to be reflected in the therapeutic dialogue. *In*

Ricoeur's terminology, this involves turning idem into ipse, that is, turning what appears to be nature (fixed character traits, idem) into something that can be changed (selected, ipse).

20 To some degree Kohut overemphasized the need for self-objects. There are good reasons to follow Ricoeur in his argument that the self is constituted not only by the other's being as a self-object (recognition), but also by other aspects of the other, aspects that concern the other as *someone other than oneself*, as sheer otherness. The other as a self-object is notably not perceived as essentially different from the self. That was one of Kohut's most important discoveries. *The other as a self-object is experienced largely as part of oneself.* Ricoeur brings balance into the account when he argues that the self is constituted *both* by affirmation and *by the other as a radically different perspective on the world and as another needy self.* Without this polarity, theory and therapy risk stalling and decaying into a one-sided pursuit of fulfilling archaic self-object needs as a kind of echo-chamber.

The points above are written in a theoretical language. How does this feel, "from within"? If we let a borderline patient speak, it will sound something like this:

"How I am? That's part of the problem, I'm so unstable. Soon I am like this, and soon I am like that. I'm changing so fast. I can be high up and way down several times a day" (deficient *idem* identity).

"Who am I? What do you mean by that question? If you can trust me? Only partially, although it is important for me to keep my word. But when I change so quickly, everything can become meaningless, and then I find no reason to show up. I often disappoint others, but also myself. I can't fulfil my plans and projects. I lose interest. Yes, they're changing, too, so I don't really know what to bet on. So it is with relationships, too. I'm bisexual and don't really know if I'm predominantly heterosexual or gay. That makes it hard to bet on someone and commit. I don't really know who I am" (deficient *ipse* identity).

"If I can tell my life story? I can, but I think it's a little disjointed, and when I tell it, I go emotional. It's dramatic, and I still live inside it, so to speak. I warn you; I have little distance from it. Besides, there's a lot that's gone. I remember absolutely nothing before school age and actually just fragments up to the age of ten" (deficient narrative identity).

"What will be the good life for me? I certainly don't know. Lots of money, vacation, sun and summer, maybe. No, I'm kidding. I don't really know because I haven't actually decided what I'm going to become. It can sound crazy when you're thirty. But that's actually the case.» (deficient projected future).

"A good life with and for others? With and for others? That is precisely the core problem. Living with others. It always breaks down after some time. We may have a great time to begin with. This applies to both girlfriends and work colleagues. But then something happens. I don't know what. It starts off quite

hot, but then we end up almost as enemies. I've been told I'm too self-absorbed. There may well be something in it. I'm often tired like hell and need something, I don't know what, to recover. Often I don't have much energy for others.» (deficient caring capacity).

"Living in a just society? Fair society? I never thought about that. Don't think that's possible. People are so greedy and envious and think only of themselves. Power-hungry people will always exploit others." (deficient group identity).

These existential dilemmas in our borderline patient can largely be understood through hermeneutics, but such understanding does not lead to any radical self-development. The person in question must be understood by *another real person* who concretizes the understanding of everyday events and interpersonal encounters through explorative, challenging, and affirmative dialogues. This person must be empathic, caring, accessible, reliable, and robust, i.e., be fit to serve as a self-object over a longer period of time. But the person concerned must also represent otherness in the sense of representing other perspectives on the world (theoretically and personally) and another needy self. It is through other perspectives on the world that the dialogue comes about, and it is the therapist's being as another needy self that sets necessary limits for the therapeutic relationship (Karterud, 2022). Psychotherapy takes place in a dialogic space where self, self-object needs, and otherness constitute the most important co-ordinates. Later we will see how this manifests itself in group analysis.

A group mind or a group self?

What relevance does hermeneutics have for the group as a whole?

Most people agree that for social systems "the sum is more than adding the parts", and that there is an over-individual level that allows us to talk about the family, the group, the company, the people, the nation, the international community, etc. But what does this over-individual level consist of? It's hard to grasp. No wonder, then, that many resorts to religious explanations: "We struggle in our individual delusions, but it is ultimately God who holds us together, who has a plan for it all." The idea of a *superindividual thinking being* is also found in non-religious explanatory models. We recall that Hegel spoke of *the world spirit* as a self-reflective being, independent of individual actors within a given culture or historical epoch. In part 1 of this book, we discussed shortly the notion of a *"group mind"*. The concept is a legacy of romanticism's notions of a *folk soul*. This idea of an animated collectivity was exploited by the Nazi ideology of "das (deutsche) Volk" and this and later abuses related to totalitarian exploitation and glorification of ethnic identity, brought the idea of animated collectivity into further discredit. Within the social sciences we find the thesis of *methodological individualism* as a reaction to collectivist explanatory principles. Methodological individualism claims that (social) actions can only be attributed to individual actors. When we say and write that *The Times* is sceptical about the government's interest rate policy, this refers to specific articles written by specific individuals where this scepticism is expressed. And even un-signed editorials are written by somebody. The danger of collectivism is that it opens for mythical, romantic, irrational, and unscientific explanatory principles and can thus be misused by totalitarian rulers. The idea of individualism, on the other hand, risks becoming too simple, too rational, and blind to collective contexts. Recall Margaret Thatcher: "There is no such thing as a society".

Foulkes' concept of matrix attempted to mediate between collectivism and individualism. Foulkes was unclear whether the matrix was animated in the sense that it contained an independent group "mind." He expressed more clearly that matrix should be understood as the conscious and unconscious communicative network that bound group members together and influenced them to such an extent that concepts such as "collective" and "individual" ceased to be opposites. *However, a communicative network lacks intentions.* So, there must be something more there. Group analysts do not say "the matrix has a problem, and it tries to get rid of that problem by isolating patient x and scapegoating patient y." No, they say that "the group has a problem ... The group is trying to get rid of ... The group flees from ... etc." Can one refer to the group in this way, i.e., the group as an actor without implying the group as animated being? This is an unsolved problem in the group literature. In theory, most therapists reject the idea of the group as a superordinated minded being, but in practice many speak as if this was a reality. Or is it just metaphorical speech, i.e., that the therapist by "the group" means *you*? It is you, Hans, Eve, Irene, etc. who have a problem that you are trying to solve in certain ways. However, if one clarifies it in this way, one has not solved the problem. One has just weakened it and changed it and turned it into individual problems (for Hans, Eva, Irene, etc.). However, the case does not concern Hans, Eva and Irene as separate individuals. It is Hans, Eva and Irene *qua group members* who have the problem in question. And thus, the problem resurfaces as a group problem, as a problem for *something* that exists on a different level than the individuals. And what is this something?

The group literature has lacked appropriate concepts for this something. The paradox is that most therapists in our time will reject notions of a group spirit, or a group mind, but nevertheless will accept characteristics such as an aggressive group, a vindictive group, a passive group, etc. What concepts can then preserve this collective aspect without falling into an over-individual animated trench?

In the 1970s Kohut struggled to conceptualize collective human phenomena. Kohut himself was not engaged, even not very sympathetic to group therapy. He was driven by a general interest of knowledge, by own personal and frightening experiences of group dynamics in professional contexts and by the relationship between people and leaders in critical situations such as during World War II. His main interest was *historical* group processes. History rolls forward, owing to collective forces. And these are not chaotic and random. They are organized and have their structure and dynamics. Kohut probably first used the term *group self* in the article *On Courage*, which he wrote around 1970 but which was first published in 1985. The term first appeared in published form in 1976 in the article *Creativeness, Charisma, Group Psychology*. The theme was the relationship between Freud and the psychoanalytic movement.

Kohut introduced it as follows:

> *"It will have become obvious to those who are familiar with my recent work that I am suggesting, as a potentially fruitful approach to a complex problem, that we posit the existence of a certain psychological configuration with regard to the group—let us call it the 'group self'—which is analogous to the self of the individual. We are then I a position to observe the group self as it is formed, as it is held together, as it oscillates between fragmentation and reintegration, as it shows regressive behavior when it moves toward fragmentation, etc. – all in analogy to phenomena of individual psychology to which we have comparatively easy access in the clinical (psychoanalytic) situation."*

(1976/1985, p. 206)

And:

> *"The psychoanalytic concept of a self, however - whether it refers to the self of an individual or to the self of a person as a member of a group or, as a 'group self', to the self of a stable association of people – concerns a structure that dips into the deepest reaches of the psyche. Indeed, I have become convinced that the pattern of an unconscious nuclear self (the central unconscious ambitions of the grandiose self and the central unconscious values of the internalized idealized parent imago) is of crucial importance with regard to the overriding sense of fulfillment or failure that characterizes a person's outlook on his life, to some extent independent of the presence or absence of neurotic conflict, suffering, symptom, or inhibitions. And I am now suggesting that these considerations concerning the influence of the basic unconscious narcissistic configurations in individual existence are valid also with regard to the life of a group, i.e., the basic patterns a nuclear group-self (the group's central ambitions and ideals) not only count for the continuity and cohesion of the group, but also determine its most important actions."*

(ibid, p. 206)

Is the group self the term that best enables reflections on the group as a living community without decaying into animating the group? What does that mean? The group self in Kohut's text refers to a "stable union of people". What we are talking about are *organized* groups and not a chance meeting between several people. The group self refers to the fact that at a given time in history, a certain number of people agreed to establish a group, i.e., to work together to realize certain ambitions and ideals. *The group self refers to the project that the group embodies.* This project is of an over-individual nature. But it does not think for itself. However, it makes specific demands on the participants, and these requirements are enacted by people in different group roles who are more or less identified with the basic project of the group self.

In the following, I will discuss the concept somewhat in depth. As the reader will notice, I accept the term and will apply it to historical and clinical analyses, but not without doubt and uncertainty. Maybe it's a whole new term (theory) we need? It could be. My choice has been to accept the concept of group self because it seems useful. It clarifies some problems, but at the same time raises new ones. It represents no definitive solution to the individual-group problem. Such a "solution" does not exist.

The hermeneutics of the group self

It should be emphasized that in this chapter I no longer explicate Ricoeur's reasoning but apply his concepts in a way to which he might have some objections. For Ricoeur, the self is linked to "the acting and suffering individual", but at the same time not *limited* to the individual as a content in the brain or in a psychic apparatus, as the other ("friends") is a necessary prerequisite for its creation and maintenance. In the case of groups ("institutions"), he speaks of "collective identities", but argues against the idea that social units have a separate existence that requires a separate ontology. Ricoeur seeks a stance between methodological individualism and collectivism and believes in finding it in a concept of the institution (group) as a *system* of distribution (of roles, rewards, punishments, etc. based on thoughts about equality and justice). As a system, the group is something more than the individuals and their interpersonal relationships, but at the same time not radically different as the system only exists as long as the individuals participate in it.

The group as a distributary system is too limiting for our purposes. It is useful for thinking about basic notions of equality and justice, notions that are not at all meaningless to group psychology, but perhaps more important to sociology, law, political science, and moral philosophy. For group psychology, it's more important to pursue the idea of *collective identity*. With collective identity, we are confronted with the personal pronoun we. We in our family, we at work, we - the team, we Norwegians, we Europeans, etc.

Ricoeur discusses the hermeneutics of the self with reference to the personal pronouns I, you, he, she, and everyone, but avoids the *we/ourselves.* Why? One possible answer is that firstly the hermeneutics of the individual self had to be formulated and discussed. Secondly, this could be a platform to develop the hermeneutics of collectivity.

And the problems of collective phenomena are large. They touch on fundamental legal and moral principles of social organizations. Within the Western modes of society, questions of responsibility and guilt are ultimately linked to the individual. In the event that a mob has maimed a victim, prosecutors will search for the person or persons responsible for the decisive beatings. The agitated group mood is, at best, a mitigating circumstance. But the reality is often complex: "It wasn't me. I was driven to participate. I was absolutely desperate. I had been sexually abused. At home, it was complete chaos. It was the guys in the gang who planned the retaliation." If it turns out that "planned" implied something more than a spontaneous action of an agitated mob, something deliberate and purposeful, the court would take that into consideration. Responsibility and blame are linked to decisive actions of both a planning and executive nature. But somewhere the court must set a line. Where? Are cheerleaders that stir up a mob to be held accountable? Is Donald Trump guilty in the case of storming the American Congress in 2021? Any "true" definition of accountability is impossible. In cases of group actions, the court cannot avoid discretionary deliberations but are nevertheless obliged to convict according to the rule of law. Either one is an accomplice and deserves punishment, or one is not. Either one is convicted, or one is acquitted.

But similar principles cannot be applied to group psychology. Group psychology must open itself to a field of collective existence in which other disciplines are forced to set limits, i.e., to a field where it is hardly possible to distinguish between individual and group, between individual and collective identity, between individual and collective responsibility. The individual self has the ability to *initiate* actions that can trigger a chain of events in the world as a consequence. The problem peaks when we are faced with concerted actions. Not when *I* do something, but when *we do something together.*

This brings us back to fundamental guiding questions in the hermeneutics of the self. We must return repeatedly to the following question, Ricoeur emphasizes: Who speaks? Who acts? Who tells his story? Who is the moral subject? What status, then, do *we* have in response to these questions? We're talking. We act. We tell our story. We take responsibility! To whom are *we* then referring? We refer to *ourselves.* Is this "ourselves" fundamentally different from "myself"?

When I talk about a group, I'm talking about this. We, unlike I, you, he, she, and anybody, refer to something common, something that unites us. What makes a group a group? All group theorists try to answer this fundamental question. Freud (1921) answered it as follows: *A group is constituted by the members taking the leader as their common ego ideal and thereby identify with each other.* My answer is different: *The group self is constituted by its members' shared ambition to realize a common project.* The concept of project includes Kohut's concepts of ambition and ideals. Groups want something. There is something to be realized, and the ambitions are guided by certain ideals. The leadership question, in my opinion, is secondary to the question of ambition and ideals. The question of leadership arises when the project is to be implemented. We face group psychology with its complicated dynamics when we concretely begin to interact, when we must organize ourselves, differentiate ourselves, agree on the division of roles, examine our resources and through this slowly begin to sense what we have actually embarked upon.

Through such an incipient realization of the group's project, the group self is becoming concretized. The members do identify themselves with the project in various ways and assume more or less significant roles. The project become personified and will thus be invested with a variety of possible meanings of a conscious and unconscious nature for the individual. For some, the group project might become an individual life project. Where, then, is the line between the individual self and the group self? It is impossible to define it sharply. The individual self and the group self are merged in some ways. For a peripheral member, the boundary may be easier to define. The person stops by for a shorter period of time and occupies a very limited role before he/she hops off and join another group. But he/she will still be involved in some concerted action.

The evolved group self is now to be understood as the concrete actualization of the group's ambitions, ideals, and resources, being expressed in an experience and realization of a purposeful and organized co-operative endeavour. It may be more or less successful, and we might talk about a well-consolidated group self versus a fragmented group self, about a vital group self or an exhausted group self. When we say that the group self wants something, we are not referring to an independent-minded being, a group spirit, but to the aspirations and ideals laid down in the project and *embodied by the group's advocates.* The realization of these ambitions and ideals demands something from the members. And these ambitions and ideals have not been taken out of the air. They refer to a tradition, and we might label it a *tradition of discourse.* If I, along with a bunch of others, would like to start a new football team that has high ambitions, we do not start with a clean slate. We must adhere to established football rules, rules for league and cup football, to financial agreements, to the existing football culture, to the Norwegian Football Association with all its advantages and shortcomings and power struggles, to UEFA, etc. A formidable number of premises have already been set. We literally must follow the rules of the game. We must submit to a discourse of football that plays with us as much as we play with it.

This discourse tradition is above the individual and interpersonal relationships. It does indeed depend on individual actors, but it cannot be reduced to them. *Thus, the concretized group self actualizes a tradition of discourse.* When we are going to realize a group project, it may come as a surprise to us that what we have set out to realize is pregnant with implicit requirements that we had no idea about beforehand. The reason why I may now repeat myself and be perceived as boring is the following: A group analytical group is one of the most difficult group projects you can start. The group's project is therapy (self-understanding and self-development) of the individual through the group process. With the concepts of therapy – self-understanding – self-development – individual – group – group processes – one situates oneself as a therapist in an extremely complicated discourse tradition. One opens for a logic and a dynamic one had hardly imagined beforehand. Gradually, one realizes that not only eight difficult individual patients demand something of one, but that something else, something difficult to define, makes its claim to one, a claim that comes partly from oneself, partly from colleagues in the supervision group, from the supervisor, from the theory teacher, from group analytical texts, a requirement to realize a particular discourse, i.e., to realize the basic ambitions and ideals of group analysis (Karterud, 2011).

However, before we move forward in a clinical direction, let me briefly discuss the group self by the same model that Ricoeur uses for the individual self. I take the therapeutic group as a starting point:

What *occurrence in the world* are we referring to when we talk about the group? Sure, we're referring to the physical nature of the group which is nine people (including the therapist) sitting in the same room. (We immediately note a significant difference if we compare it to people. A person has *a* body to which the self is attached. A group has many bodies.)

It is to this physical "object," nine people in a circle, that we *attribute* a group self.

The group has *numerical identity.* Let's call this group as Group 1, as opposed to other groups that I run (Groups 2 and 3).

The group has *qualitative identity.* It is similar in some ways to other analytic groups, but clearly different from a football team as a group.

The group has *uninterrupted identity.* I would say it's the same group, i.e., Group 1, although none of the members who started it are members anymore. Some of them are remembered by someone, but that is no prerequisite. I still write my minutes in a protocol labelled Group 1.

The group has an *idem identity.* I can rightfully describe the group with the same type of adjectives as I describe people. The group is warm, caring, cautious, considerate, a little leader-dependent and aggression-inhibited. Or it may possess other characteristics.

But does the group have *ipse identity* ("we-ness")? Can the group promise something *qua* group? Can the group keep its word? Can it be true to its ideals? To answer these questions, we must take the detour about the group's existence. Most people will agree on the group's existence when one can point to it as a physical object: "There it is. As you can see, the group now has a meeting." But does the group exist when its members have left? *It obviously does not exist as a complex physical object anymore which can be identified in time and space, but I would argue that it exists as a group self.* It exists as a mental representation in each participant. It still demands something from its members. As a mental representation, it is still present and cannot be clearly distinguished from the personal self. Through its presence, individuals process their experiences between each group meeting. The same goes for the group analyst who writes minutes between each session and contemplate the dynamics. What makes the group self a reality and not *just* a fantasy or mental representation? The group exists in the sense that *the group self is a reality as long as the members of the group keep their promise to the group.* And this applies to all organized groups, to families, school classes, businesses, and nations. The group as a reality is contingent upon (at least some of) its members do show up when they are called upon. By showing up, you confirm your loyalty to the promise you once made about membership in the group. This promise is a commitment in relation to the ambitions, values, and norms that the group stands for. *Through the group members' ipseity (the wish to live together and declaring loyalty), the group self is constituted as the shared project that binds the group members together.*

The main difference between a group and a person is that the group has no body, and thus no brain as a means of thinking and no limbs to initiate actions. Can we then speak of a group self in the same sense as we have done previously, in terms of "power to act", "capacity for self reflection" and "keeping one's word"? No, not in the same sense. That would be animating the group. But we can talk about the group self in a *comparable sense.* Language gives us ample opportunity for it. Are we not saying that "the White House has decided" and that "the Church keeps its promise"? Nevertheless, in accordance with methodological individualism, there are reasons to maintain that concrete actions that require a brain and a body are performed by individuals. However, these individual actions are conditioned by a collective and *performed on behalf of the collective.* Since the group self lacks brain and body, it must express itself through *advocates.* Permanent advocates, who perform structural functions for the group self, assume significant *role positions.*

But can't we now say that the difference between person and group is not one body versus no body, but one body versus many bodies? When the group separates as a physical object, it does not cease to exist as a physical object, but it undergoes a temporary fragmentation. A whole becomes nine separate parts and then heals again next week. What is the group's spokesman doing with his body vis-à-vis the group, if not to lend it? *By acting as the group's spokesman, I let the group self speak through me.* In this way it is legitimate to say that the group acts, that it is able to keep its promise, etc. In this sense, we can talk about the *ipse* identity of the group without resorting to an assumption of a separate spiritual existence.

The group's *narrative identity* causes us less trouble. By analogy with the individual, the group's history as a narrative mediates between its *idem* and *ipse* identity. We can describe the group's history of creation, what project it has set out to realize, how the character of the group is shaped through negotiations (cf. Dorothy Whitaker's theory of group negotiations and group norms, Whitaker & Lieberman, 1964), and how its current status is to be understood as a dialectic between its character (as limitation and possibilities) and the requirements arising from the nature of the project.

The concepts of matrix, the social unconscious, and the group self

The concepts of matrix, the social unconscious and the group self are overlapping, partly complementary and partly competing concepts. They try to grasp much of the same thing, what human collectivities consist of. By the concept of foundation matrix Foulkes (1973) referred to the conditions that all humans share *qua* being an exemplar of the *Homo sapiens* species, such as the abilities to think, to communicate, being able to relate to other fellow beings, to co-operate, sharing a common language, etc. When people interact in smaller and larger groups, these abilities are there "silently" in the background. Foulkes described it as a *"pre-existing, relatively static part"* of a general overarching matrix, as *"a firm pre-existing community or communion"* (cited in Hopper & Weinberg, 2017, p. 13). In any given group, the foundation matrix will merge with the more specialized dynamic matrix which concretize the very nature of that group, for example, if it is a scientific committee, a cult, a school class, or a therapeutic group. Hopper and Weinberg (2017) include in the foundation matrix the basic conditions that coin large collective projects such as nations, civilizations, and religions. The matrix refers to a certain structure that defines a particular group. Most groups are not chaotic. They are structured through a web of established communicational patterns. In the depth of the group, we will find more or less hidden norms and rules which may be loaded with contradicting emotions. Understood in this way, there is no contradiction between the concept of matrix and the group self. Matrix will refer to the structure of the group self in the same way as personality refers to the structure of the individual self. This structure is not a thing, it is a dynamic system of biological and mental forces. As for the individual personality, the dynamism of the (group) matrix is mainly unconscious. By that way, the world might go around rather smoothly. We do not need to think that much. We just do it, what is expected from us in the diverse group roles which we occupy. However, when we do something "wrong" we will encounter the boundaries of the system and which (unconscious) forces that defines and protect the system.

Earl Hopper has been the leading authority for the concept of the social unconscious through a series of articles, books, and conferences (Hopper, 2003, Hopper & Weinberg, 2011, 2016, 2017). His efforts have expanded group analytic theory considerably. Yes, there are massive unconscious processes at work in groups. Hopper's work illustrates the complexity of the group self. When we emphasize the group as a common "project", the concept may seem rather bleak and cognitive. However, it is necessary to have in mind the *core self aspect* of the group self, which consists of the emotional power that group members bring with them and which are activated in the group. Of course, group members are not solely "project managers". They are living beings who come with their entrustment and enthusiasm but also with their rage, envy, rivalry, jealousy, thwarted needs for revenge, shame, guilt feelings, as well as their love, empathy, care, and playfulness. Without their emotional involvement (and entanglement) their reasons for group co-operation would turn out to be empty words. The phenomenology of this emotional involvement in therapeutic groups will be explored in the last part of the book.

However, the concept of the social unconscious is not unproblematic. Firstly, it needs a wider concept of the group self to be meaningful. The social unconscious is after all an unconsciousness of something. Groups are organized ways of co-operation, and it is these co-operative efforts that are suffused by unconscious mental forces. The question is if we should rather speak about *unconscious group processes*, rather than *the* social unconscious, as a noun. Is it, strictly speaking, meaningful to say that, for example, the Catholic Church *has* an unconscious? Is it not more appropriate to say that unconscious group processes are operative within the Catholic Church, for example, related to the denial of massive sexual abuses?

An asset of the discourse on the social unconscious is its emphasis on pathological aspects of collective systems, about unprocessed collective crimes and traumas and the effects upon the citizens. To a lesser extent, one has been concerned with the ordinary "fabric of society".

National identity is a phenomenon we can situate at the intersection of the foundation matrix and the dynamic matrix, loaded with unconscious signifiers. However, group analysis has had relatively little to say about phenomena like national identity. The concept of the group self makes it clearer: National identity is maintained by myriads of actions and events. Children and youth learn about it in school, they learn the history of the nation and are taken to the celebration of national markers (in Norway, 17 May), they learn the language of the nation, what separates us from them, and flock to the television sets as "our sports heroes" fight the others. The national elite makes sure that the people participate in such national celebrations. Money is allocated to local orchestras, events are widely covered in the media, leaders at all levels engage by embellished dignity and speeches are held in which the people are admonished not to forget the crucial moments in the history of the nation. For Norway it was the great Viking era, the following four-hundred years of submission and domination by the Danes, it was the fathers of the Constitution of 1814, the secession from Sweden in 1905, the role of national intellectuals like Henrik Ibsen, the unity in the war against the Germans during 1940–45. And above all, it is the significance of the Constitution. The Constitution is the text that holds Norwegians together as a nation. It says how we should fundamentally align ourselves in this country, what is us. It says that Norway is a free and indivisible kingdom based on the ideas of a liberal democracy and that "freedom of speech should take place."

The main difference between the concepts of matrix and group self is that the group self is invested with values and meaning, while matrix refers to more impersonal forces. It might be illustrated by way of the war in Ukraine after February 2022, a war that had an enormous impact on all of Europe and in many ways became a game-changer. It turned out that the differences between the Ukrainian and the Russian forces were formidable in terms of motivation. Ukrainian soldiers were fighting for their families, friends, shared values, and a sense of national identity that were supported by the entire West. Ukrainian victories on the battlefield were being cheered in Western media and heads of state were lining up to show their solidarity in Kyiv. Ukraine's struggle became a struggle for Western values of liberal democracy. It touched on the very foundations of the European group self. This realization mobilized enormous political, economic, social, and emotional forces in the West. At the same time, one saw more clearly the differences between the European and the Russian group self. Broadly speaking, the latter is autocratic and fear-based, while the European is democratic and trust-based. It was a lesson that partly originated from group dynamic studies in the United States in the 1950s and spread quickly to Europe, that industrial groups (and the individuals within them) functioned better through trust-based leadership than through authoritarian and fear-based leadership. This insight gradually permeated (to varying degrees) Western democracies. Through trust-based leadership, one says yes to the idea that a high degree of autonomy should take place and that free and open communication in a group can release prosocial and creative forces that everyone can benefit from. An authoritarian and fear-based group, to the contrary, favour submission and corruption, paralyze creativity and cause moral decay. The group self falls apart. Vladimir Putin has appealed to Russian greatness in the Middle Ages and under the Tsarist rule to gain support for his regime and war project. But Russian soldiers have been reluctant to fight for this project, fleeing by the hundreds of thousands out of the country.

The brief analysis in this paragraph on national identity makes use of concepts such as personal and collective identity, *idem* and *ipse*, loyalty, the notion of the good life for and with others in just institutions, contained in a narrative. We unroll a story with deep roots in history. A similar narrative can be constructed about the group-analytic group self. It demonstrates how the concepts of matrix and the social unconscious need the overarching concept of a group self in order to explain group phenomena properly.

The group-analytic group self

What we might denote the group-analytic group self was born in the late 1940s when Foulkes gathered around him a group of colleagues who began to meet regularly. The group had different purposes. Partly it was a counselling group, of friends and colleagues but it also had therapeutic aspects. It sought to look at its own dynamics and allow for more personal openness than was customary in professional groupings. It discussed theory, and not least the future of group analysis. The group's theoretical anchorage was Foulkes' first textbook from 1948, and through discussions within the group, Foulkes gained a group of followers that increasingly identified with the basic and still emerging ideas of group analysis. It was this group that in 1952 gave birth to the Group Analytic Society (GAS) *which was the first organizational expression of the group-analytic group self.*

At this time, group analysis had a unifying set of ideas, enough people who identified with these ideas, a clear theoretical and organizational leader, and an organization that members could rely on. An identification with this base committed them to develop and disseminate the theory in practice, to new patients and new colleagues.

This is what an organized group requires: Some grounding ideas, ambitions for something to be accomplished, criteria for membership that also define the group's boundaries with the outside world, as well as role differentiation (board, leader, members, etc.). We are now facing a *consolidated group self.*

But this group self also contains its tensions and contradictions. How consistent are the grounding ideas? Are the ideas sufficiently relevant to the social reality they address? Are the ambitions realistic? Does the group have sufficient resources? Is the group able to deal with internal contradictions resulting from role differentiation, such as conflicts of authority, rivalry, jealousy, and envy? Does the group succeed sufficiently so that it achieves respect and recognition from the outside world?

As we recall from Part One and Part Two, Foulkes consolidated his leadership in the 1950s and 1960s through tireless theoretical, therapeutic, educational, and organizational activities. Important milestones were the establishment of Group Analytical Practice (1951), the Group Analytic Society (1952), the journal Group Analysis (1967) and the Institute of Group Analysis (IGA) (1971). IGA laid the foundation for a formalized training in group analysis. With this, new tensions arose within what we now can denote the *group-analytical movement*: How would the division of tasks be between IGA and GAS? Who harboured the essence, or the soul or spirit, of group analysis? Would the IGA become more prestigious and drain resources from GAS? Next came the expansion in Europe. Group analysis was no longer a London phenomenon. GAS became GASi (Group Analytic Society International). There were tendencies towards rebellion against "English imperialism". This resulted in the formation of EGATIN (European Group Analytic Training Network) which sought to move the centre of group analytical training away from London.

We see a movement from a single organizational expression in GAS in 1952 to a multitude of associations, institutes, and journals across Europe. Can we still talk about *one* group analytical group self? Yes, and this is, in my opinion, an essential part of the strength of the concept of the group self. This concept is able to summarize a historical movement that has a clearly definable starting point, and which slowly spreads into a more loosely organized diversity. This diversity is characterized by cultural and local peculiarities, but the differences are overshadowed by the similarity that is grounded in a commitment to what we might call *the spirit of group analysis*. In broad terms, it is the same basic project that one tries to realize in countries such as Norway, Germany, England, Greece, and others. The training institutes in Oslo, London and Heidelberg have the same project, and the training candidates from these institutes also seek to realize the same project in the specific groups they create. They seek to realize a special form of group culture, *the specifically group-analytic discourse.*

A specific group-analytic group is thus an actualization of the group-analytical group self. The extent to which the individual group analyst succeeds in this project, by letting tradition speak through him, depends on many factors, the most important of which are his/her personality, his/her own group analytical experience, how well he/she has learned the theory, the quality of the supervision and his/her skills (and luck!) in selecting appropriate patients. Of course, "letting tradition speak through oneself" does not imply being a group-analytic parrot. A competent group analyst has appropriated the core ideas in a hermeneutic sense, i.e., personalized them and integrated them into his/her personality.

Considering the diversity of psychological phenomena at work in a group analytic group, there is no one-to-one relationship between theory and practice. It is not the case that there is one "correct" intervention to be found. Rather, there are many relevant options (including silence) at any given time. The individual group analyst therefore has ample opportunity to cultivate his or her personal group analytic style. When an individualized practice nevertheless can be labelled group analysis, i.e., being a particular expression of a general category, it depends on the extent to which the general principles of group analysis prevail across individual characteristics. *It is in this sense that we can say that the tradition speaks through the individual group analyst (with all the paradoxes and limitations that tradition carries with it).*

What contradictions exist today within the group-analytic group self, and which are sources of unrest, debate, and development? As I have discussed previously, there are controversies concerning the theoretical foundation, for example, which theory of individual psychology is best compatible with group analysis: Ego psychology? Object relations theory? Kleinian theory? Self-psychology? Jungian theory? Mentalization theory? Modern personality theory? In this book, I have voiced my personal view that the dominant ("mainstream") theoretical basis is somewhat old-fashioned and thereby weakens the relevance of group analysis for a broader range of clients. I have argued for a return to the descriptive and clinical Foulkes who adhered to "egotraining in action", and to develop this legacy through modern theories of evolution, hermeneutics, the self and personality. I have further discussed the consequences of such a theoretical reorientation for the understanding of the group-as-a-whole, through the theory of the group self. These are ideas that, of course, will challenge other actors with invested interests in the group-analytic group self. And so it will always be, that parts of the ideological foundation for an institution or a group decays and expires, and that significant advocates of the (old) group self oppose more radical change.

There are also contradictions about the identity and delimitation of group analysis. Is group analysis tantamount to standard group-analytical psychotherapy, or is group analysis a theory of social phenomena in a broader cultural sense? Personally, I have expressed some scepticism towards the socio-cultural version of group analysis, for example, about the explanatory values of concepts like the matrix and the socially unconscious. At least some of the phenomena one wishes to elucidate and explain by these terms, I believe, become clearer through the concept of the group self and its historical-narrative grounding.

The most important challenge in our time (2024) is probably the relationship with the outside world. Many group analysts are concerned about this. Expressed by modern words: Can group analysis "deliver"? And more specifically, deliver what to whom? The big question is what it can deliver to public mental health care. A justified doubt has arisen here about the relevance of group analysis and the demand has decreased. Demand for training has also decreased in several countries. The average age of group analysts is rising. There are more rivals than ever. This does something to the group self. The project we once had and which we were proud of, isn't it worth so much anymore? Does group analysis primarily have relevance for a smaller segment of clients and for health personnel seeking training who can see a therapist in private practice? What about more tormented clients from "the people"? Has something gone wrong? Has group analysis slept in the class?

Theoretical modernizations A summary

Earlier in the book, I justified the claim that group analysis has stalled a bit, both theoretically and practically, and that it needs a modernization that can give new meaning to the slogan "egotraining in action". In this Part Three, I point out the resources inherent in an evolutionary perspective combined with a rethinking of the nature of the self, and thereby the group self. I highlight that:

- The self is two-dimensional and by no means identical to itself. The core self is found in all higher-ranking animals, while the self-reflective self is unique to *Homo sapiens*.
- Unique to *Homo sapiens* is also the capacity for shared intentionality, which is the emerging prerequisite for an experience of a *"we"*.
- In evolutionary history, language evolves in tandem with more complex group formations, based on collective intentionality that gives rise to a more *complex we*. The group agrees upon crucial elements of language, like signs, concepts, metaphors, grammar, and inference rules which paves the way for narratives, and utterances can thus appear like something "objective" that forms the basis for normative self-reflections. Thus, the human group becomes spiritualized.
- The self-reflective self gives birth to self-consciousness, a theme that has preoccupied philosophy for millennia.
- I highlight the tradition from Hegel, via Schleiermacher, Dilthey, Heidegger, Gadamer, Habermas, and Honneth, to its culmination in the work of Paul Ricoeur.
- In Ricoeur's hermeneutics, interpretation integrates understanding and explanation. For example, an emotional arousal can be explained, while at the same time it can be attributed a meaning.
- The interpretation of texts is based on literature with narrative structures: "What would we know about love and hate and about moral feelings, and even what we call *the self*, if this had not acquired linguistic expression and been articulated through literature?" The understanding of human actions is similar.
- Self-understanding is therefore not something one achieves through solitary contemplation. Self-understanding must take "a detour about the world."
- Philosophical reflection also favours a two-dimensional self: a kind of identity based upon "same-ness», and which is closer linked to the core self, and another kind of identity that can be named self-hood, which is closer linked to the self-reflective self. Narrative identity integrates these dimensions of the self.
- The primary need of the self is friendship and friendship is based on reciprocity. One takes care of the other as oneself, and oneself as the other.
- An ethical goal can be formulated around the good life with and for others in just institutions.
- Self-psychology also highlights the self's need for self-objects (friends). In addition, the self needs the other as sheer otherness.

- The story of being borderline dramatizes the existential dilemmas associated with the hermeneutics of the self when the developmental needs of the self become thwarted.
- The group self was coined as a concept by Heinz Kohut in 1976. However, it caught little interest as an alternative or supplement to the concepts of group mind and matrix.
- I propose that the concept of the group self remained undeveloped because it was not subject to a hermeneutic analysis a la the individual self.
- The group self is formed by the members uniting through a common project.
- The group is embodied by the group's advocates.
- Like the individual self, the group has numerical identity, qualitative identity, uninterrupted identity, and *idem* and *ipse* identity that are bound together by narrative identity.
- The group is a reality as long as the members keep their promise to the group. A group demands loyalty.
- The group members' different relationships with the group's project supplies the group with strong emotions. This is discussed in detail in the next and last part of the book.
- With the above-mentioned concepts, the group-analytic group self is described, an ambitious project that could only be partially realized in the 1900s, owing to conceptual limitations of the time.
- A specific group analytical group is an actualization of the group analytic group self. Tradition speaks through the individual group analyst, with all the paradoxes and limitations that tradition carries with it.

I should emphasize that when I use the term "modern" it is in a Hegelian sense, not as a word for what is modern in a fashion-like way or modern in the sense that it is a way of speaking which is valid for our time in contrast to sometime in the past. Modern in a Hegelian sense comes with a truth-claim, that "the modern spirit of group analysis" has reached a higher level, for example, it is closer to the truth, is closer to things "as they really are", has a higher explanatory power, is more coherent, conveys a higher construct and predictive validity, etc. The modern spirit of group analysis is a way of conducting philosophical, empirical, theoretical, and clinical discussions that rest upon certain grounding principles. In the first three parts of this book, I've tried to explicate these principles and thereby laid the ground for what really counts for the clients of group analysis, i.e., that the theory "works" when it is guiding the practical wisdom (Aristotle) of the group analyst who must deal with the living (group) world.

In this volume I've limited myself to the topic of group analysis in a more restricted sense. Only to a limited extent have I discussed the flaws in early psychoanalytic theory and their consequences for the course of the psychoanalytic movement (group self). The evolutionary dawn of consciousness is also described rather cursory. So is the theory of primary emotions (according to Jaak Panksepp) in its full complexity and significance, from the level of neurotransmitters to the phenomenology of feelings. Even the theory of mentalization is mentioned only briefly, as is the theory of personality and personality disorders. I have discussed these topics in detail in a series of previous books and articles (Karterud 2015b; Karterud, Wilberg, & Urnes 2017; Karterud 2017; Karterud, Folmo & Kongerslev 2019; Karterud & Kongerslev 2021; Karterud 2022; Karterud 2023). These texts might be important for some readers who want more details about the theory in its totality. In particular it concerns the details of the dawn of self-consciousness from the perspective of mentalization. This theory binds together philosophy and psychology. In Hegel, self-consciousness was a philosophical concept. Axel Honneth is the modern representative of the Frankfurter School which influenced Foulkes in the 1930s. Honneth (2012, 2021) has extended the concept of recognition ("Anerkennung"), which is crucial for self-consciousness, to a social-psychological construct. However, Honneth miss the depth-psychological aspect of recognition which is mirroring in a Kohutian sense and being minded in the sense of Peter Fonagy. From these pillars it is possible to rise a theory of man and his groupishness. This theory should also be the foundation of a theory of larger groups, for example, state formations. Frances Fukuyama goes to a great length in founding his theory of "The origins of political order" (2011) on evolutionary reasoning, for example, to legitimize political structures that might counteract man's proneness for nepotism. However, his reasoning about evolution rests upon gene calculations more than any evolutionary account of the individual-group relationship.

The theoretical ramifications mentioned above are important for the major theses in this volume about the philosophy, dynamics, and therapeutics about groups. I claim that a theory of the group self is essential in the same way that a theory of the individual self is essential for a profound understanding of man's being in the world and his sufferings that compel him to seek a therapist. When S. H. Foulkes got the idea back in 1940, in Exeter, to establish a therapeutic group, his ideas about the nature of the challenges he then would encounter, was of course very fragmentary and the conceptual resources that was at his disposal were limited. Since then, I maintain, the driving force in the development of group analysis has been the tension between the nature of mental pain, its manifestation in a therapeutic group, the analyst's theories about this connection and the adequacy of the discourse which the analyst promotes. The ego-psychological starting point of Foulkes had its clear limitations, and it was only "natural" that post-Foulkesian group analysts sought to integrate viewpoints from different schools of object-relational theory. I argue that the Kleinan approach was a step in a wrong direction, while supporting the more empirically sound approach of Donald Winnicott and colleagues. However, this approach also has its clear limitations. Its benefit was that man became liberated from the prison of a psychic apparatus driven by the motor of libido economics and that internal and external relations to other people came to occupy the main stage. However, in this discourse tradition, the acting and suffering individual, for example, the primacy of the self tends to disappear. As I will demonstrate in the last, practical part of the book, a knowledge of the vicissitudes of the self and its manifold configurations is paramount to a proper understanding of what really goes on in groups and the ever-changing life therein.

Part Four

Modern group-analytic psychotherapy

By the term group-analytic psychotherapy I mean a broad approach to group psychotherapy that extends from group analysis in a more classical sense to mentalization-based group therapy for severe personality disorders. The typical arena for classical group analysis is private practice. In therapeutic institutions of different kinds, and in outpatient departments of public health services, we find a range of group psychotherapies that modifies group analytic principles because of context restrains and membership peculiarities. It is important, in my opinion, to maintain group-analytic reasoning even in modified, or hybrid, groups. The therapist should not change theory, but she should change her technique. Technical flexibility requires a good command of general group-analytic principles but will also imply that:

- Modern personality theory is taken seriously.
- That the therapist explicitly considers levels of personality functioning when it comes to composition of groups.
- Therapeutic technique should be adjusted according to the boundary conditions, for example, the "amount" and type of personality problems in the group, if it is slow-open or closed, if it is heterogeneous or homogenous, if it is long-term, short-term, or focused, if the therapist is in control over the boundary conditions, etc.
- Technical variation should be adjusted to the need for structure, which implies how much "leader" the therapist should be. In classical group analysis will structural initiatives from the therapist be minimal.
- The therapist, and the group, might try to approach a more profound group-analytic discourse, as an ideal, but should not despair if that is not possible. The best should not be an enemy of the good. Therapists needs guiding ideals. Group therapists should therefore conduct a range of groups constrained by different boundary conditions, in order to acquire practical wisdom (Aristotle!).

DOI: 10.4324/9781032696027-4

In "Mentalization-based group therapy" (Karterud, 2015b), I have outlined principles for how group analysis can be modified when the challenges come from severe personality disorders. In the present book, my case is group analysis in a more classical sense. What unites the different approaches is a common theory of what a group is about. For example, how does a group come into being, what is the project, how does the structure evolve, how do the group norms become established in the matrix and the group self? Which norms are crucial for therapeutic groups? Should the therapist be explicit about these norms, if so, in which ways? Or should the group develop these norms by itself, aided by the therapist? In which way should the therapist mark his/her authority? What should the members discover "by themselves"? Good answers to the questions above depend on our theories of group development. Group analysis aims at developing groups that are able to perform a group-analytic discourse. What does that mean?

Let us start with theories of group development in general and from there proceed to development of groups that master a group-analytic discourse.

Group dynamics and group analysis with emphasis on developmental phases

Group dynamics for group analysis corresponds to the importance of psychodynamics for individual psychology and psychotherapy. However, textbooks on group dynamics are most often written from a *social psychological perspective*. They deal with development phases of groups, about groups' need for territory and boundaries, about group roles, norms, authority issues, group cohesion, communication patterns, the importance of group size, about groups as socializing agents, about conformity and peer pressure, about leadership, productivity and creativity versus demoralization and stagnation, about decision-making, about the relationship with the outside world, about groups in larger organizations, about the relationship between groups, etc. A group analyst explicitly or implicitly takes a stand on all these problem areas. In what way, hopefully, will emerge from this text as it develops. It is recommended that students in group analysis study these basic works, for example, the classical text of Forsyth (1990) where definitions and social psychology research literature can be consulted. The topic of group developmental phases is particularly important for group analysts. I have therefore chosen to review this topic in a bit more detail.

Most people agree that groups have a development trajectory that to a certain extent can be compared to the individual. Groups can evolve from being simple, primitive, dependent, and vulnerable, to sophisticated, nuanced, independent, robust, and productive. Not all groups follow such a line of development. Many groups perish at a young age. Others solidify in different patterns, some because maturity is simply not the goal, such as in criminal gangs and or extremist cults. Others stagnate because they are paralyzed by unmanageable internal and external conflicts. It is noteworthy that we describe groups with the same adjectives that we describe the individual: dependent, vulnerable, robust, productive, etc. With this mode of speaking, we are referring to the group as a group, not to an aggregate of individuals. We are talking about the group self. What observations are we relying on when we say that the group self is immature, primitive, and fragile versus mature, sophisticated, and robust? These are observations and measurements along several dimensions: for example, leadership dependency (Lewin et al., 1939), group cohesion (Braaten 1991), communicational patterns (Bales & Cohen 1979), group norms, tolerance for affects and differences, degree of black-and-white thinking (Karterud 1989b), the group's mode of boundary regulation, its conflict-resolving ability, etc.

The analogy with the immature individual self is striking: the immature group self is authority-dependent, harbours a group cohesion characterized by ambivalence, an inflexible communication pattern, display rigid and inconsistent norms, limited tolerance for emotions and differences, tends to primitive thinking, struggles with its boundary regulation, and has limited conflict-resolving ability. It is clearly justified to speak of a (multidimensional) development from *immaturity to maturity*. For groups, too, there is a process of education and civilization in the romantic bourgeois sense (*"Bildung"*), from the inarticulate, vulgar, and ruthless to more considerate, thoughtful, and formed forms of social intercourse. When we use normative concepts such as immature/primitive versus mature, we are also saying that we are taking ethical and moral stances. We weigh the group against some ethical goals and the moral norms we believe are essential to achieving these goals. If we endorse Paul Ricoeur's ethical goal, "to realize the good life, for and with others, in just institutions," we must ask ourselves to what extent the group contributes to the advancement of such a goal. Can it balance notions of the good life with a caring companionship with others and organize itself in a way that does justice to its members while simultaneously educating them in justice? An overarching question then becomes the following: Is there any necessary steps in the development of an immature group self into a mature group self?

This was an important research topic in the golden age of small group research, in the period from about 1945 to well into the 1960s. Classical studies were conducted by Lewin and colleagues (1939), Stock & Thelen (1957), Whitaker & Lieberman (1964), Bennis & Sheppard (1956), Gibbard, Hartman, & Mann (1974), Slater (1966), Tuckman (1965), Hill & Gruner (1973), among others. Lacoursiere (1980) attempted to summarize these studies into a general theory of group development in the book *The life cycle of groups*. Regarding this literature, one should keep in mind that many studies revolved around self-developmental groups with American students in university settings. Tuckman's theory (1965) has a special appeal since it summarized crucial research findings in a simple and almost suggestive way through the headings of *forming, storming, norming, performing, and adjourning*. Tuckman's theory in simplified form is shown in Table 4.1 (from Forsyth 1990, p. 77):

Table 4.1 Five stages of group development

Stage	Major Processes	Characteristics
Orientation (forming)	Exchange of information; increased interdependency; task exploration; identification of commonalities	Tentative interactions; polite discourse; concern over ambiguity; self-discourse
Conflict (storming)	Disagreement over procedures; expression of dissatisfaction; emotional responding; resistance	Criticism of ideas; poor attendance; hostility; polarization and coalition formation
Cohesion (norming)	Growth of cohesiveness and unity; establishment of roles, standards and relationships	Agreement on procedures; reduction in role ambiguity; increased "we-feeling"
Performance (performing)	Goal achievement; high task orientation; emphasis on performance and production	Decision making; problem solving; mutual co-operation
Dissolution (adjourning)	Termination of roles; completion of tasks; reduction of dependency	Disintegration and withdrawal; increased independence and emotionality; regret

Source: Forsyth, D. R. (1990). Group dynamics. Pacific Grove, California: Brooks/Cole Publishing Company

As we see, this is a *general* group dynamic theory. Most group therapists will experience this as a useful overarching framework but will seek to understand the processes in a more psychodynamic language and according to the *special tasks* that psychotherapeutic groups have, i.e., self-understanding and self-development.

In *the orientation stage*, the members of a psychotherapeutic group are generally more anxious than the members of more instrumentally task-oriented groups. This is of course related to the fact that the members of a psychotherapeutic group are more anxious and insecure than the average population. This is precisely why they apply for membership in such a group. But it is also related to the nature of the task. Self-understanding and self-development, what is it? How do you go about achieving that? What is expected of me? What can I expect from others? And above all, what can I expect from the "leader"? Other groups, by comparison, may seem very simple. A football team, a bridge club or gardening together offer simpler purposes and defined roles. People approach a psychotherapy group with unclear ideas (partly infiltrated by negative prejudices and scary rumours) about having to open oneself up and expose one's weak, vulnerable, and shameful sides, but also with the hope of a restoration of the self. One meets with a *fundamental ambivalence*, on the one hand with a *fear of retraumatization* but on the other hand with a *readiness for idealization* (hope). Often it will be the case that the fear of retraumatization concerns the other group members and that the readiness for idealization is linked to the therapist. Throughout, there is *more at stake* in a psychotherapeutic group. It is not something you can constantly sign up for and off, as in a course of chess. In the orientation stage, therefore, there is an intense conscious and unconscious exploration of the other group members and the leader. Who are they, what are they, are they to be trusted, are they dangerous, can I co-operate with them, what is it possible to talk about here, in what way can you talk about things, what rules apply? According to Gustavson & Cooper (1979) and Stone (1996), this phase is particularly characterized by so-called *unconscious planning*. To get answers to these types of questions, group members may set up special tasks or "traps" for the therapist and the others. Test situations are created. To test out who you are, I must try you out. I must see in practice how you react. Can you tolerate despair, helplessness, humour, stubbornness, rebellion, and anger? At the same time, there is an intense quest for affirmation through equality. "How are we going to approach this, we don't get much help from him there (the therapist)? ... Can't someone start? ... Are you also coming from the north? ... Do you feel that way too? ... Do you know XX? ... Have you gone to psychotherapy before? ... How exactly do such groups, Doctor X, work?"

The best psychodynamic theory for the initial stages of psychotherapy groups is found in the work of Whitaker & Lieberman (1964). From the outset, we are talking about conscious and unconscious *negotiations*. "How are we going to figure it out with each other, how are we going to become a *we* that collaborate on a *project*? We haven't even chosen each other. That's what the therapist has done. Why has he brought in this guy to my right? He seems rather unappetizing and scary. The one on the left, on the other hand, seems pretty nice. How is this going to go? Maybe it pays to lie a little low in the terrain to begin with?" Many group therapists will agree that basic assumption dependency (in Bion's terminology) is what predominates in the orientation stage. The group members tend to perceive themselves as insecure, helpless, ignorant, and dependent and find that all competence, knowledge and wisdom are localized to the therapist (defensive idealization).

In *the conflict stage*, on the other hand, basic assumption fight/flight predominates. Now criticism and dissatisfaction are expressed. The target of dissatisfaction can be anything and everyone. It easily takes on a scapegoat character. It implies all against one, that the victim is given few real chances to defend himself and will get blamed for the miserable state of affairs. It is during this stage of conflict that individuals prone for projective identification find the most ammunition for their ideas. It's as if the group needs an "object" that can contain everything contemptuous, and to which a unified aggression can be directed. However, it is not "everything and everyone" that is the *typical* measure of dissatisfaction and criticism. It is primarily the group here and now. And besides: The criticism is basically constructive and necessary to lead the group on to the next stage of cohesion.

The criticism has many sources. In part, it is a matter of disappointment towards the (defensively) idealized therapist. The content of the criticism is often that he/she is too passive, gives too little advice, explains too little, gives too few guidelines for the work of the group, speaks too cryptically, and the like. Hence the realization that "here you don't get much for free". Words about co-operation is actually a reality! "But how am I going to co-operate with the two of them to my right? One doesn't say anything, and the other has expressed attitudes and opinions that don't suit me very well." In the conflict stage, the testing of each other has come so far, and a certain measure of safety has been established through the experience that one's worst disaster fantasies (retraumatization) have not occurred, so that members dare more directly express criticism of each other and the group, a criticism that was initially disregarded or displaced. The battle is now about what kind of norms (morals) should apply in the group. Mine, or yours, the therapist's, ours? But ours, then, how do we define ourselves? The battle about norms is closely linked to rivalry for leadership. The therapist can symbolically be "deposed" and replaced with a leader recruited from the members' own ranks. A recurring theme in connection with norm formation and leadership is so-called "turn-taking". Turn-taking means that the group organizes itself in such a way that everyone gets their turn, on a roundabout, and that time is fairly distributed. Turn-taking is a strategy that aims to solve moral and emotional dilemmas related to differences, especially with regard to talkativeness versus silence, favouritism, envy, jealousy, and justice. Turn-taking is structured justice to nullify the foundations of these painful contradictions. One (of many) problem with turn-taking is that the scheme must be administered. It requires leadership. In group analysis, the therapist has refrained from this leadership, and in the vacuum thus created, alternative leaders can be sucked in from the group. In mentalization-based group therapy (MBT-G), on the other hand, the therapist assumes this leadership and spares the participants conflicts that he/she assumes will be too difficult for the group members to resolve.

As typical as controversies over fair distribution of time and attention is the controversy over fixed seats (alternative leaders can occupy the "therapist's chair"), about sanctions against those who do not show up or arrive late, about confidentiality, about interaction outside the group, about what emotions and what topics should be allowed in the group. In the orientation phase, there is a *submission* to the therapist's assumed goals and intentions with the group. In the conflict phase, there is a movement towards *owning the group itself.* The "therapist's group" is becoming "our group." This is a movement that requires struggle. And it requires "deviants". Without deviants and norm-breakers who challenge tacit norms that have already been established, or who are in the establishment phase, there will be no public debate in the group about norm establishment. The result can then be tacit norm establishment (unconscious negotiations and submission) for which no one takes responsibility, conflict shyness and hence a consequent lack of tradition for conflict resolution.

In *the cohesion stage*, the basic norms of the group are largely established. The group now relaxes more, is more conciliatory and can let in more jokes and laughter. A community has been established. The word *we* are starting to have a meaning. This community is not necessarily based on millimetre justice but can allow differences and different people to assume different roles. The group has often got its "gatekeeper", its negotiator, and its enfant terrible. One further begins to come to terms with the therapist's role. True, there is still a lot to say about him/her, but he actually makes some constructive contributions! In the wake of a growing sense of community in psychotherapeutic groups follows an increasing exposure of the participants' "weaker" sides, i.e., admitting vulnerability, helplessness, shameful actions, and shameful needs. When this is listened to and accepted in the group, it paves the way for strong experiences of reciprocity and closeness, which in turn reinforces the sense of community. In American literature, it is often said that the stage of conflict is followed by a stage characterized by *intimacy.*

It should be underlined that extreme cohesion is not a goal of psychotherapeutic groups. Extreme cohesion is relevant for group projects akin to hazardous expeditions. Here one must be willing to sacrifice everything for the group. One for all and all for one! In psychotherapeutic groups, it is important to promote differences, tolerance for different thinking and affect expressions, for contradictions and a challenging dialogue.

In *the performance stage*, psychotherapeutic groups are characterized by the fact that most group members have learned and identified with the main principles that the therapist stands for. The demand for turn-taking has lapsed. The group can move more freely between different topics and different actors. Members have learned to explore fantasies, to emphasize emotions, to see connections between the past and the present, and that the group's here and now takes precedence over "there and then." The therapist is perceived as an important resource and is often subject to a new and deeper idealization. Members are beginning to realize what therapeutic groups can be used for and what they *can't* be used for. There is a growing realism to therapeutic objectives. At the same time, there is a shift from symptom preoccupation to preoccupation with self-understanding and relationships. In the performance stage, there is also a recognition of time. The group is starting to get a history. The present is compared to the past. "Do you remember what it was like in the first place? As you have developed! In the old days, you were terrified when there was an argument in the group."

The future is beginning to take shape. "I plan to quit sometime next year, but first I have to do something about my fear of not being liked. I just have to dare more."

The resolution stage is not a necessary stage in all psychotherapy groups. Some groups end, but others can be "perpetual". In slow open group analysis, individual members quit, while the group continues. Early on, the group may have had premature terminations in the form of dropouts. Mostly these are scars in the history of the group. Something went wrong. The first regular termination, on the other hand, is a milestone. The first person has finished. He/she quits because he/she has come to the end of the road. The goal of the therapy may have changed along the way, but it has been satisfactorily achieved. Group psychotherapy is useful! For the first time, there is the experience of a *terminating process*. One does not end abruptly. Terminating takes time. Things need to be worked on. In the termination phase, many things are seen in a new light. The time perspective changes: *"If I had started over, I would have done certain things differently. And occasionally, I wasted time. Strange that I shall never see you again. That you have endured me. If it hadn't been for you, Kari, during the most critical period, I wouldn't have persevered. I am so grateful for everything you have given me …"* Recurring reflection, regret of missed opportunities, pride on one's own behalf, gratitude for what one has received, uncertainty about the future, grief at separating, these themes will naturally coin the terminating process. Although "naturally", there are abundant forces at work to downplay the importance of a terminating process. Here, too, the first time the phenomena occur, it is the therapist who must work to *make* these themes a "natural" part of the process. A group that has been through its first good termination has learned something new and valuable. This capital can be utilized at the next crossroad, and then the therapist can presumably lie lower in the terrain.

Is there any regularity in how long these stages last? No, the duration varies enormously and depends on the purpose of the group, the therapist's technique, and the members' self-structure. In typical time-limited groups of 12–20 weeks duration, parts of the therapist's technique are designed to guide the group quickly through the developmental stages (MacKenzie 1990, Piper et al., 1992, Lorentzen, 2014). The therapist becomes more directing and makes active suggestions on what to do. One might try to get the orientation stage done at the first meeting. The therapist encourages a presentation round, is actively directing in this round and uses every opportunity to emphasize educational points that can strengthen the alliance and co-operation in the group. During the second meeting, any conflicts about the group form should be processed and the cohesion stage should be in the making. Most meetings should belong to the performance stage. Time-limited groups are focused groups. The focus may be, for example, unresolved grief. The group should rapidly be brought to a level where one can concentrate all forces on the focus and not get stuck in, for example, rivalry between some group members or different factions in the group. It is also important to focus early on the group's termination. Once cohesion is established, which can become quite profound in such groups because one quickly shares intense pain, loss, and grief, the focus will also include how to say farewell to those one has connected with in the here and now. How is *this* termination and *grief* dealt with, compared to what therapy was sought for?

As I have emphasized, by and large a group analyst acts *non-directing*. No recipes are given on how to get through the different stages. On the contrary, it is a point that the group finds its own way through these stages, not directed by, but assisted by the therapist when necessary. Nor is it the case that a group's development is linear, like climbing the steps of a ladder. The group can periodically fluctuate between dynamics belonging to the orientation, the conflict, and the cohesion stage. There are no studies that have investigated the typical length and interrelationships of stages for group analytic groups. Based on my own experience and from many years of supervising candidates in group analysis, I would say that the orientation stage in group analysis typically will take some months, and that the orientation and conflict stage should be completed within the second half of the first year. During the first part of the second year, the cohesion stage should be well established, and during the next half year, a group analytical culture (performance stage) should have been established. Some training candidates will fail with this process. The group doesn't settle down properly. During the second year, there is still a lot of *turnover*, little security, scepticism and distrust of the group, a lot of absence, a recurrent fear that the group will collapse, criticism of the therapist and his/her style, and testing of boundaries. These are signs that a group analytical culture has not been achieved. These signals may indicate that the therapist needs more self-treatment, theoretical studies, and supervision.

If one has a lot of early dropouts in a new group, one can quickly end up in a vicious circle. Dropouts leave a general sense of failure. Dropouts often end suddenly. The emotions associated with them thereby become difficult to process. For each dropout, the therapist must bring in a new member. Generally speaking, new members cause a (at best temporary) group regression. The group revisits early stages of development. New members also need to orient themselves, find out about the group and consider its norms. The relationship with new members is *always ambivalent*. (Let me interject an apropos here to the debate over immigrants. Expressing concern, discontent, and criticism of immigration is not necessarily "racism". It's something that occurs in *all* groups if one is willing to see it.) There's always someone who mislike the newcomer. A new stage of conflict is inevitable. Frequent dropouts and frequent newcomers can lock the group into a perpetual lap dance on topics that belong to the orientation and conflict stage. This is the fate of many groups in psychiatric institutions (Karterud 1989c). Such groups are nevertheless useful when orientation/disorientation are important therapeutic topics, such as psychosis and borderline conditions (Kibel, 1981). At the same time, one must be aware of the limitations of such groups.

What drives a psychotherapeutic group forward? There is an interaction between the need for self-understanding and self-development and the desire and need for belonging. Gradually, fear of retraumatization will diminish in the group and the prosocial forces of the individual, inherent in primary emotions such as exploration, love, and play, will be stimulated. These needs manifest themselves in different ways and at different times in different group members. Some will be impatient to move forward. The tendency to submit and be cautious in the orientation phase will be perceived as inhibiting. In the group, polarities become crystallized and represented through different group members. Role positions characteristic of each stage appear, and the group negotiation so well described in Whitaker & Lieberman (1964) take place through disputes of a wide range of themes. The group moves typically from a set of "restrictive group solutions" to a set of "liberating group solutions." Agazarian (1994) emphasizes refractions between subgroups. Scapegoats, outsiders, rebels, latecomers, rivalrous therapists, system critics, conformists, subgroups, and the like are not something one unfortunately have to take into account in analytic groups. In such role positions lies a welcome source of development and growth. It is enshrined in the therapist's guidelines for composing an analytic group. The main principle is *differences* with respect to personality styles. One might as well say *otherness*. Group analysis is about to create a fertile arena for exploring self versus others. It is through the others, also in the sense of otherness, that the self develops. To pinpoint it, a homogeneous group consisting of menopausal women with depressive disorders is a poor starting point for group analysis. There is too little otherness.

S. H. Foulkes was less concerned about theories (and practical implications of) group development. The textbook of Schlapobersky (2016) repaired this lacuna in group analytic theory. His chapter on group development refers to a wide array of studies and authors. I agree with his warning of any simplistic conception of a linear development of groups. Group development is certainly a complex affair. However, the reader may notice that the theoretical position in this book is more coherent than that of Schlapobersky. I argue for a view that definitely highlights a development from immaturity to maturity in analogue with individual personality development. However, it is not linear. Without a valid theory of group development, it is hard to say something meaningful and coherent about a concept like the *discourse of group analysis*.

The boundary conditions of group analysis and the group analytical situation

In the previous chapter, we discussed development in psychotherapeutic groups in more general terms. In this chapter, we will discuss the *particularities* of group analysis. Even before sitting down in the group's first meeting, the group analyst has made several outlines that set important premises for the group's development.

The group analyst abstains from the role of "leader" of the group analytic dialogue but assumes the full role of leader in the sense of *dynamic administrator* (Behr & Hearst 2005). This means that the group analyst is responsible for ensuring that the group has a defined, pleasant, comfortable, and undisturbed location. He/she must protect the group and defend the boundaries of the group's physical "home". It goes without saying that his/her phone is silent, that strangers do not enter the room, and that one is not constantly disturbed by noise in nearby rooms.

It also belongs to the therapist's role as dynamic administrator to make sure that the right number and comfortable chairs are lined up. There is a group analytic rule that the number of chairs corresponds to the number of members. The chair is there even if a member is absent. Furthermore, it is the therapist's task to convey messages (for example, about absence) to the group.

The group analyst determines the time of the group and a semester schedule. It is explicitly stated in the pre-treatment interviews that one expects the group to be prioritized above "everything else" and that the members arrange their holidays at those times when the group also has vacation. In terms of time and frequency of meetings, the standard is 1.5 hours once a week. The group analyst begins the meetings on time and concludes precisely. It takes a lot of drama to go beyond allotted time.

The composition of the group together is not least important. Through the composition, the group analyst signals the importance of differences about gender, age, life experience, personality, and mental disorders. But it also signals similarities about what is possible to work with in groups. An old slogan has been "differences in formal diagnoses and personality, but similarities in ego strength". An often-unnoticed aspect of the group analyst's work with group composition is that he/she *minimizes the risk of violence*. Violence and coercion (e.g., suicide threats) exist on the margins of many social environments. It sets limits on what is possible to explore. Group analysis work with *internal* violence and coercion, and the group analyst must ensure that this does not have its parallel in external reality.

The time perspective is an exceedingly important boundary condition. In most cases, group analysis has no time limit. Anyone can take the time he/she needs. It is made clear in advance that group analysis is *long-term psychotherapy*. Personally, I use to say that treatment under a year's duration serves no purpose. One should expect around two to four years.

Important is also agreements about price and method of payment.

In pre-treatment interviews, the group analyst should review the following norm expectations: that you meet regularly, that you meet precisely, that you pay punctually, that you are expected to have a duty of confidentiality with regard to the information you receive about others in the group, that you do not associate with other group members outside the group sessions, that you strive for honest, free and open communication, that the group does not have any kind of agenda but that strive for a free-floating group conversation, that group analysis is a form of therapy in which the group is the most important agent and that it is not about individual therapy in group, that the ordinary group size is seven to eight members, that new members are admitted after someone leaves, that you should attend the group until you have by and large solved the problems for which you sought therapy and that you commit to at least a couple of months of termination phase after you have announced to quit.

The above boundary conditions are important guidelines for the group and help to define the *group-analytic situation*. It is within this framework that the chances are greatest for a group analytic culture to develop. The group-analytic situation consists of a fruitful interaction between a certain set of boundary conditions and a special kind of dialogue. In the initial stages, the group analytic situation will have its clear limitations. In favourable cases, it will slowly open up and bloom. The group analyst has then succeeded in "recruiting" several of the members to a core group that has understood and identified with the most important norms and attitudes of group analysis. These norms and attitudes are ultimately derived from the ethical foundation of group analysis, which is *self-understanding and self-development consistent with a good life for and with others in just institutions.* To cite Mullan (1987): *"group therapy is an ethical way to change patients psychologically".* And: *"group psychotherapy owes a large part of its success as a treatment method to the morality inherent not alone in the patients and therapist but in the process itself"* (Mullan, 1991).

The group analytical culture and the group analytical discourse

Is it possible to say something more precise about what characterizes a good group analytic culture? Above all, it should be anchored in *autonomy*. The group started when the group analyst gathered a certain number of strangers who were invited to join a relatively unclear journey. The group self starts as a project in the head of the analyst. He/she must recruit members for this project in such a way that it no longer becomes his project, but the group's. Through development, the group must come to owning *itself*. The norm expectations (commitments, no social interaction, etc.) that the therapist explains each participant before the group starts will initially be accepted with a good portion of submission. At the first boundary violation (which may well come in the first session), these norms are put to the test. The group's first reaction is often to turn to the therapist as the "leader" and expect an authoritative and normative action from her. However, group analysts should refrain from speech acts that "sort things out." Foulkes should be mentioned as a reference here. He was said to be "a master of the unfinished sentences", by utterances "that were hanging in the air". The group analyst's recommendations should have been clarified on beforehand. When it comes to *living practice*, the group must figure it out on their own, assisted by the group analyst as a dialogue partner. As long as the group struggles to figure out its way of working, the group analyst should *prioritize group interventions* over individual interventions. It's a common mistake for therapists to jump too quickly on individual psychological modes of understanding. In the initial stages of groups, it is to recommend that the therapist concentrate on the dilemmas that the group must solve *qua group* in order to develop further. These dilemmas must be lived out in a dramatized form. As early as possible, the group's quite special reality character must be established. *The group must exist on the border.* On the border between the inner and outer world, on the border between fantasy and reality. In a sense, it's an illusion, but at the same time real. Actions and events may be given enormous symbolic significance. A trifle is not just a trifle. A glance is not just a glance. A glance in an analytic group can have enormous consequences. Failure to appear may involve a formidable betrayal. Through his use of language, the group analyst orchestrates the group and through his stubbornness, he holds on to key dilemmas and doesn't let them go until the group has resolved them. The therapist's norm expectations are cast in flesh and blood when they are put to the test in dramatized group conflicts.

When the first late-coming takes place, the group analyst must be vigilant. How does the group react? The same with the first no-show. Often it is enough to point out that the event is *not* discussed in the group. When the event(s) *are* discussed, the group will differentiate itself. From being a gray mass that leaves that kind of thing to the "leader," to encompassing differentiated views that tend to range from an anarchist laissez-faire attitude ("I thought this was a place of freedom and not a military camp") to the strict executioner who requires cadaver discipline. Some will take on a mediator role and some will impatiently demand a "decision" "to finish the case so that we can move forward" (*"We have more important things in store than such trifles"*). *"What does this confidentiality stuff really mean? Can't I talk about the group at all? But what if I talk to my wife about my experiences." "No socializing outside of the group. What does that mean then? What about the waiting room? Should you sit there dumb as oysters? Is it allowed to drive to and from in the same car? Or the same tram? Are you going to pretend you don't know each other?" "Can you talk about absolutely everything in this group? Absolutely everything? There hasn't been much talk about sex until now. Nor about lies and deceptions". "It's impossible to show emotions here when it causes people to want to quit."*

Through such confrontations, the group develops what Ricoeur (1992) denotes *practical wisdom*. This means that the norms – commitment, confidentiality, separation, honesty, respect, non-violence, free and open communication, reciprocity, etc. – are not perceived as rigorous injunctions, but are discussed and practiced with regard to the uniqueness of each situation and with a growing recognition of why one should have a set of common shared norms and what these are good for.

When the group owns its own norm base, the group analyst can relax from the role of being a moral head and police officer. Once the group has established a good group analytic culture, i.e., reached the performance stage in Tuckman's terminology, the development is somehow complete. There are no more stages to go through. It corresponds to the idea that democracy is the highest level of political social organization. There is no more "advanced" stage than democracy (Fukuyama, 1992). Within a group-analytic culture, it is no longer about elevating the group to something radically new, but, like democracy, about allowing its potentials to unfold, preserve the culture, nurture it, and repair it in the event of setbacks. It is at this stage that one can say that the group self is organized around the project of group analysis. The group self is now founded in the group's embodied experiences of developing and managing a self-reflective community. It has its genesis in an emotionally charged story that can be told (narrative perspective) and its timeliness in a characteristic form of communication characterized by a specific normative basis and a specific cognitive and emotional style. This is what group analysts have traditionally called the *matrix*.

What specifically characterizes a good group analytical culture? From attendance registrations, one can see that there is little absence and latecomers. That kind of problems have disappeared. People stay in the group for a long time (several years). The replacement of members is slow (between one and three a year). Morale is high. The group is highly appreciated. It is perceived as meaningful. Participants can observe a positive development in themselves and others. Dropouts occur very rarely. The group handles boundary issues smoothly. The group analyst can lean back and concentrate on his job as an analyst. The group has learned the free-floating group conversation way of working. It oscillates between the here-and-now, the past and the present outside the group, with an emphasis on the here-and-now.

But perhaps more importantly, it has learned to oscillate between the inner world, the group as the "intermediate world", and the "real" outer world. It has realized that group analysis is radically different from regular social interaction. The group is a laboratory, and this statement takes on many meanings. The group is more open to the dream world. It has learned the language of dreams and recognized that there are many layers to what is going on. The most interesting thing is not reality itself, but how to relate to, and thereby change, social reality. Counselling is therefore toned down in the group. Instead, it is filled more with dream material where the dynamics of the individual and the group merge. The members begin to have their projects concretized. Such projects can often be formulated based on *model scenes* (Lichtenberg et al., 1992).

Example 1: *During the first year Gunnar tells stories about two somewhat older and tired parents and himself as an only child. On Sundays, they often went on road trips and visited relatives and friends. These were also often elderly and childless. While his parents were inside, Gunnar sat in the back seat of the car, bored and waiting. Eventually, this "sitting in the back seat, waiting, in boredom" became a meaningful metaphor for several areas of his life. His therapeutic project eventually became "getting out of the back seat." This became urgent when he realized he had placed himself in the back seat of the group as well. We see how model scenes, personal projects and meta-phors merge. The group is a psychotherapeutic group, but it is also a car. Other members (and the therapist) sit in other chairs, but these chairs are at the same time the front seat of the car. In a dream, Gunnar takes the group to an island near the place where he grew up. On a rock, the therapist sits in an authoritative position behind a desk and Gunnar approaches devotionally to present an application. Someone points out that he maintains a respectful distance in the group as well. Does this have anything to do with the position in the back seat? This is how past, present, dream and social reality are entangled.*

A group-analytic culture is also characterized by a greater capacity for humour (Lewis, 1987). The members (and therapist included) allow them-selves more joking and laughter. This is related to the group's ability to con-struct and utilize metaphors and change perspective on what is going on.

Within a group analytic culture, in my opinion, one should not only allow oneself, but one *should* involve oneself in sequences of "individual therapy in group". When done properly, this reinforces the group analytic culture. The other members can observe therapeutic sequences in which the therapist plays out a larger repertoire: the way the therapist speaks, her tone of voice and attunement, empathy in practice, how the therapist in the dialogue goes straight to the points, exactly what the therapist emphasizes, how she con-nects the past with the present, the inner world with the group and the external world, which central dilemmas and conflicts are highlighted, how this unfolds in the transference(s), and not least the therapist's formulation of the challenges the person faces. Through such expositions of the therapist's (empathetic) understanding of the individual, group members gain a kind of understanding which they gradually make their own. These processes illus-trate above all the therapist's clear position on *the needs of the self*, i.e., the self's need for affirmation and recognition, for dignity and reparation, for idealized others, for equal fellowship as well as otherness. This fuels the group's struggle to figure out dilemmas such as what an offence is; whether one can own the feelings involved; whether it is legitimate to talk about revenge; about who should take precedence, I or the others; about what one has the right to expect from others; whether one exaggerates or not, and not least how it is possible to reconcile and forgive others and escape from cycles of revenge and avoidance.

Within a group analytic culture, an understanding of what self-development entails and the role of the group and therapist as necessary others (self-objects) also begins to dawn. This is also clarified by the therapist's interventions. For example, when the therapist recognizes therapeutic advances. Self-development manifests itself by new qualities.

Example 2: *Vera was an only child and grew up in a close-knit and over-involving family. She went her own way early on. The interest of others was mostly perceived as attempts to control her and get her to accept her allotted place in the family drama. The therapy was characterized by intense emotions and an almost shocking honesty and unsentimentality with regard to the other group members and the therapist. Towards the end of her treatment, she says that she now experiences the therapist differently than before. She now experiences his interest as care, a word she had previously frowned upon. Caring she had seen as camouflage for power plays. During the termination phase, she recounted episodes from home where she engaged differently with the children. Instead of arranging and managing them, as she used to do, she gave herself more time, listened to them more, talked more with them about other things, comforted them, yes, gave them more care. The therapist nods and says that it is nice to hear, that she has been able to overcome the self-protection she had to take on while growing up, that she has been able to take in the group's and the therapist's interest as care and that she is now able to pass this on to the next generation.*

The group begins to realize that its members (including the therapist) can be "used" for many purposes. It's not just a place that's different from other places, where you can speak out openly, be honest, display emotions, etc. The group is also populated with potential fathers, mothers, siblings, cousins, maids, bosses, and buddies, who you need for a shorter or longer time to fulfill internal projects. A group is a place for *multiple transferences*. At the same time, one and the same group member has several transference relations going on.

Example 3: *Albert had a confusing childhood. He was an only child with a distant and withdrawn father and an anxious and obsessive mother with pronounced paranoid traits. Retreat into his own fantasy world was a prominent self-protective strategy for Albert. Specifically, he avoided people by sitting up in trees, like during brake times at school and in the neighbourhood at home. In the group, he immediately adopted an outsider position. Metaphorically, with reference to his model scene, this was referred to as him sitting in his tree in the group as well. Several years passed before he dared to climb down. He was then supported by a fragile idealizing transference to the therapist, a twinship* *transference to one of the members and occasionally transient experiences of mirroring. Another group member suffered an intense maternal transference from his side that manifested itself in scepticism and accusations of dishonesty and manipulative intentions. A third group member embodied troublesome male rivals.*

In the drama that plays out in the group, *all* transference manifestations are important. Not just self-object transferences. Self-object experiences helped Albert coming down from the tree and start getting involved with other people. After many years in the group/tree, he could see that there was someone down there who probably wished him well. At the same time, the group was populated with frustrating others, some who resembled his mother and some competing peers. The process of change consisted of strong upheavals and conversation with these frustrating others that he might eventually perceive as well-meaning and not persecuting. Self-understanding and self-development require not only affirming others, but also different others with whom one can measure oneself and define oneself in relation to. In this respect, the group is a unique medium.

The analytic group self is a fragile plant. It is put to the test in every meeting. *This fragility is a characteristic of its being.* Had it been robust and predictable, it would not have been group analytic, but the core of a fixed working group that follows strict rules and leans on well-defined roles. At each new group meeting, one has no idea what is going to happen. Do members dare to explore new mental territories? Do they dare to be honest and authentic? Are they able to maintain faith in the group as a significant and creative community? Trust is based on numerous experiences of "small" events in the group. When one group member affirms another, there is friendship and care in practice. If this action also confirms a significant group analytic value, one can say that the action simultaneously confirms the group self. And if the group functions poorly for a period of time, it has the potential to heal itself. *It is my contention that it is through participating in the group's self-healing and self-creating processes that the individual repairs and creates him/herself.* This is said in other words, and with other theoretical references, but in accordance with what I perceive is the essence of Foulkes' vision of group analysis.

What one might call the *group-analytic discourse* is thus a distinctive self-healing form of dialogue, governed by some particular boundary conditions, and characterized by:

- norms that respect the needs of the self.
- a free-flowing group dialogue ("multilogue") that revolves around self-understanding and intersubjectivity.
- a group dialogue in which the group analyst is not the "leader", but the analyst.

- commuting between the here-and-now, past, and present.
- commuting between the inner world, the group, and the outer world.
- having no tacit taboo areas.
- displaying mutual empathy and care.
- having courage to explore conflicts.
- accepting and analyzing multiple transference manifestations.
- an ability to create and work with metaphors.
- playing with a sense of humour.

On the use of vignettes

The text that follows is illustrated with abundant clinical vignettes in order to convey a feeling of what group analysis is all about and to concretize theoretical issues and technical challenges. With reference to Ricoeur (1981b), I would like to remind the reader of the character of these vignettes as *texts*. Once written and published, the vignettes escape my (the author's) control. In their essence, they are ambiguous, and the reader cannot ask the author for in-depth commentaries and supplementary information that might provide evidence for alternative or "more correct" interpretations. The vignettes stand there as independent "objects" that can adopt completely different meanings for the reader than the author intended. In the vignettes the reader will encounter many named people, several groups and one (?) person called the "therapist". Are these people *real* people? Do these vignettes refer to real events? Or are they fictional? Are vignettes *fiction literature*? The reader receives no unambiguous answer to this and must live with a corresponding uncertainty. *The vignettes are small stories intended to serve educational purposes.* Whether they refer to actual events, paraphrased events, or poetry is of secondary importance. My clue has been for them to be *realistic*. If they haven't happened, they *could* have happened. Nor do the vignettes aim to be "representative" of a certain therapeutic style. For example, I have not tried to create a "balance" between the number of "good interventions" and "good groups" and the number of "bad interventions" and "bad groups". The vignettes are literary illustrations whose purpose is to illustrate theoretical issues. When I say that the vignettes are realistic, I mean by this that they are *referring to a group analytic experiential world*. They refer to experiences I myself have had during several thousand group analytic sessions with a large number of people over the course of about 40 years. They also refer to experiences I have had as a supervisor for many training candidates and as a supervisor for practicing group therapists. It is not the case that "good interventions" refer to experiences in my own groups and that "bad interventions" refer to experiences with training candidates!

Some notes on dynamic administration

The group therapist's most important administrative actions concern composition of the group. There is no golden rule here. It's all about the group's boundary condition. Is the therapist planning for "pure" group analysis or, for example, for a group composed of a variety of personality disorders within national health services? If the last option is the case, I would accept most kind of characters, including (non-psychopathic) anti-socials and quite a lot of substance misuse. I would accept tiny motivation and rather poor initial alliance. These features are part of poor personality functioning. The first task of the treatment will thus be to augment motivation, strengthen the alliance and handle substance misuse and other (self-)destructive acting out. To achieve such goals, one might need an additional psychoeducational group and initial supplementing individual counselling. Therapists should be pragmatic. Local circumstances vary enormously. In some instances, only gradually will the group become the main therapeutic agency (Karterud, 2015).

When it comes to more classical group analysis, assessment of level of personality functioning (DSM-5) is of outmost importance. Most therapists do that rather impressionistic. However, candidates in group analysis should undergo a more formal training in personality assessment. Seasoned therapists with profound theoretical knowledge and long-lasting clinical experience may assess clients correctly during a first seemingly fleeting interview. If in doubt, one should engage in a trial individual psychotherapy. That might also be crucial for motivation and alliance, for example, with respect to narcissistic vulnerabilities. Personally, I might advocate group analysis after, for example, 15–20 hours of individual psychotherapy. By skilled personality assessments, the analyst can compose the group according to his/ her own preferences. The analyst should also bear in mind, and explain to patients, that one might be suited for group analysis in general, but that the analyst must balance this particular group with respect to personality characteristics.

Nobody should be persuaded to group-analytic psychotherapy. To the contrary, if the motivation is poor and there are other options, patients should be advised to abstain. Group analysis is in many respects a frustrating kind of treatment that presupposes a high motivation. Many patients will experience situations where they feel neglected, misunderstood, abandoned, disrespected, or hurt. There might come periods when they experience the group as awful. Why do we believe that exactly this patient is able to work through such periods without dropping out? What does the patient him/herself think about such scenarios? How is his/her record with respect to frustration tolerance?

When the therapist has judged a patient as suited for group analysis, I personally present him/her with a written contract that summarizes the most important boundary conditions (confidentiality, etc.) for the group. We discuss what free and open communication will imply for the patient. The therapist should underline that even as he/she will know details about the patient's life history, he/she will not tell the group about it. The patient should find his own way into the group.

Example 4: *Ben, a 35-year-old real estate agent, had chronic problems with his girlfriend. He couldn't break up, but on the other hand he couldn't move in with her. Besides, he quickly got into arguments with other people and tended to isolate himself in his spare time. His secret passion was sexual intercourse with horses. He had no problem telling the therapist about it, but how would the group react to something like that? The therapist emphasized that the way new members present themselves is entirely up to them. At the first meeting, the therapist would welcome him, but the rest was up to him. The therapist would not say something that the patient had entrusted to the therapist in advance. It took our zoophile real estate agent about half a year to dare to talk about the horses. Amazing how the group took it! They were curious, but basically accepting. As one said: "Yes, that was something special, I admit that ... But tell me ... how do you actually perform that?"*

Group analysis is usually a one-therapist endeavour. Co-therapists should be an option for groups with more severe personality disorders. However, the lonely group analyst needs a space for reflection. I use to recommend his/her records. Instead of reflecting with a colleague before and after the group session, the analyst reflects through his record writing. Personally, I write nearly one A4 page. That is how I "mind the group". It is an important investment. The text fuels my thinking about the group between the sessions and new thoughts appear when I re-read the text before the next group meeting. Above all I'm curious about (cfr SEEKING!) what the last session has set in motion in the minds of the members. Of special importance are their dreams, and in particular their group dreams, as I will discuss in a later chapter.

Medication is another issue that the group analyst must deal with. Optimally, group analysis is a medication-free project. However, the real world is complex. It is almost inevitable that some group members use some medication or misuse alcohol or illegal drugs.

Example 5: *Chris was a 43-year-old married bank assistant. Two years before his group therapy, he had been hospitalized for a major depression. After discharge, he had received supportive therapy at a mental health centre (MHC). From there, he was referred to group analysis. He was then on a quite high dose of a SSRI. In the assessment interviews the psychodynamics of his depression was discussed, and the group analyst explained why he should discontinue the drug during his group treatment. He entered a lively group that challenged him during the first meeting. To the next meeting, he reported the* *following dream: "I was at Tivoli and went into a 'shaker'. I could recognize some of the other group members in there. The session was tougher than expected. It was a relief to get out of the machine, but at the same time I felt more alive than before." The dream was interpreted as a group dream. He had literally been shaken in the group but had obviously benefited from it. Gradually, it became apparent that he had problems with emotional awareness, emotional differentiation, and emotional expression. He was happy to comment on what was going on in the group with an intellectualizing distance. This was pointed out repeatedly by other group members and the therapist and he was reminded that antidepressants often exacerbated poor emotional consciousness. After six months, he, in consultation with the doctor at the MHC, began to gently reduce the dose. After three quarters of a year, he began to be more and more annoyed by events in the group. In one meeting, he told of two recent rage reactions that had 'shaken him'. The therapist interpreted these reactions with reference to some triggering circumstances of his depression and his personal development in the group. As the systematizer he was, he compiled lists of the most important people in his life and reviewed his emotions in relation to these. After a year, he had quit his medication and told he hadn't felt so good in many, many years.*

In group analysis, there is a rule that other and potentially competing treatments should preferably not occur. But in the real world, one often encounters "extraordinary" situations. There are no rules on how to deal with these and who should initiate what.

Example 6: *John (27) was a talented student but seriously addicted to alcohol. During his group analysis, he fell in love with a girl that challenged him in a positive way. His alcohol misuse became related to ups and downs in this relation. His girlfriend was also in therapy. Her psychologist offered to incorporate him into couples therapy. The group analyst has no objection to this. The psychologist and the group analyst discussed the dynamics of each other's therapy by phone. The couples therapy lasted for a year and contributed positively to John's development.*

Example 7: *Emma (32) had a severe personality disorder, obsessive-compulsive disorder, sexual identity confusion and periodic cannabis abuse. After several years in the group, she developed a negative therapeutic reaction. The relationship between the group analyst and Emma deteriorated. He confronted her about the cannabis abuse and almost demanded that she quit the misuse, but she couldn't see anything wrong with her marihuana smoking. She eventually reported signs of increasing decompensation. The group analyst considered the group treatment destructive, and, on his own initiative, he contacted a psychologist who offered to take over. Emma (and the group) was then served a fait accompli, that she had to quit the group. She was offered a* *termination period of two months. During this time, she was recommended to work in parallel in the group and with the psychologist.*

Example 8: *Sue (33) had a paranoid and borderline personality disorder. At times, she was lost in psychic equivalent thinking. She repeatedly complained about the therapists' ineptitude, how banal the group was and that she received far too little attention. One day she informed that she'd gotten herself an individual therapist, one hour weekly. The group was relieved. It was thought that this adjunct would take away some of the pressure and accusations against the group. But the devaluation continued. The only difference was that group therapy was now also compared to a gratifying (body-oriented) individual therapy. However, despite these chronic reproaches for poor and inadequate group therapy, Sue showed up steadily. She was the group's most stable member! The group therapists never got the impression that the individual therapist shared Sue's devaluation of the group. He thought that this was Sue's own project and if she attended the group punctually, she should be allowed to follow her own path. The individual therapist was not contacted. In the third year, after one year with combined individual and group therapy, a change occurred. Sue became more active in the group, more conciliatory and could appreciate the community of peers. She could also report that her relationship with her boyfriend was significantly better and that, after 5 years of rehabilitation, she now wanted to go back to her job in the tramway.*

What if the "collaborative" therapist contradicts the group analysis? This is a tricky problem. I have no hesitation in warning against therapists whom I know conduct a kind of psychotherapy that is contrarian to group analysis. It concerns directive therapists who neglect the relational aspect and who create submissive patients who do not dare to speak freely about how they react to the therapist's behaviour. Such therapists often have too simple explanatory models and therapeutic strategies based on practical solutions, homework, training regimen, emotional blowout, etc. Such treatment programmes clash with the group analysis' emphasis on patient and long-term self-understanding and self-development in an intersubjective field. But group analysis can also come on a collision course with more psychodynamically oriented individual therapists. It is easy for a therapist to get caught up in the imaginary world of a patient who feels overlooked and hurt in a group and then play along in the illusion that the patient and the individual therapist constitute the ideal couple and that the patient should preferably leave the group. Some therapists are also sceptical about group treatment in the first place. Telephone contact is important here. Any contradictions between individual and group therapy should also be discussed openly in the group.

How to handle longer absences from patients in the group? There are no clear rules here either. Occasional absences do not pose any problem. The chair is left standing, and the patient must pay for the times he/she is away. However, in the event of a longer absence, it may be a matter of giving the person in question leave. Reasons for such leave may be childbirth, somatic illness or mental decompensation, studies or work out of town. Questions about such leave must always be considered individually. Where is the person in his trajectory? Just started, or towards the end? How crucial is the competing project to his/her future? Does the leave taste of an escape? The needs of the group must also be taken care of. If we are talking of longer leaves which counts several months, the person may be advised to terminate but to reapply at a later occasion.

What about therapist absences and scheduled days that fall on holidays? Group analysis in the Nordic countries takes place once a week and the process can easily be halted if several meetings lapse. Personally, I use to run groups on Mondays. The therapy is then affected by Easter Sunday and Pentecost, for example. I compensate for this by moving to Tuesdays these times. If I get hit by a moving holiday (for example, the first of May), I don't do anything about it. If I run the risk of two meetings in succession being cancelled, I try to arrange a compensatory meeting. If so, this must be planned well in advance and preferably be on the semester overview that is distributed to the group. The therapist has the same obligations to the group as the patients. The group should be prioritized over other things. As a practicing group analyst, one must forgo the possibility of impromptu vacations and participation in numerous congresses. Personally, I have an absence of two to three sessions a year, owing to congresses and vacations. I do compensate for these personal restrictions with a long, two months, summer vacation. Sometimes I have had study periods abroad of a couple of months' duration. My groups have then been run by reserve therapists who have been diplomaed group analysts. This has gone complication-free. Of course, such an arrangement presupposes mutual trust between the therapists and that great emphasis is placed on mutual information before and after the leave. Some choose to solve the problem of the therapist's occasional absences by having the group meet on their own. This is, in my opinion, an emergency solution. I would clearly prefer a substitute even in occasional absences.

Following these comments on dynamic administration, we now move to the therapist's role as a group analyst.

Handling the orientation stage

There will meet a group of seven to nine anxious people to the first meeting of a new analytic group. The therapist included, and that is no shame. If it's his/her first analytic group, it's natural to be anxious and insecure. It *is* a difficult situation. He/she faces high and unclear expectations from the participants and perceives his/her own performance anxiety. At the first meeting, the reality is that the group analyst already knows the participants from the pre-treatment interviews. He/she has selected the participants based on professional considerations and with the belief that these individuals have a fair chance, together with the therapist, to develop an analytic group. I find it reasonable that the therapist starts with this fact. That he/she opens the group by welcoming everyone and saying something about the fact that he is the only one in the room who knows everyone from before, that everyone has received a briefing on what group analysis is about, but that this has been very summary and that there is certainly a lot of uncertainty out and about in terms of what this entails in practice and that people certainly are curious about who the other group members are. Another option is to welcome everyone and leave it at that. When I prefer the former, it is because it signals that the therapist is willing to take an initiative and be helpful in getting things started to begin with, that he immediately problematizes the overarching theme of "what is group analysis" and that he suggests that the best way to get started is to get to know the other group members. The problematization of "what is group analysis" is no invitation to an intellectualizing discussion. If so, it should be commented on by the therapist after some time, indicating that one may need some practice to figure this out. The question "what is group analysis" should rather hang in the air. It's an overarching theme that the group members (and the therapist!) will grapple with for at least a year. What characterizes group analysis in contrast to other groups, from regular socializing, a group of friends, to the discourse in the family group and groups in the workplace?

Sooner or later, someone will initiate a presentation round. It's about getting to know each other. "What was your name again, what's your background, have you been to therapy before?" Such rounds of presentation vary widely. The first two who present themselves usually set a kind of norm about what to say, what information you emphasize and how much you say about yourself. Some may dislike such a round of presentation. If so, one is already in the process of discussing goals and meaning. The attitude of the group analyst should be friendly and supportive. A group analyst, above all, is no sphinx. Answering questions with exalted silence is a caricature of group analysis. The group analyst should be a model in terms of kindness, empathy, tolerance, respect, and analytic ability to see and translate complex issues to a common sense here and now language. He/she should, so to speak, through the power of his/her own example, recruit a majority of the members on to "his/her side". In the orientation phase, the group analyst should be somewhat more active than later, somewhat more educational and, above all, more group oriented. The main task in this phase is to help the group become a group and facilitate its development, preferably without compromising anyone. You don't cure any of the participants in the orientation stage!

The orientation stage in group analysis is about getting to know the other group members, accepting the other group members, getting to know the place and the significance of the boundary conditions, getting to know the therapist better, getting a certain idea of what group analysis is all about, contradicting the worst fantasies about retraumatization, and establishing a sense of security and trust. As previously mentioned, there will initially be a submission and defensive idealization of the therapist and an experience of oneself as vulnerable and incompetent. The group will often resort to restrictive group solutions at this stage. The therapist should be patient and not push to make the group "swinging". On the contrary, he should be a mouth-piece for reactive fear unless expressed by other group members: "I can well understand the desire put forward by several in the group to display more emotion and be more direct. On the other hand, it involves more risk. What if one is not taken care of? What if you're hurting someone? It would be strange if such a concern is not present in the group." In the following, I review some examples from the orientation phase.

Example 9: *It is the first meeting of an analytic group. One person has not shown up and a chair is therefore empty. Two of the participants (a man and a woman) find the empty chair disturbing. It would be best to remove it. They scoot over at the therapist who has so far said nothing but a brief introductory speech. The therapist does not answer as he has not been given a clear-cut question. He awaits what the group does. The two activists are rapidly stepping up. "Yes, if no one minds, I'll remove the chair," says one. Just as he's about to get up, the therapist says he thinks the chair should stand. The chair belongs to a group member who may have been delayed for natural reasons. Moreover, it is a good group analytic principle to be careful about acting, but rather try to understand one's own reactions to situations that arise in the group. The therapist adds that he can well understand that an empty chair at the first meeting of the group evokes emotions and action impulses. In his quiet mind, the group analyst notices the immediate exclusion tendency within the group. Nor does he interpret the obvious challenge of the therapist's (administrative) leadership. Instead, he marks leadership and in a pedagogical way.*

Example 10: *It is the second meeting of a training group. One of the members begins by mentioning that she discussed a difficult case with another group member during lunch and wishes to share it with the entire group. She comes up with a longer story and eventually gets some comments from the others. At this point, the therapist is not very concerned with the content of her story. Instead, he says the conversation during lunch, which was the starting point for the story, raises the question of how group members should regulate their interactions outside the group. In ordinary groups, it is easier to keep distance. In group analytic block-training it is more difficult. Whether you want to or not, you'll encounter each other outside the therapy sessions. This leads to a lively discussion. One mentions that he had asked the members of another group how they (who were more advanced) practiced this. After a while, the* *group analyst presents a metaphor. He says that one might think of the group as a boat that is still in port. The boat is about to embark on a long journey. Where it will end up, one does not really know. Besides, the crew doesn't know each other very well and is not quite sure what kind of equipment one needs. It may then be natural to ask the crew of other boats for advice.*

Example 11: *It's the first meeting in an analytic group. The therapist opens with a short welcome speech. After some silence, a short presentation round follows. Then silence again. The silence is commented on, and some say they have decided to be a little hesitant. The therapist now comes up with an interpretation in which he says that the hesitation in the group probably is related to the fact that each individual is concerned about whether, with all their weak points, they are accepted or will be rejected in the group. There follows a sequence calling for rules and leadership. Can one bring bottled water here? How early can one come? How should the payment be made? Should one pay for longer absences due to illness? Robert says he's starting to feel cheated. On the one hand, he pays and on the other hand, he is largely left to his own devices. Some say sarcastically that the therapist makes himself rich in nervous people. There was a noticeable increasing polarization between the therapist and the members during this first meeting. It may be related to the fact that the therapist came up with an interpretation at a very early stage. Did members felt undressed and put in a different cubicle ("with all their weak points") than the therapist? Why is he here? Primarily to make money?*

At the beginning of the next meeting of the same group, Arlene recounts a dream she has had since last time: "I was on my way to London in a plane. The plane crash-landed. I survived but had to stay in a hotel. The hotel was fully booked. No ordinary rooms were available, but I could spend the night in a hall full of urinals." How to deal with such a dream? It was the first time a dream was told in the group. The group was full of other issues. No tradition of working with dreams had been established. The therapist nevertheless decides to go straight to the point. After some comments from members that "it was a strange dream" and "I don't understand dreams," the therapist says he thinks it's related to the previous group meeting. He believes the crash landing is a metaphor of the defeat in her life that led her to group therapy. She survived but needed help. She arrives at a place packed with people and is directed to the toilet. The therapist said he believes the hotel represents the group. Last session she was caught off guard by how many people there were and that aroused a fear in her that here, too, as in several other places, she will have to settle for piss. The therapist goes on to say that this is a general dilemma in the group: How to make room for oneself when there are so many here. Quite surprisingly, seven more dreams are now being told! And the content is no trifles: One dreams that he eats up all the earth and all the water. Another that his thumb begins to grow like a balloon, filling the entire room and pushing him into a corner. A third that the parents are asleep and that a monster comes through the door. A fourth that he lies basted and tied to a railroad track and that the train is coming. A fifth that some drug dealers get into his apartment and slit his throat. A sixth that his teeth fall out and that he is unable to speak or eat. A seventh that there is someone after him. The therapist feels rather sweaty. How to deal with all this? Was it wrong to "give" Arlene something, i.e., attention and the interpretation of her dream, so early in the group's history? Immediately, seven hungry others showed up. How to saturate these? After a while, the therapist says the following: 'This was a lot at once. Unfortunately, we don't have time to deal with all these dreams one by one. Merged, we can possibly glimpse a common theme that has to do with greed, punishment, and persecution. It may have to do with the situation in the group. Here you must share with seven others. It can arouse a fantasy that if you don't cover up your own greed, you can be severely punished." But afterwards, the therapist wondered if he had come out a little high. It was probably wrong to make these interpretations early in the first and second meetings. Perhaps he should slow the process down!

In the latter example, the therapist relates to typical topics in the orientation stage ("will the others accept me?", "how greedy can I be with seven others?"), but the way he does it seems to increase anxiety. When it comes to the choice of interventions, it should be guided by the main task of the orientation stage, which schematically revolves around mentalizing the following experiences: *'This is roughly how a therapeutic group look like. This is how other members of the group look like. This is how the therapist works. What I feared most didn't happen. Possibly this can turn into something. I think I'll give it a go."* In the orientation stage, people are still sitting on the fence. In the conflict stage, they sign up more and say that *if they are going to participate, they want to be involved in deciding how it should be.* At the norming stage, these negotiations are carried out and a tacit agreement is concluded on grounding norms and obligations of the group. Other metaphors for the same thing: The bait the group analyst has held out through advertising and individual interviews is tasted in the orientation stage. Some spit it out and become dropouts. Most people swallow it. At the stage of conflict, it is kneaded in the stomach. At the norm stage, it is taken up into the bloodstream and becomes an integral part of the person.

When the therapist is to guide the group through the orientation stage, he must reconcile general group dynamic processes with what is specific to group analysis. In the latter example, the tab is kept a little too high. The interpretations are a bit Tavistock-inspired. They are a bit bombastic and somewhat plunging. Initially, a simpler style is preferable. The anxiety level is high enough during the first meetings. Don't increase it further. When someone comments on silence and says that they have decided to be a little hesitant, the therapist may nod and say that yes, it is a somewhat unfamiliar situation and indirectly encourage the participants to find out what is unfamiliar and how it can be more comfortable to be here. If a dream is told in a group already at the second meeting, one should rather emphasize this fact (now a dream is told in the group for the first time) than interpreting the dream for the individual. Rather: What is it like to hear such a dream? What are dreams? How can we work with dreams in this group? In the orientation stage, the participants nibble a little in the bait. It's nibbled at different themes and sampled a bit until they sink their teeth in, take a chew, and say "listen, now it's time to move on".

Handling the conflict stage

In some groups, the conflict stage begins immediately and runs side by side with topics from the orientation stage. Groups of professionals can be competitive from the very beginning. The members have their identity as more or less high-profiled therapists or leaders to take care of. In the following, I discuss examples from the conflict phase.

Example 12: *In this group, members had their passports signed quite early: In the third meeting, Tom is harshly criticized for being too intellectualizing. The therapist asks how Tom feels after this criticism. But this concern is not neutral! The therapist's comment is perceived as him taking sides in the conflict, i.e., for Tom. The "backseat therapist" Greg shows up and asks Elsa, who led the attack on Tom, how she feels. Elsa breaks out in a dramatic cry. She has felt neglected and overlooked, and especially by the therapist. She mentions several episodes. The therapist is somewhat puzzled because he has experienced Elsa as the most competitive in the group. It begins to dawn on him that there is a significant need for mirroring here. Elsa has tried to show how good she is but has perceived more criticism than recognition. The therapist does not say anything about this but listens, like the others, on her despair and reproaches. In the fourth meeting, the group members direct their anger at Elsa. Several members find her guilt-inducing. They want to be deprived of the blame she puts in their laps. This is followed up by differentiation and literally clearer rules. Laura tells Elsa that she doesn't think it's a good idea for them to drive together to and from the group. Laura adds that she is struck by the similarity between her upbringing family and the group. They were nine siblings, and the family was characterized by a distant and privileged father who everyone had to comply with. The therapist thinks (but doesn't say it) that it is now safer for the group to direct their aggression at the therapist/father.*

In the conflict phase, the therapist faces many challenges (Indrehaug & Karterud, 2015). First, he should demonstrate that he can tolerate aggression. He doesn't break down if anger is directed at him. Nor does he counterattack (if he manages to control his countertransference). He does not punish those who are rebellious. He is not conflict-shy and does not avoid conflicts in the group. He thinks about the surfacing anger in its proper context, which is the following: After a phase of careful exploration of what this is all about, the group members now say a tentative yes to the project. But on certain conditions. And these terms are different for each member. It deals with topics such as autonomy, relationships with authority, relationships with like-minded people, who decides what, the ranking between members (can someone be the therapist's favourite?), security and trust. It is also about finding out more about what group analysis is all about.

Example 13: *In a private group, the conflict phase starts in the seventh meeting. Symptomatically, Ben has notified the therapist since last session that he is resigning, and the meeting starts with the therapist informing about this. Ben has tasted the bait and spit it out again. However, Ben's defection is drowned out by Walter's topic that will fill the entire meeting. By next session, the group collides with an important football match and Walter asks if they could move the group. The therapist is a little taken aback, hesitates a little and says vaguely that in principle it might be possible. The rest of the group is quite benevolent. After a few minutes of reflection, the therapist says it was a tedious conflict, but that the timing of the group is stuck. Sorry for that. He explains the reasons, that it is not possible to change the timing and that Walter gets to choose. The therapist's clear message is perceived as a relief for the group. An intense discussion occurs with a high temperature. It is about motivation, about the individual versus the group, about responsibilities and obligations and about one's impact on others. Walter goes into negotiations. How about a little group and some football? Half and half? It is rejected. A strict group ethic is underway. But what about Erik's absence in the fourth meeting? Erik explains about job demands. Erik makes suggestions for group rules. It provokes even more. But Vera forces the group to embark on the difficult art of trade-offs. She says she won't come next time. Her four-year-old daughter has a birthday. The daughter has asthma. Crying, she tells of desperate and anxious vigils during pollen season. Next week, she cannot disappoint her daughter. The group bows out but has nevertheless done a significant piece of work. After the therapist clarified the boundary conditions, they performed that kind of discussions that build a group.*

Before next session, the therapist receives the message that Vivi has also resigned. She, too, spat out the bait. The temperature last time seemed to be too hot. The group is clogging up. In the ninth meeting, there was a new round about roles and power in the group. Two have now quit and the therapist is asked if there will be new ones. Yes, it does. The therapist says he is working on the case. Nora says it's important for everyone who's coming and that she thinks it's reasonable for the group members to be involved in deciding that. Vera reacts and says that Nora is far too direct towards the therapist, even almost rude. He is the leader and has the right to decide. The therapist comments that it is his responsibility to select new members for the group, but that

Nora raises an important topic about what lies in the therapist's role in the group. There is a dialogue between Nora and Vera about this. About the therapist's way of responding, about false and genuine authority, about leadership, whether the therapist is a member of the group or not, whether the members are completely powerless, etc.

Example 14: *In another group, the conflict phase also starts in the seventh meeting. Members are in the process of differentiating themselves. Initially, Ruth joyfully shares that she has been feeling much better. She used almost no anxiolytic medication the last weeks. Marlene follows up, saying that the last week was her best in a year. However, then Lene comes in and talks about her despair. She has been on sick leave for two weeks, does not feel better at all, but is forced to start working again. She is exasperated and hopeless. She speaks of suicidal thoughts. She initially had some hope attached to the group, but it's over. She can't bear to take in other people's problems. How's it going to go? Everyone gets tired of her. How long will her boyfriend endure? The therapist says that "it can be difficult to find one's place in the group and start trusting others that one doesn't know very well. For some, the first period can be like a honeymoon. Then there might come a reaction of disappointment. Lene is the first to express such disappointment in the group." Marlene protests, "That's not true." She has expressed disappointment before. Now she feels overlooked, yes zeroed out. The therapist confirms, yes, she's right. Sorry, Marlene had indeed done that. After a few days, the therapist receives a letter from Marlene stating that the last group meeting and especially Lene's suicidal thoughts triggered strong anxieties in her. It made her recall her sister's suicide. It still hurts, and she doesn't know if she can bear to talk about it. She will not come to the next group meeting. The therapist tells the group that he has received a letter from her, that he will call her and that the group can discuss the contents of the letter when she turns up. Anxiety is spreading in the group. The therapist must several times assure that he will call her. Lene becomes very flustered. She says she believes Marelene's absence is because of her. Joe tries to bring in a different topic, but the group keeps returning to Marlene and the therapist. The therapist is reproached that he did not contact her before the session. Lene reacts with strong crying and anger. After a while, Holger comes in and tells how extremely upset he is. It boils inside. He feels cheated. Now he doubts if there is any point in anything. Everything is hopeless.*

Example 14 clearly displays the *disappointment reaction* that is often an essential component of the conflict phase. Initially, a defensive idealization takes place that produces a temporary recovery ("best week in a year"), but which can be followed by a painful de-idealization that in this case is accompanied by despair, crying, hopelessness, suicidal thoughts, and rage. Here, the therapist should cling to the chair as best he can and ride out the storm. The most important thing is to keep one's composure, don't start defending or apologizing, but maintain the boundaries and allow members to react and speak out. In this case, it was a relief for the group when Marlene arrived next time and told her tragic story of a schizophrenic sister who killed herself.

A significant dynamic point of disappointment reactions is that the group members realize that they must take more responsibility themselves. The disappointment reaction spurs the discussion and the upheavals that *must* come about what kind of group this is going to be, about boundaries, roles, obligations, and responsibilities. In an analytic group, different therapeutic processes take place at one and the same time. On one level, the individual gets to tell about herself, relieve herself, ventilate and receive support and encouragement. At another level, one participates in a self-structuring process through the construction of the group self. On this second level, here and now, one plays out one's dependence, defiance, greed, envy, and longing for freedom of responsibility, in conflict with one's own and others' needs for co-operation and community, structure and predictability. At the same time there is activated a nascent longing for a medium to grow in. The challenge for the group now is to create this medium by enabling dialogues between the manifest level (narratives about themselves and the group) and the underlying level at which unconscious forces are at stake.

Handling the norming stage

As we have discussed, the orientation stage and the conflict stage are not clearly separated. It happens that an incipient analytic group can go straight into high-temperature conflicts. When it comes to establishing norms, the group analyst has laid down rather strong guidelines through the pre-treatment interviews and the contract. Norm questions therefore also arise in the orientation stage. However, the great battle of norms takes place in the stage of conflict. When the worst tumult has settled, the group enters a phase where there are some lengthy negotiations about the norms and where these are tested in practice. The group then begins to acquire a structure. That is, rules and routines get sedimented in the matrix as established communicative routes. Maps and terrain don't have to be constantly reinvented. Now it is about making these rules and routines appropriate for the project that group analysis is about. The therapist influences this process by expressing or tacitly accepting certain norms and rules and by challenging others that he/she believes are inappropriate. Moreover, the therapist shows the way through himself as an example.

As already mentioned, the norm controversy often starts with topics that connect the group's boundary conditions with conflicts between individual and collective needs. Typically, this applies to latecomers, absence, socialization outside the group, contact with the therapist outside the group (letters, telephone calls and requests for consultations), confidentiality, permanent seats in the group and the like. The therapist has had his/her say in the pre-treatment interviews and it is important that he/she now relinquishes the role of chief of police. On the other hand, he/she must pay close attention to what is going on in the norm formation process and help to problematize norm issues. If the group shy away from open discussions, *that* should be said. Sooner or later, the therapist will mark *his* boundaries. If a person has so much absence that treatment becomes meaningless and the group suffers from it, the therapist must be clear: Either you follow up, or you quit. Many therapists hesitate too long to put their foot down. This applies in particular to patients with severe personality disorders who simultaneously may appeal with a marginal existence without any social network. If that person loses this group as well, what then? And what about all the possible plausible reasons put forward to legitimize great absenteeism? In such cases, anything but focusing on the person's relationship with the group is a flight. The therapist must hold the person and the group firmly on to this topic and endure accusations of coldness and mercilessness.

In essence, the norming stage is above all the stage for the group members to unite. It is during this phase that one commits in practice to membership in a community. The orientation stage is "see and hear". The stage of conflict is disappointment, autonomy, anger, and rebellion. The norming stage is *wanting to create and belong to a community and conduct the necessary concrete negotiations on its basic rules.* In this phase, the prototype elements of Dorothy Whitaker's group focal conflict theory (Whitaker & Lieberman, 1964) can be observed. One sees the typical oscillation between provocative wants and needs on the one hand, reactive fears on the other and how contradictions are sought to be resolved through negotiations about what can be said and done and in what ways. Within this terminology, generally accepted norms in the group are to be regarded as *group solutions.* Some norms are fundamental to the group self, yes, they are an inherent part of this group self. Others are more superficial and have a shorter lifespan. The following triad is a fundamental set of norms: to meet regularly, to put feelings into words and not to use violence. A highly temporary norm may be the following: Sexual feelings and fantasies should not be talked about in this group.

Example 15: *It's the twentieth meeting. Chris has been silent after he was criticized for his late coming and self-centredness. What about the group, he was asked. After a while the therapist points to Chris' silence. The controversies are brought up again. Roger says that he experiences Chris as a rock singer who only wants to play to full houses and who cannot stand half-empty premises. It reminds him of a previous cohabitation with an ambitious, sexy, and intellectual girl. It became overly turbulent with alcohol abuse, acting out, and her extreme self-centredness. There was no place for him there, just her* *inflated ego. Later, he missed her. It became empty and he cried afterwards. The therapist wonders if there really is such a contradiction between the magnificent and mirror-seeking part of oneself and being part of a community, a group. Siri now tells of her jealousy towards what she experiences are three couple formations in the group. These couples have basked in each other's eyes, she claims. She herself stands outside. She goes on to talk about her own intense need to be seen. Especially by her father who "left her" when her ten-year-younger brother was born. She is ashamed to feel and express the intense need in herself. Several nods movingly. Slowly, Chris comes back on stage. He is surprised that latecomers are associated with self-centredness. But it is true that he has always had big plans. He's kept a lot of them to himself. They were not suitable to share with others. They could possibly make him hazy sometimes, sorry for that.*

Let's summarize this in a more theoretical language: Irritation with late coming is a reality factor from previous meetings. It is understood as individual self-centredness and grandiosity. The group solution is to punish the "sinner" by ignoring him. The solution is broken up by a simple remark from the therapist. An interpretation by the therapist leads to greater acceptance of mirroring needs. The "culprit" acknowledges grandiose traits and participates in a group discussion of shame. This group solution ("it's ok to talk about reprehensible sides that most of us have"), is better than isolating a person (Chris) in the group. It's a more "enabling group solution" than the old restrictive one.

In the norming stage, the group analyst should help the group to relinquish restrictive group solutions and establish a set of group solutions that are consistent with the needs of a group analytic culture. Typical of a good development in the norming stage is that members dare to take more chances by opening up and exposing themselves. When the group can respond constructively to this, it leads to experiences of mutual closeness and care.

Example 16: *This group had a hefty start, but gradually calmed down. In the twelfth meeting, the tone is more low-keyed. Initially, the conflict between loyalty to the group and the desire for sharing is discussed. What the group analysis evokes in one is so hard to bear alone. Is it allowed to share experiences from the group with a husband or cohabitant? Gordon tells of a growing sadness. That he has failed in his project of being a straightforward and nice guy and helpful to others. Tim agrees. He's found himself fumbling the last few sessions, doesn't really know what to say or do. Sadly, he tells of a distant father, of never really getting together, that what was between them could hardly be called a relationship. Eric talks about his "nervous breakdown" five years ago. About how terrible it was. That he almost turned crazy. There was no one to lean on, no one to share the gruesome experience of "unravelling." Esther tearfully talks about her move from north of Norway at the age of 12.*

About everything she lost, everything she still misses, and about her family's long-standing roving existence in eastern Norway before they finally took root again. Marit tearfully talks about her artist parents who were constantly on tour. She was placed with her grandmother. She tells of confusion, outbursts of anger and crying. Oh, how she longed for dad! Through the acceptance of these stories, members create the community that makes it easier to bear the immeasurable sadness and loss that they harbour.

In the norming stage, the therapist's authority is often restored after the disappointments during the conflict stage. It is the beginning of a new and more durable idealization. Idealization of the therapist is an inherent part of the creation of norms. Even if the formation of norms takes place mainly in negotiations between the members, the therapist is always present as the ultimate guarantor. Idealizing the therapist and the group goes hand in hand. Idealization makes the group project worth striving for. It becomes invested with hope.

Example 17: *In the tenth meeting of this group, participants begin to discuss how they experience the therapist. There has been something reassuring about him. Initially, many were afraid and uncertain. Espen tells of an intervention that he was greatly impressed by. That it was possible to have such an overview! Other times, the therapist had spoken more cryptically, but when Espen digested it, it also gave rise to lots of thoughts and new angles on things. Several members are now starting to talk about their relationship with their fathers. Towards the end, the content becomes more and more aggressively charged. Eva talks about her revenge fantasies vis-à-vis father after his divorce from her mother. Wish she called him and scolded him while he had intercourse with the new chick. Moreover, that she punctured the wheels of that lady's car. Gun talks about how annoying it was to constantly have to pay attention to dad, be quiet, not interrupt, and walk on tiptoe when he slept dinner. Terje talks about the rage inside. It's so big he could tear apart, that his chest being sheathed to pieces. In his mind, the therapist is grateful for the idealization of himself. That's what allows the group members to experience and reflect about this rage. The group has taken a new and important step forward in terms of what it is able to talk about and process.*

When does the norming stage end? There are no clear boundaries. It gradually merges with the performance stage, which in group analysis is tantamount to an established group analytic culture. One should also keep in mind that group norms are not something that is up and settled once and for all. They must be confirmed and reproduced through normative acts. If no one upholds the norms, they will decay. Also, within a group analytic culture, the group has its ups and downs. In regressive periods, it's as if it's forgotten how the group previously handled complicated issues. It must go through a new and hopefully short-lived norming phase. Typically, this happens in connection with the intake of new group members.

Example 18: *The group had existed for eight years but had replaced half of its members during the past year. Lene, the first of the newcomers, had an avoidant personality disorder and abundant social anxiety. She was constantly on the verge of sick leave. At the beginning of a group meeting, she says in passing that she was absent last time (without giving notice) because of "the annual meeting" with some friends in her hometown, who meant a lot to her. No one comments on the message. Later, Lene addresses the problematic relationship with her boyfriend and wants the group's views on it. After a while, the therapist says that right now he thinks that theme might be a dead end. He thinks it will be more constructive to examine the problematic relationship that Lene and the group have with each other. Lene seems to have some difficulties with complying with the agreement and the group has difficulty bringing this up with her. Per says that he thinks Lene is perfectly OK. Considering how much Lene struggles, he thinks it's nice that she can occasionally provide herself with something good. The very latest say they have no opinion. Do you have to take a position on such matters? Lene becomes upset and tells the therapist that now she's getting "pissed off." It's like she's done something wrong. Moreover, the therapist is unfair. She has no more absences than others. The therapist says after a while that the group's problem seems to be that it places the therapist in the role of chief of police and that this is related to a refusal of responsibility among members about obligations and reciprocity. This leads to a long discussion about the old versus the new members, about responsibility and the desire to avoid an "adult role" in the group, about fairness, a comparison of absences and about different reasons for absence.*

By this, we have arrived at the group analytic culture. The presentation will now change shape. The group analytic culture is the final stage. There is no higher goal. One should stay there and cultivate its therapeutic possibilities. From now on, I will discuss the most important tasks of the group analyst in a thematic way with special emphasis on the consummation of the therapies. But before I conclude this section, let me comment on Foulkes' slogans like "trust the group", "leave it to the group", "serve the group", "follow the group" and the like. I appreciate these attitudes but will add that Foulkes underestimated the therapist's active role in the process of "serving the group". I would like to add, *"build the group."* The therapist should actively assist the group in its developmental process. Therefore, therapists should ask themselves what the group might need to move forward *qua group*. Does it need some new members, members that bring in "something else"? Does it need more pedagogy? Does it need more trust? Does it need more tolerance for differences? Does it need its members to dare to challenge each other more? And how can the therapist act constructively about this?

The dramaturgy of group analysis

Group meetings in the initial stages of group analysis are unpredictable, laden with intense emotions and contradictions. The group analyst must improvise as best he can and try to keep the anxiety at an acceptable level. As the group settles down, the group analyst should direct herself according to a group analytical dramaturgy. The purpose of this dramaturgy is to optimally stage the group's inner world in its present moment. Each group meeting is composed of phases. A typical course is the following: Initially there is an open or covert negotiation on the topic. Then follows an exploration of the topic. Then an associative turn of the topic into something relevant to the group as a whole. Then an actualization of the topic here-and-now. The emotional temperature and commitment are now at their highest. Then follows a reworking of the topic. Towards the end of the meeting, there will be a downplaying of emotions and conflicts. Let me interject that not all group meetings follow such a pattern. Some may have several sequences. In other meetings, one fails in processing the themes and the group ends with open and emotionally charged conflicts. In still other meetings, there is no actualization here and now.

Aligning oneself with a group-analytic dramaturgy means the group analyst's interventions should align with the group's current phase. It requires a certain musicality. Initially, one should remain hesitant. A common mistake is that the therapist comes on board too early in a commitment to a single member and the topic he/she brings in. Rather, wait and observe what the group makes of it. If you intervene at an early stage, this should be in a way that promotes communication and interaction. The group analysts' activity should be at its highest after the topic has been digested in the group for some time. That's when his/her expertise comes into its own. The therapist now has a wealth of material for interpretations that can convey a deeper understanding of what is going on: the group's initial negotiations, who has taken which positions, how the topic has become entangled in the ongoing group process and how the group members have gradually become actors in a drama that seems to unfold according to a hidden text.

Example 19: *The group is in its second year. For a long time, a tension has built up between Carol and the therapist. Carol has been critical and devaluing in relation to the therapist and opposed when others have idealized him. She is a mental health worker herself and is quick to say that what happens in the group is quite common and highly ordinary. The group meeting in question begins with casual talk about the upcoming Christmas. Relationships with parents come into play. Olav, who until now has emerged as a very controlled and intellectualizing person, begins to talk about his relationship with his father. It follows a tragic story of a stubborn and headstrong man who pulled out of his family, moved on his own, cultivated his quirks, and eventually* *became paranoid psychotic. Olav was the only one who conceded to him at the end. It's a long monologue, but the group is captivated by his story. Towards the end, Olav cries quietly. One of the members of the group is absent and the space next to the therapist is empty. Ann gets up and sits down next to the therapist. She says she felt so guilty. She saw her father in the therapist. Sad and abandoned. She talks about her guilt. Crying. Actually, dad was OK, he just had so awful lot to do. They were seven siblings. What could reasonably be demanded from him? At this point, the group is full of emotions. Carol breaks her ice. Sobbing, she begins to talk about the difficult relationship with her father. She had adored him. He was brilliant. The way he could declaim! The way he could read fairy tales! But at the same time so brutal. He could spank her for the smallest reasons. Other times, there was a real beating. So demeaning! She had to push him away. She had to harden herself. Now is the time for an interpretation. The drama is still intense here and now, but at the same time open for reflection. The therapist says, "And here you've steeled yourself with me. Kept me at a distance with constant criticism. So that I wouldn't mean anything to you. You've shielded something important and vulnerable that could be destroyed again if it turned out that I was as brutal as your father."*

It belongs to the group analytic dramaturgy that the analyst is concerned about *scenes*. At the best, they condensate key conflicts of the individual with analogue conflicts in the group here and now. Example 19 displays a nice example. There is a breakthrough of intense and repressed emotions related to a core intrapsychic conflict which reverberates with concerns in the group as a whole while at the same time being reflected and invested with new kinds of understanding. Such scenes are group analysis at its best. They are definitely "moments of meeting" in the sense of Daniel Stern (2004) and they integrate new waves of emotion consciousness, attachment and augmented mentalizing.

The group analyst should also be concerned about scenes in a less dramatized way. In early stages of a group, the group discourse may be coined by a tendency to accept generalizations and opinions about this and that. It is a defensive style that should be challenged. In MBT it's labelled pseudomentalization (Esposito et al., 2021). The analyst may intervene by asking for concretizations. Where, when, and how did it happen what the individual is talking about. In other words, what was the scene? Who said what to whom in what way? A group must learn to explore scenes. It does not come by itself.

In the following chapters, consideration of the dramaturgy of group analysis will accompany discussions of therapeutic interventions. I will start with the areas where there has been the greatest development in recent years, and which are inadequately incorporated into group analytical theory and practice. It's about the basic components of personality: emotions, attachment, and mentalization.

Emotions in group analysis

The most important component of patients' symptoms is *unmentalized emotions* (Karterud, 2022). By unmentalized is meant that the person's emotional reactions in the past have not been symbolized, verbalized, accepted, expressed, and processed in a conciliatory dialogue with others. It's about emotional memory traces, which, when activated, lead to painful self-states that the person is unable to transform through his/her own mental activity and that he/she would rather just get rid of. If the defence mechanisms do not manage the job, they can be supplemented with behaviour: over- or under-eating, drugs, self-harm, suicide attempts, violence, social withdrawal, etc. *Mentalizing unmentalized emotions is the foremost task of psychotherapy.* First and foremost, it is about FEAR (Karterud, 2022). All clients have a devastating fear of something and most often of something in themselves. *In psychotherapy, fear is alleviated through the processes of corrective emotional experiences and their mentalization.* Thereby, fear is deconditioned and replaced by other emotions like acceptance, forgiveness, reconciliation, love, etc. Fear will often be embedded in shame (which is the fear of decline in social dominance/acceptance combined with fear of being ejected by the group which in turn arouses separation anxiety). It is the fear of having blamed oneself, that one has been scornfully exposed, that one is a nobody; it is the desire to be invisible, the wish that things have not happened and the self-reproach after the *fait accompli*. Fear can also be part of guilt (which is the self-reproaching fear of having hurt others, and a desire to repair). But most important it is the fear of losing control of oneself, one's other emotions, so that others (and oneself!) will see how vulnerable one is, how hurt and angry one is, how scared, how vindictive, how jealous, how longing, how rejected one feel, how sad, how self-absorbed, etc. *This is what group analysis is basically all about. Always. At every meeting.*

The art of group analysis is to assist the group in finding the best possible balance between emotional activation and collective reflection. This is the main challenge for the therapist when he/she is sitting there. Is the group now within a well-functioning window in the sense that significant emotional reactions can be expressed? In principle, the group may be underactivated, that is, flat and boring. It's just talk. People are defensive and talk in a pseudomentalizing way (see *Esposito et al., 2021* on pseudomentalization in groups). Or the group may be overactivated so that raw and unmentalized emotions fill the room and cause someone to run to the door. In both cases, the therapist should "take action." Underactivation testifies to a defensive group and the therapist should say something about what he/she thinks the group is defending against, or make a general comment at the group level, like noting the present lack of emotional depth. Overactivated groups should be stopped. The fighting cocks should be separated, and the therapist should actively engage in getting the other group members on the field in an attempt to reflect on what has been enacted. Therapists differ in terms of how much emotional temperature they are comfortable with. Common mistakes are that they accept both too much empty talk and too much blowout without intervening. Too much empty talk slows down the therapeutic process and too much blowout can hurt and offend too much, leaving wounds that are not processed and possibly leading to dropouts. Finding a good balance here is not easy. We are now talking about *the art* of group analysis. In the vignettes that accompany this text, there are many examples of strong emotions and emotional breakthroughs: "I've never been so angry before." "Then I noticed how deeply distraught I was." "I'm terrified of losing you." "It was horrible to be rejected at the last meeting."

A group must be taught a group analytic discourse. Foulkes simplified it when he said that group analysts must first and foremost be patient, "let the group deal with it." Left to their own devices, groups will reproduce what is common social discourse, and that has little to do with group analysis! Common social conventions will cover-up emotional reactions. During initial phases, the therapist should come up with *repeated interventions of an educational nature*, along the lines of: "emotions are important"; "emotions are of the most important things the group should work with"; "emotions are often something we try to avoid"; "emotions are complex, one emotion can cover up another"; "to know an emotion, one should feel it"; "how much anger can we endure here in the group?"; " jealousy is a difficult emotion"; etc.

How individualized should the therapist be about emotions? A group learns through concrete emotional experiences. The group members learn to challenge each other. They learn this through the therapist as a model. Especially in the initial phases, the therapist should stop at obvious emotional events in the here and now. He/she thus signals that emotions are significant, that this is primarily what the group must learn to explore. (Put more technically: *A group analytical discourse is a collectively mentalizing discourse about emotional dynamics*). The group analyst should stop and point out: "Can we stop a little there, it seems that Kari is reacting to something". The therapist stops, points, and says that we should be curious about this (SEEKING) and seeks to stimulate collective reflective explorations. In such exploratory processes, individual and collective defences will emerge. Kari: "It was nothing, just move on." The therapist should keep the theory of emotion consciousness in mind. Does the person have the capacity to *feel* emotions, or does he/she feel only bodily agitation, stomach ache, etc? Can they put their feelings into words? Is it fear, sadness, anger, jealousy, loneliness, abandonment, or what? Can they think about these feelings? Is he or she able to contextualize these feelings in the present and past? Can they find a good expression of these feelings here and now? How does the group collaborate on this? The group analyst should occasionally take the lead in such work, partly by demonstrating how exploration can be performed and partly by commenting on defence strategies that prevent further exploration. In this work, he/she can use all possible means: "Shall we stop a little here". "John, you seem to have reacted to something." "How did you feel then ...?" "What's the feeling like?" "What's in your legs?" "If your legs got a voice, what would they say?" "How strongly did you react?" "What made it so strong, do you think?" "It seems like this is uncomfortable for a lot of people here." In a good group, these attitudes will be internalized in several of the group members and become part of a group culture that explores emotions without much lead from the therapist.

Theories of group analysis have traditionally emphasized negative "affects" like fear, shame, aggression, hostility, envy, jealousy, obsessions with revenge and destruction. There has been a neglect of prosocial emotions, like CARE (love and empathy), PLAY (joy), and SEEKING. In fact, they are more important for group cohesion than RAGE and FEAR. The analyst should be a model for these emotions in accepting them, being interested in them, and sharing the empathy and joy. When prosocial emotions are mobilized, they are accompanied with a deeper motivation for change.

Attachment in group analysis

Foulkes (and to a certain extent later group analysts) overlooked the theoretical and therapeutic resources inherent in attachment theory. Today, we would rather say that *group analysis, "properly" performed, can be regarded as a long training in more secure modes of attachment.* When people start, most are fearful and insecure, they hesitate to open up, talk about themselves, and often struggle to relate constructively to other group members. They are also afraid to connect; for example, they resist allowing the others and the group to hold profound emotional significance for them. Each one enacts their attachment pattern. The more distanced try to keep the others at a distance emotionally and often intellectualize their relationship with the others. They find what's happening "interesting". Those who are over-involved bring intense emotions, and the group dynamics swiftly assume a dramatic tone. The disorganized, who should preferably attend more structured groups, feel left out for longer periods of time, and display a profound ambivalence about becoming a member "for real", whatever that really entails. To a large extent, patients' attachment patterns can be identified by how they behave in psychotherapy (Talia et al., 2017; Talia et al., 2022).

The vignettes in this book illuminate the intricate journeys individuals embark upon to become more open, sincere, and trusting. They learn to better connect with their feelings, share more openly, show empathy towards others (and themselves), and foster an honest attitude in seeking help during distress, all without unnecessary dramatization.

Group analysts should use the resources of attachment theory in an open and pedagogical manner. First, group analysts should now and then use the very word attachment. He/she should reinforce it when a member mentions it for the first time, and he/she should definitely mention the phenomenon when it is actualized in the group. That is primarily before holidays and when someone terminates. How do members respond to such events? Does it matter to them? Some would say "I couldn't care less. It's nice to have a little break. There are other things in life too." Others will say "it's going to be terrible, how am I going to survive". In this way, the attachment pattern of each individual is actualized, and it can be understood and explored here and now. Members with a distanced pattern are often challenged by other group members: "But are we completely indifferent to you? Don't you care? Don't you feel anything?" For the vast majority, it will be a goal to make the attachment pattern more secure.

The most important tasks of the group analyst in this context are:

1   to be concerned with the phenomenon and in a pedagogic way help the group to explore and understand it;
2   clarify to each individual the challenges he or she has with regard to attachment;
3   be available as an attachment figure ("it seems like I don't mean much to you, Henry, could we talk a bit about that?" or the opposite "it seems that it means a lot to you what I think and feel about you"); and
4   commenting on attachment events when they actually occur ("it's been hard for you to open up in the group, Helga, but now you made it about a difficult topic. What was it like for you?" or "now that you're about to quit, I think it's important to reflect about what the group has meant to you").

Mentalization and mentalizing failures in group analysis

I have repeatedly mentioned that Foulkes summarized the essence of group analysis with the slogan "ego-training in action", that he was ahead of his time, but at the same time bound by the concepts of his time so that his elaboration of what that meant was limited. The full scope of "ego-training in action" require new concepts, such as the core self, the self-reflective self, mentalization and unmentalized emotions, the hermeneutics of the self, self-object needs, otherness, oneself as another, and intersubjective competence. But above all, we should talk about mentalization. Unmentalized emotions which the individual has been unable to process on his/her own become activated in the group. Someone might touch upon these unprocessed emotions, perhaps tangentially and without fully grasping their depth. Yet, this initiates a ripple effect that impacts other members, leading to what Foulkes described as communication at progressively deeper levels. Faced with these phenomena, we can talk about a matrix, a social unconscious and Bion's

metaphor of "thoughts waiting for a thinker" which I would rather para-
phrase into *"emotions waiting for thinkers."* But these concepts can also
obscure some of the essentials of a collective mentalizing process. Foulkes'
texts sometimes give the impression that this process "goes by itself", that
there are forces in the matrix and the social unconscious that just express
themselves, and that the group analyst acts as a kind of conductor of these
forces. A modern view attributes a far more active role to the group analyst.
The development of a group analytic culture that leads to a group analytic
discourse that in turn leads to it being able to mentalize previously unmentalized emotions, hinges on the group analyst. He/she must cultivate this
culture, champion it with warmth, acceptance, respect, and authority, and
model appropriate responses to self-object needs and failures, especially
amid the turbulence of powerful emotions within individuals and the group.
For the group members, such sequences will provide a series of possible
corrective emotional experiences (Pines, 1990).

In principle, we can differentiate between generally poor mentalizing abilities, specific mentalization issues in limited areas ("blind spots" or isolated
symptoms), and mentalization failures during challenging (typically interpersonal) situations. Generally, poor mentalizing ability manifests itself
through statements that are trivializing, denying, deprecating, projecting,
black-and-white-like, irreconcilable, arrogant, concretistic, evasive, schematic,
clichéd, and that have a non-reflective denomination: that it's obvious, that's
just the way it is, that there's no reason to nag more about it (you just have to
pull yourself together). In a well-functioning group, the members challenge
each other when faced with such statements. And if they don't, the therapist
must show the way. Challenging low levels of mentalization is an essential
part of the process of group-analytic psychotherapy. The members are there
because they want to develop and eventually, they get a better understanding
of what this is all about and what it requires. They eventually realize that they
are not moving forward by belittling, denying, and dodging. They react when
they see it in others, and they will hear it when it shows up in themselves.
They learn to measure this process, aided by the therapist, against the ideal of
a free exploratory discourse.

The lower the level of personality functioning, the more often the group
member will experience mentalizing failures in everyday life but gradually he/
she will understand the importance of talking about it in the group. He/she
acquires a space where the mentalizing failure can be processed. Here, too,
the therapist has an important model-creating role about uncovering in detail
painful interpersonal events and thereby clarify the person's intersubjective
experiences. First, the therapist should encourage detailed explorations and
demonstrate the importance of going in depth. Usually, people give in too
easily in such work. They often "buy" the person's story and are quick to
identify with them. "Agree, mothers are anxious and overprotective";
"Damned, so little respect you get. Tell them"; "Your chick is extremely

jealous; sure, you shouldn't quit?" Principles from MBT (Karterud, 2015b; Folmo et al., 2017; Karterud, Folmo & Kongerslev, 2020) suggest that the therapist rather should intervene by, for example, "can we stop here and go back and hear what exactly happened between you and ..." The devil is in the details, and it also stimulates the ability to reflect instead of merely characterizing others. After a detailed review, it is about understanding whole interpersonal sequences, one's own involvement in them and the implications of what follows in the aftermath of events, that is, how to get back into mental equilibrium. How long does it take, and what is it that person doing? Reflecting, talking to a friend, crying, taking a shower, going for a walk, cutting oneself, overeating, listening to a record, scolding one's neighbour, getting drunk, or? The manual for MBT-G (Karterud, 2015b) discusses in depth the therapist's role and intervention options in such cases.

Good groups commute between there-and-then and here-and-now. Often, what is happening out there will also show itself here-and-now. It should be welcomed. Gradually, patients will become more open about their vulnerabilities in the group. This allows the therapist to explore even better what is happening in and with them. When it happens in a dramatized way in the group, it becomes a golden opportunity to deal with mentalizing failures here and now. It often manifests itself through anger, intransigence, attacks, withdrawal, and silence, screaming and crying or someone running to the door. Again, I refer to the MBT-G manual for a detailed discussion of such events. The main principle is that the therapist stops and takes control of the situation, that the actors who are at odds with each other stop with mutual offences and that the therapist puts them in parentheses and brings in the other group members that the actors are "forced" to listen to. What the therapist then tries to promote are reactions to what has been going on, but no suggestions for a solution to the conflict in question. What thoughts and feelings have the others had while listening? The actors should calm down, they should hum themselves because at the moment they are in a psychic equivalence mindset from which nothing good will come. By listening to others, they can gradually become aware of some other perspectives that put their own reactions into relief. Here it is literally a question about "seeing oneself from the outside". Once the actors have calmed down, the therapist can relax his grip and lead a reflection on what happened here and now and what made it all so strong that the actors lost their temper.

While group analytic literature brims with examples of mentalizing failures and their devastating outcomes (see Schlapobersky, 2016; Barwick & Weegmann, 2018), a significant gap remains: this literature lacks a clear theoretical and technical grasp of mentalization failures. The British group analytic literature is somewhat locked into object relational concepts where one tries to explain the phenomenon through reference to "part-objects", death drive and projective identification. However, that kind of theory seldom suggests constructive coping strategies for the therapist. Throughout this last part of the book, I suggest alternative theoretical and technical pathways that, in my opinion, make group analysis a flexible practice that is also capable of dealing with individual and collective mentalizing failures.

On modifying group analytical principles

Addressing mentalizing failures in the immediate moment, as discussed in the previous chapter, serves as a prime example of deviation from classical group analytic principles. Technically, it is akin to the use of "parameters" in psychoanalysis, i.e., use of "non-analytic" measures that should be terminated as soon as the crisis is over. The group therapist takes more responsibility and lead in exploring external and internal events. However, this should not be understood as parallel to parameters in a classical sense. Through participation in exploring events, the therapist helps to train the group. In a mature group, participants do much of this on their own. Mentalization failures in the present moment are more challenging. It tends to put everyone out and favour a *collective* mentalization failure, owing to a rapid escalation of FEAR. This is what Bion (1961) attempted to depict in "Experiences in Groups." Collective mentalization failures are linked to group composition and boundary conditions. When these change in an unfavourable direction, should the group analyst also change his/her technique? In my opinion, yes and no. Group analytic psychotherapy should be a flexible practice ranging from classical group analysis to MBT-G. The first with little leadership and structure, the latter with a higher degree of leadership and structure. Between these two, there exist hybrid forms (Kalleklev & Karterud, 2018). Therapists shouldn't alter their core beliefs but should adjust/tailor their methods, doing more of one thing and less of another, especially when working with groups comprising individuals with significant personality issues (Karterud, Folmo & Kongerslev, 2019). A flexible group analyst will adjust his/her style according to what happens. If the group has difficulties in getting through the conflict and norming stage, the group analyst should stay there and be more active and not act as if the group has already developed a group analytic culture. Being more active means being more educational and working more directly with self-object failures and mentalization failures there-and-then and here-and-now.

MBT-G is a strategy that should be chosen if all group participants have serious personality problems (Karterud, 2015b). The therapist takes a more active stance, is more pedagogic and creates a structure where self-object failures and mentalization failures are explicit targets for the group. Turn-taking is staged, and the therapist tries to go in depth, together with the group, in the exploration of significant events. The manual for MBT-G demonstrates how this can be done technically. This take will prevent chaos and retraumatization, but it can make the group quite rigid, un-vital and un-playful. MBT-G therapists are often uncertain about when and how they can unravel the structure if there is potential in the group for more autonomy. This uncertainty is natural if they lack general group psychotherapeutic experience and training. Thus, some kind of group analytic training should be mandatory for MBT-G therapists. Similarly, many group analysts are unsure how to deal with self-object failures and mentalization failures in classical group analysis, if they lack theory and experience with MBT-G. Optimally, the extremes should stimulate and challenge each other!

Empathy and care in group analysis

Empathy and care in group analysis are complicated themes. An outside observer may easily find a group analyst uncaring. Group members can recount the utmost distress, show their bottomless despair, appeal for advice and help, or they can act destructively towards each other, and the therapist seems to do little about it. Quite often, we may also hear reproaches from patients that we are distanced and disengaged. Group therapy represents a formidable challenge to the therapist's capacity for empathy and care. One might think that ideally, when comparing to individual psychotherapy, one should grasp the principal features of each member's self-structure, their self-states during the group's interactions, and the overall group dynamics from moment to moment. A "complete" understanding is, of course, impossible. In any situation, there are one or more actors in the foreground while other group members stay in the background. The foreground will naturally catch the therapist's attention. From time to time, he/she might look around the group and wonder what the transactions mean for the more passive members. Occasionally, the therapist will also ask about it: "I wonder what this means for you, Emma". But the reality is that the group analyst must navigate in a sea which is both foggy and unpredictable. Situations can quickly change character and thus significance for each member.

Considering how complex a group analytic meeting is, it goes without saying that the risk *of empathic failure* is great. In the self-psychological literature, it is often underlined that empathic failures (in individual psychotherapy) are inevitable. In group analysis, this must be highlighted in capital letters, and I have dedicated a later chapter to the theme. Empathic failure is often experienced as *neglect*, like being overlooked, "zeroed out", not being considered, not being protected from reckless treatment by other group members, that the group analyst has not tried to remember and understand, etc. In reality, the group analyst's dilemma is unsolvable. Group analysis *is* a conglomerate of conflicting interests and needs. If one supports one party in a conflict, the other may rightfully feel let down. There are different and sometimes conflicting interests and needs between the individuals in the group, between subgroups and between individuals/subgroups and the group as a whole. How do we navigate in such waters? What interests and needs should take precedence? Put bluntly: Should the individual be sacrificed on the altar of the community or vice versa?

The group analyst's main strategy is the following: *Make it a problem for the group*, problematize it, but do not try and solve it. However, group analyst doesn't quite get away with this. He is also a participant, arguably the most influential one, within the group. He makes several choices along the way. He might focus on Peter instead of Hans. He points out aspects of Peter's relationship with Erna, not with Else. He takes the initiative to change the subject after a break in Tor's story. He *doesn't* ask how Ragna is doing. He should be able to justify such choices and respond when challenged (and not sink into the role of a sphinx): "Why did you interrupt me there?" An answer like "it got quiet, and I thought you were done" is only a partial truth. Something more should be added, like: "I was also waiting for an opportunity to bring Else on board. The group has a problem with Else from last time and it is important to move forward with this." Such reasoning can be elaborated on, and it says something important about the therapist's mindset, values and priorities and it helps shaping the group's culture. The therapist says implicitly and explicitly: 'Yes, I am aware that there are many and sometimes conflicting interests and needs out and about. In this particular situation, I considered this to be most important because ..." In principle he could also have added that "I see now in retrospect that I misjudged the situation. I didn't realize how strongly you Erna reacted right then."

Does the group analyst have guiding principles when needing to prioritize between varying demands/needs? When he is reticent in the opening phase of the group, despite a strong appeal for help from a group member, he prioritizes the group over the individual. In my opinion, this can be justified by reference to the therapeutic potential *of the group* and to *the time*. A restrained group analyst implicitly says the following: *"You approach me with your distress, and I don't give you the answer you want. I refer you to the group and the group process instead. I strongly believe that this is just as good for you, and it is certainly best for the group as a whole. I'm keeping a close eye on what's going on. We still have a long time left in the meeting. If you don't get on with your problem in this way, I have you in mind and I might raise your topic later."* For this to be an ethically valid justification, the group must de facto *have* such therapeutic potentials. If it doesn't, you refer the painful individual to a new defeat. Technically, this is a significant problem for groups in, for example, psychiatric institutions. There, too, therapists may wish to escape the expert role of feeding a dependency group. They may hesitate in direct answers and say implicitly or explicitly "but what if you turn to the group". But this "group" to which one refers may be non-existent. It may be a "pseudogroup" that is maintained thanks to forces in the system that cause participants to come together (Karterud 1989c). A pseudogroup is not constituted through an independent and voluntary decision-making process on the part of the participants and it is characterized by a lack of common norms and a fragmented and unpredictable group process. What, then, is the individual being referred to? Many group analytic "techniques" *presuppose* that the painstaking preparatory work required to create a group analytic culture has been carried out. *Then* references to the group makes sense. Within *such* a culture, there is a potential of empathy and care to draw on. The group analyst also has the advantage that he/she can observe the neglect and lack of empathy of the other group members and the individual's reactions to this and make this subject to processing if the group is unable to cope with it on its own.

The priorities of the group analysts are highlighted if the needs of the group and the individual become incompatible. If it is not possible to process a negative therapeutic reaction, it is the individual who must go. Fortunately, this rarely happens in a well-composed group. But such a boundary situation also sheds light on more ordinary situations. Group analyst will lean towards prioritizing the group. And on the grounds that what is good for the group in the long run will turn out to be good for the individual. However, it is problematic to *define* "what is good for the group". In some cases, an active and in-depth interpretational work with one person in the group may be what is best for the group as a whole. In other cases, it will be best for the group if the therapist refrains from engaging with a single member. Deciding what is best for the group, therefore, is not easy. It requires long experience and an intimate understanding of what the group's needs are.

Empathizing with the group requires understanding the group's core objectives. The group's project in our case is to realize group analysis, i.e., to create and maintain a group analytical culture through which the individuals in the group can understand and develop themselves. Empathy with the group presupposes that the group analyst has a thorough understanding of the nature of this project. He/she must have experienced it him/herself and have knowledge of its dynamics. It requires an ideal prototypical conception on the part of the group analyst whereby he/she can measure the group's current struggles. It is such comparisons that allow a group analyst, when observing a group, to say to himself: "This group still has a long way to go. Here there is quite a gap between the group culture as it actually is and the way I want it to be. For the group to get closer to my ideal type, stronger refractions are needed in the group so that the group's hidden conflicts and inherent distrust can be processed. *The group needs someone to dare to challenge more.* I cannot dismiss that this person might be me!" That's how, in relation to a project, one can articulate a group's needs.

The same goes for caring for the group. The group analyst caretakes the group by upholding boundary conditions, incorporating new members, minding the group between meetings, enhancing his own theoretical and technical skills, undergoing supervision, and consistently embodying his role as a group analyst.

Transferences in group analysis

There have been controversies over the concept of transference since Freud launched it in 1905. In this book, by the concept of transference, I mean the following: *Distinctly personal ways of experiencing and relating to other people in a therapeutic setting, which are cultivated and reinforced by this setting, and which may be covered up in daily life by social conventions.* This definition states that transference is a technical term, that is, something that only makes sense within a therapeutic relationship. But the phenomenon itself, that each individual experiences and relates to other people in distinct personal ways, makes itself felt in all human situations. The therapeutic situation is constructed in such a way that it reinforces the depth structure by which the individual organizes his or her experiences. It does so by urging individuals to abandon common social censorship, to be fully honest, and to dare to see beyond their own defence mechanisms. In daily life, the opposite usually happens. You cover up what you feel deep inside and think and play with in the social conventions that apply. The definition is consistent with the views of Stolorow et al. (1987). Transference is an *intersubjective phenomenon*. It is promoted by certain contexts and muted by others.

Stolorow et al. (1987) emphasize that transference is to be understood as a set of invariant principles that organize the experience of others and that transference is not repetition compulsion from childhood, not defence mechanisms nor does it represent a distortion of reality. Personally, I think it is important to emphasize that transference *is* based on childhood experiences, that it *can* have a defence function (e.g., keeping others at a distance to avoid retraumatization, cf. Example 19), and that in some cases it must be characterized as distortion of reality. But transference cannot *be reduced* to repetition compulsion and defence mechanisms.

The therapeutic significance of transference is based on fact that pathogenic features of the individual will always reveal themselves, in the relationship with, i.e., in the experience of, others. If the therapist behaves in a particular way, the patient's relationship with him/her will assume a stronger and stronger transference character. Thus, pathogenic characteristics become an ingredient of what is happening here and now. They can be studied here and now and worked through here and now.

Transference is often categorized based on a presumed etiology, such as «maternal transference» or «paternal transference», or as «positive» or «negative» transference, or according to psychosexual stages, such as "oedipal" or "preoedipal." More important is the distinction between transference in the traditional sense and *self-object transferences*. Self-object transferences are experiences of archaic self-object needs of mirroring, idealizing and/or twin-affirming type which become associated with the therapist. Stolorow et al. (1987) denote other transferences *"repetitive transferences."* The problem with the nomenclature here is that self-object transferences are also repetitive. The most important difference between these two main types of transferences is that in self-object transference, the individual wants to receive something *from* the other (mirroring, being part of an idealized relation, being affirmed by equality), while in traditional transference, the individual wants to do something with the other (punish, hit, kill, shut out, have sex with, compete with, etc.). Better terms would therefore have been "other-to-self-transference" and "self-to-other-transference". Because of the established terminology, I will henceforth denote the transference categories as self-object transferences and other-transferences.

In psychotherapy, it is important to awaken self-object needs and connect these to the group, to the therapist as a person and to the therapeutic process. It took a long time for psychoanalysis to grasp the essence of self-object needs and when Kohut formulated it for the first time (1971) he was strongly criticized and attempted marginalized as "non-analytic". In retrospect it is not difficult to understand the heat of this controversy since the theory of self-object needs undermined the foundation of the psychoanalytic personality theory of the time. The theory of self-object needs presupposes a theory of a primary love ("CARE") and that loving empathy is one of several prerequisites for good personality development: "Man needs friends" (Ricoeur) and "Minds are minded because minds mind minds" (Fonagy). When this need is awakened in the patient, the therapeutic relationship becomes invested with a new intensity and vulnerability. Let me add here that different transference types can coexist and that they can alter in a figure-ground configuration. For a period, idealizing self-object transference may be in the foreground. In other periods, other-transference may be in the foreground (e.g., experience of the therapist as stingy and self-absorbed).

Transferences represent stable and distinctive patterns in how we experience ourselves and others, and they change slowly. Transference should be distinguished from situational emotional reactions. Anger in response to perceived offence is not transference. However, such anger can become *part* of a transference relation if, for example, it is taken as yet another confirmation that the therapist does not want one well and initiate old revenge and protection strategies. Thus, there is no clear distinction between "normal reactions" and "transference reactions". Reactions must be examined in their intersubjective context. In particular, care should be taken not to attribute irrational motives (transference) to the patient in situations where the patient's reactions can be explained as a reasonable response to the therapist's behaviour.

An important difference between individual and group psychotherapy is that groups allow the cultivation of *multiple and simultaneous transferences.* Also in individual therapy, several transference conditions may be cultivated and processed. Maternal transference for one period, paternal transference in another and possibly sibling transference in a third. Occasionally, one can also observe how maternal transference can shift to paternal transference within one and the same hour. In the patient's inner world, parallel processes are likely to take place. In group analysis, such parallel processes are given more favourable terms since they can connect with different people in the group. Thus, one can have a maternal transference relationship of an idealizing type to the therapist, parallel to a fatherly submissive transference to one of the other group members, parallel to a sibling-rivalry transference with two other group members, in parallel with a twin self-object transference to yet another group member.

A common belief is that group psychotherapy "dilutes the transference." This is an imprecise statement. In any case, group analysis does not aim to dilute transferences. Quite the opposite. Group analysis aims to provide the transference with broader growth conditions. What is often meant is that the transference pressure on the group therapist may be decreased compared to what happens in individual therapy. This is precisely why, it is said, groups can be a good option for patients with personality disorders. But what actually happens when group therapy might have a greater holding capacity than individual therapy is that the individual experiences support from self-object transferences to fellow patients that help carry him/her over crises in the ambivalent relationship with the therapist. Reactions to disappointments and setbacks do not become as much a threat to the treatment itself.

It is also claimed that individual therapy has its strength in a more detailed and comprehensive processing of transference relationships related to early authorities such as mother, father, grandparents, preschool teachers, and the like. Group psychotherapy, for its part, reportedly has its strength in a more extensive processing of sibling transferences. That might be, but it should be added that the intensity of transference depends on the therapist's working style. There are individual therapies and therapists who do not work "in the transference", but who avoid it and strive for a "rational" collaboration with the patient to identify and solve problems. Likewise, it is possible to run groups that minimize the transference manifestations. Group analysis is a type of treatment that not just permits, but practically demands, the complete utilization of the therapeutic potential found in multiple transferences. How this can be done is the topic of the next chapters.

More about self-object transferences

Let's start with a clarification of the difference between (everyday) self-object functions and self-object transferences. Self-object functions are everyday events and experiences that have the effect of confirming and vitalizing the self. A therapeutic group is usually rich in self-object functions. One is recognized, greeted, listened to, understood, and commented on. One recognizes oneself (affirmatively) in others and one listen to moving stories and people of respect. By self-object transferences, however, we mean that *archaic*, i.e., early, basic, and undifferentiated, self-object needs are aroused which become associated with people in the group. Everyone needs to be seen and heard and respected. However, once mirroring self-object transference is established, it is vital to be seen and heard in a *special* way.

According to Kohut (1984), self-object transferences constitute the key to therapeutic growth and development. They bring to life self-object relations that have stalled healthy development. Archaic self-object needs have been displaced, expressed indirectly and covertly, and have been covered up by compensatory and defensive character traits. When archaic self-object needs reappear, in the transference, a second chance is given. A chance to complete a development that has gone off track. *It is when a patient is literally held in a self-object transference that he/she gains the courage and strength to confront defensive and destructive aspects of him/herself, as these are expressed, for example, in other transferences.* The great advantage of group analysis in relation to individual therapy is that much of what the patient and therapist talk about "there and then" in an individual therapy, i.e., topics that do reveal themselves in the relationship between them, are evident in the lived life in an analytic group, i.e., here and now. So much more becomes visible in a group. But to take in what the individual previously has denied or externalized, but which others can see, the individual must be provided with new resources. These resources can be found in self-object transferences.

Let's break this down systematically, starting with idealization. I have previously characterized the initial idealization as defensive. The reason for this is to underline that it is not a matter of self-object transference. Why isn't it? Because this idealization mainly is a manifestation of defensive character traits of a *submissive* nature. This submission has a clear defensive function. The fear of the group situation and the other members makes the individual sacrifice his own autonomy for the purpose of being protected by an external authority. Submission is the price he pays. As previously mentioned, this stage is usually short-lived. The aggression expressed at the end of this stage is important. Partly it is a belated showdown with authorities one didn't really had to submit to, and partly it is a reckoning with one own cowardice.

It is after the stage of conflict, in the norming stage, that one sees the first seeds of true self-object transference of the idealizing type. Most group members are unconsciously searching for someone or something that can confirm the small hope of change in them. This hope is beautifully expressed by the Norwegian poet Olav H. Hauge in the poem *It's that dream* (translated by me):

It's that dream I'm carrying
that something wonderful should happen,
that something must happen –
that time should open up
that the heart should open up

that doors should open up
that mountains should open up
that springs should flow –
that the dream should open up,
that early some morning we should slide
into a road that we didn't know existed

Idealization often manifests through subtle recognitions and compliments, such as "Nice to see you" or "This is actually a rather pleasant room", "I like the atmosphere here", "thank you for supporting me last time", "now I feel like there is a community here", etc. Like other kinds of transference, idealization is not something that is reserved for the relationship with the therapist. However, by virtue of his role in the group, he finds himself in a special position. His role is de facto the one that most closely resembles the parenting role in the family and therefore stimulates the archaic idealization that belongs to the *idealized parent imago*. In the norming stage, the therapist is carefully scrutinized with regard to idealizability. Emerging signs of idealization are expressions of admiration of aspects of the therapist. It can be his/her education or appearance or clothing, but preferably something that relates to his/her function as a therapist. For example, the therapist's memory, patience, or empathy.

Example 20: *In the twentieth meeting, the therapist was unusually lucky with an intervention. It concerned Lotte's vague story about her mother and their upbringing in the north. It was hard to grasp the meaning of the story. Along the way, the therapist's associations began to wander towards her own summer experiences as a child, especially about the geography and flora of the summer resort. The experience was unusually strong and after a while the therapist says that "it may not have any connection with your story, but as you spoke, I began to envision beautiful summer flowers". Lotte is immediately shaken. She begins to cry and tells of her mother's great passion of flowers. She was widely known and admired for her flower beds. Lotte was very proud of this. This revealed a new (and idealizable) facet of her mother, who had previously been depicted as drab, self-effacing, and guilt-inducing. The therapist's intervention made a strong impression on several group members. In the next hour and repeatedly thereafter, the intervention was referred to as "magic". Did the therapist know about it in beforehand? Was it a coincidence? Did the therapist have unique abilities?*

How should the therapist relate when his abilities are assumed as magical? Satisfied but curious! The therapist should stimulate conversation on the subject. By all means, he/she should not downplay the experience to an everyday realistic plane through trivializing explanations. *In the unconscious, the idealized parental imago has magical abilities.* When the therapist is experienced and referred to as magical, the kind of bridge is being built between unconscious beliefs and the here and now that is needed for the group to become an *illusion-reality*. That is, illusion and reality simultaneously. The "reality" is that group analysts *don't* have magical abilities. But when group analysts are assigned characteristics inherent in an archaic idealized parental imago, he becomes invested with magical abilities. As previously mentioned, many therapists become uncomfortable when they are subjected to idealization. The main reason is that idealization activates the grandiose self of the therapist. As a defence against this, the therapist might do a series of actions, consciously and unconsciously motivated, where the message is variations of "now you exaggerate, this was not so special, I am not that special". *But members want the therapist (and the group!) to be special.* It is a therapeutic blunder to actively frustrate this desire.

Candidates in group analysis often struggle with idealization. In part, as therapists, they are still a bit clumsy and fumbled and harder to idealize. However, the knot lies in their personality. Trainees struggling to establish a safe and stable group-analytic culture, often face challenges assuming idealizable parenting roles. They tend to be overinvolved and engage with the group on an equal footing, i.e., patients and therapists become too similar, or they put themselves in an authoritarian and withdrawn position from which they deliver interpretations that often have a critical touch, i.e., that they become too distant and critical.

Should one never "reality-confront" an idealizing self-object transference? Put bluntly, no! So-called "reality confronting" happens by itself. In group analysis, the therapist is publicly exposed in ways that most individual therapists will squirm away from. In psychoanalysis, the therapist even sits outside the patient's field of vision and analysts make great efforts to avoid meeting their patients in other social contexts. Group analysts, on the other hand, make their mistakes and stupidities in the public eye and are publicly discussed and criticized by their patients. In group analysis, idealization is put to hard trials. In group analysis, it is more relevant to ask patients who have developed a strong idealizing self-object transference what it is like for them when the therapist gets a hard time in the group. If you dare to do that, there will surely surface historical material about conflicts of loyalty and how embarrassing it was when father or mother made a fool of themselves in public.

To the idealization also belongs curiosity about the therapist as a person. Here too, it is important to avoid reality confrontation. Let the process play itself out.

Example 21: *Laura tells in a meeting that somehow it has turned more difficult in the group. It has to do with the feelings towards the therapist. She experiences him as a kind and caring uncle. But she would much rather go to the movies with him and go on a cabin trip than meeting in the group in this* *"artificial" way. This ushers in a long sequence about the therapist. Ingrid speaks of her tumultuous and confusing feelings of love for the therapist from a while back. Everything else didn't matter. Knut shares fantasies about being adopted by the therapist and his wife. Laura is convinced that he is married, has two or three children and a dog. It is especially nice that he has a dog, it is so cozy with walks in the field. The atmosphere during this sharing is quite light-hearted. Else: But I thought we decided last year that he's not married! Morten admits the same fantasy as Knut. Einar says he has thought that maybe he and the therapist could become friends and socialize after finishing the group, "but probably he won't." Knut comes in with several meta-comments defending the therapist's "blank role" "so that the fantasies and feelings can come out freely"(!)*

The degree of idealizing self-object transferences varies from patient to patient, and it also varies greatly when it appears during the course of treatment. Patients who drop out have either not developed any idealization or it occurs because of a traumatic de-idealization after disappointments and/or violations in the group. It is important to know the difference between authority submission and idealization. They may appear similar, but an experienced group analyst knows the difference in the same way that a carpet expert knows the difference between real goods and cheap imitations.

Example 22: *Frank, a married banker in his 40s, was referred for group analysis because of recurrent depression that did not respond to medication. Initially, he expressed great respect for the therapist and was overtly grateful for the opportunity to join the group. For a long time, he referred to the therapist as a "psychiatric expert." He asked for comments on things he had read about anxiety and depression, asked the therapist to offer his "professional views" and called for "expert advice". Initially, he was puzzled, but later grew more frustrated when he didn't receive the responses he sought. As the story of his father came to the table, the behaviour became more understandable. His father had been a strong, charismatic, and wealthy pater familias who managed the family as a strict executive president. If you behaved well, there were expensive gifts. If one behaved "naughty", the children and his mother got to hear it. The father was the axis of the family that everything revolved around. As the submissive behaviour in the group declined, it was not idealizing transference that emerged. Instead, Frank's repressed grandiose self surfaced, mirror-hungry and highly vulnerable to criticism and rejection.*

Compare this to the following (extreme) **Example 23**: *Nina suffered a severe bulimia with a lot of shame. She was a devoted Christian and had prayed to God for many years to get well. The image of God was strict. God looked into most corners of her soul and was not gracious. In the group, she posted about her sinful thoughts and sinful desires and gave God the right in his* *harsh judgement of her. In daily life, she had long inner conversations with God. After about four years of group analysis, she was able to allow herself a somewhat more pleasant and relaxed life. One day, she shares with the group that the therapist's voice has started to blend with God's. She no longer really knew who she was discussing with, was it God or the therapist? She adds that it may not be so strange as she has gradually become more impressed with the therapist. He is incredibly wise. The other patients interfere and say, yes, he's not too bad, but comparing him to God is a bit too much. The therapist, on the other hand, says the following: 'It's nice to hear that I've started to have an impact on you which is comparable to God. Your God has been terribly strict. When my voice is heard, perhaps God will also listen to it and become more conciliatory. By the way, I think the fact that you've gotten better about yourself lately is related to what we are now talking about."*

Dreams often signal the onset of idealization as much as they can attest to its absence.

Example 24: *It's meeting number twenty-four. Tina starts by telling a dream she has had since last time: "I'm in a marina and I jump into a boat that's there, but the boat overturns. I fall into the water and am terrified of drowning (can't swim in real life). But I get my backpack and boots off and float up to the surface and get on land." Tina believes that the dream is related to the previous group meeting when she took the plunge and talked about shameful experiences as a child, when she was beaten by her parents. It was like revealing a family secret and she was afraid of being dismissed. But she was accepted! "It's possible, you don't drown if you talk about your past," she says. It was as if she had received ballast from the group. Ingrid then tells her dream: "I'm in a big city and persecuted by a man who hits me with an iron rod. I fear being killed. However, I get into a hotel and run through the corridors there. But no one comes to my rescue. It's a nightmare." She waked up crying for a long time afterwards. The therapist compares these two dreams and says that both are in some ways about the relationship with the group. Tina seems to have found something here that prevents her from drowning, while Ingrid has no experience of anyone coming to her rescue. Ingrid's experience makes it more understandable that she has been away a number of times and that she has talked about quitting. The therapist adds that he hopes Ingrid stays in the group and that she too succeeds in finding something here that can protect her from destructive forces. Ingrid responds by talking about her anxiety, self-insecurity and desperation. She flutters from one to the other. Can't find what she's looking for anywhere. Everything crunches. She knows she has creative abilities but can't take advantage of them. Two weeks later, Ingrid calls and says she's quitting. She has chosen to start in a different kind of therapy. Tina, on the other hand, is entering an intense dreaming period. In the following months, she talks about how she wakes up at night, writes down her dreams,* *cries and works with them. Several with sadistic content. In parallel with this, she admits to sadistic thoughts about punitive acts towards another "hyper-caring" woman in the group. The therapist believes she permits herself this due to the rooted idealization.*

In group analysis, it is common to have fairly long summer vacations. Personally, I use to finish in the middle of June and start again at the start of school, i.e., in mid-August. The group's absence puts idealization to the test. In the following example, the absence has caused some to resign, and the idealization of the therapist and the group has been shaken.

Example 25: *It's the first meeting after an extraordinarily long summer vacation of two and a half months. During the summer, the therapist has been notified that two members have quit. Discouraged, the therapist tells this initially and Jan replies that he has also wondered about quitting. He was on vacation this summer and experienced anxiety attacks again. He doubts whether group analysis helps. The group analyst starts to question his own approach/project. The idealization of Foulkes falters as well as his belief in his own abilities. However, Astri comes to the rescue of the group. She tells of decompensation this summer, that she became depressed and was bedridden for a long time. "I think it was related to the group's absence as I got much better as the time for the group approached. I need you!" Nils talks about improved social competency. It used to be a nightmare to say hello to new people. This summer has simply been fun. And Fredrik says that "sexual life has returned". Thank goodness the therapist thinks.*

Does idealization have its price?

Example 26: *Six months in, Tom frequently speaks about his idealization of the therapist. Finally, there is a grown-up man who takes an interest in him and whom he can admire. He has missed that all his life. But does he have to perform anything to be liked and accepted? Will it also restrain him? Somewhat later, this becomes linked to a homosexual ambivalence: Does the therapist demand recompense from him? Does Tom have to satisfy him sexually?*

An advantage of group analysis is that it allows de-idealization of the therapist without it becoming a serious threat to the therapeutic bond. If the therapist has failed (in the patient's eyes), the group may still be available.

Example 27: *Six months later, Tom is in a critical period. In a group meeting, he spends a lot of time talking about how miserable things are. He has dropped out of his studies. He's drinking a lot, having suicidal thoughts, and is more confused than ever. He fears that the therapist will throw him out of the group. The therapist is also perceived as cold and dismissive. He is compared to* *the distanced stepfather who occasionally did beat up the kids. But the group steps in. Tom gets a lot of sympathy and support. The other recognize themselves and they care about him. Next time, payday, he has "forgotten" the money. But he rides over the crisis.*

A process of change often requires a de-idealization of (aspects of) the parents. The de-idealization takes place in parallel with the idealization of the therapist or others in the group. In the following example, Ivar begins to see his mother with new eyes.

Example 28: *Ivar was seen as the group's reliable "teddy bear." He was faithful, showed up regularly, and was never involved in the group's tumultuous conflicts. He had few things of his own to say, but always paid close attention and gradually became more and more concerned with comparing his own parents with what he heard from others and through what he experienced in the group. After two and a half years, he occupies most of the time during a group meeting. It revolves around his schizophrenic sister. The whole family has recently been summoned to the local mental hospital. For the first time, the word schizophrenia was mentioned and that the prospects for the future were bleak. It had been terrible. It reinforced his anxiety about his own mental health. In the family there was a large hereditary burden. His grandmother and four of his mother's nine siblings had been admitted to psychiatric hospitals. He was also very worried about his youngest brother (21) who was still living at home. The brother was socially clumsy and difficult to get along with. Ivar reacted more and more to the way his mother treated his brother. She treated him as a doll, it was like she wanted it that way. She did nothing to get him out and become independent. Ivar himself encountered increasing problems with his mother. There was something about the way she related and talked, that he reacted to more and more. She also felt criticized for the slightest thing and was upbeat. "It shouldn't be like that, should it?" he asked the group.*

As can be seen from these examples, idealization is a multifaceted process. How it should be handled depends on *the context*. We will return to this in the chapter on interpretations. Let me conclude with an example that illustrates how the therapist can confuse idealization with (need for) mirroring transference.

Example 29: *In this group, the therapist had been diligently working to reintegrate a patient who had been absent for a while due to decompensation. The group was concerned about this patient and the therapist had claimed that there were strong forces in the group who wanted to expel him. It was a tumultuous meeting in which members felt that the therapist did not take their misgivings seriously and that he blamed them unjustly. At the next meeting, Belinda tells the following dream: "I'm with a friend who is excited about her* *own creative projects. But suddenly I find myself sitting on the roof of a tall house. I get terrified of falling. Then I see a man on a ladder, repairing the gutter. I think that I can possibly save myself by jumping down to him, but at the same time I fear that I might tear him with me in the fall and plunge into the abyss."* The therapist interprets the dream as her trust in him having been weakened due to the events of the previous meeting and that she now fears that he is not able to contain her in the therapeutic process. This makes sense for Belinda, but not for Bess. Bess runs on with reproaches against the therapist in a way that surprises him. She has been depressed for a long time and cried a lot in the group. Isn't she in a depressive position where she too is afraid of harming the lifebuoy/therapist? Gradually, he realizes that it was not the case. Bess' project seemed to be to get the therapist admitting that he was unreasonable and that she (and the others in the group) were right. Cost what it will. The therapist should admit his guilt and apologize and through this give Bess (and the others) redress. Bess did not harbour any idealizing transference. She experienced rather a violation of her grandiose self.

Compared to idealization, *mirroring transference* is more difficult to handle in a group. It is related to the following conditions: It is more difficult to create and maintain the illusion that one is the therapist's eyestone in a group. Moreover, search for archaic mirroring in a group may cause envy and destructive attacks from other group members. The principle known as the Jante Law in Scandinavia also holds true in analytic groups: "You shouldn't think you're any better than us!" In the following group dream, it is said bluntly.

Example 30: *Karen says she has dreamt "that the group was in a swimming pool. I went on the water, but I only reaped 'Jante reactions' from the others!"*
Mirroring self-object *functions*, however, are abundant in analytic groups. People are taken seriously, listened to, confirmed and the like. But the archaic grandiose self causes more trouble. To prevent the group from stifling hints of grandiosity, proactive measures by the therapist are necessary. He/she should comment on tendencies of envy, contempt and ridicule and support the one who ventures into the perilous terrain of grandiosity. It is particularly problematic that the desire for archaic mirroring most often is directed at the therapist. When the therapist supports the group member who wants to be the therapist's favourite, it can easily be (mis-)understood as a confirmation of exactly what the other members fear and hate. In the wake of this, intense feelings of jealousy might follow.

Mirroring transference relates to the grandiose self and carries vulnerability to offences and triggers of narcissistic rage. In the following example, firstly a budding grandiosity is dismissed, then it is acknowledged to some extent and then follows recollections of offence and narcissistic rage.

Example 31: *Frederick says that over the past week he has thought that maybe he has been afraid of success and of having a good time. At school he was often highlighted and often gained positions of trust and at work and with women he could pick and choose from offers. But he then began to shirk away and take things less seriously. He had never had the same job for more than two years. He has now realized that by this way he would never achieve his goals. The group responded mainly with criticism and irritation. Frederick's problem was a "luxury problem". As the group is about to change its theme, the therapist says: "Is it really the case that Frederick is the only one who has ambitions in this group"? Rolf now begins to talk about his failures at work, Anne about her quite ambitious plans, and Birgitte, the group's left-wing enfant terrible, eventually comes in and tells about her shameful innermost dreams of becoming a "nice lady", elegant, formed and cultured. Anne, who was a human resources consultant at a large firm, had sought therapy for somatization and dissociative symptoms. She could have seizures at home where she crushed everything around her but had amnesia for what she had done. At this point in her treatment, she is rid of her somatization and tells the group that she has never felt as healthy as now. At the next group meeting, she says that last week she had a tantrum (without amnesia!) where she hit her husband and told him to go to hell. The reason was that he didn't listen to her and ignored her. The group discussed the need for attention and respect. Oscar, an intellectualizing taxi driver, told (finally!) about his rage at his girlfriend. She kept walking two steps ahead of him. This, and a number of similar situations were degrading. Through the discussion in the group, he could see how he partly "constructed" the situations himself by putting himself in second place. The associations went to his dad. When Oscar was a kid and trying to say something in a family party, dad could say sarcastically "but listen to the small tuff!" It felt as if someone had knocked his legs out from under him.*

On the other hand, it's not easy to let go of a grandiose position. One risks shame and humiliation. If one is cornered, one will defend oneself with teeth and nails, like attacking despicable weaknesses of others that at the same time represent despised aspects of one's own self.

Example 32: *Susan had been in individual therapy with the group therapist for several years before joining a new group from the start. It wasn't long before she established herself in a self-appointed co-therapist role. Numerous comments and interpretations did not get her out of this position and "down among the other group members". The position was linked to an arrogant and destructive devaluation of the other men in the group. They got their ears fluttered for their awkwardness. The therapist (with whom she was an ally in her own eyes) was the "only masterful man in the group". He was knowledgeable and successful. The other men were seen as unsuccessful and impotent. Nobody dared confront Susan, and the therapist inwardly grumbled. All attempts to* *turn the problem to herself fell on stone ground. When she left after a year, the therapist breathed a sigh of relief. In the subsequent meetings, the men were noticeably more active! The topic was speech difficulties at school, about traumatic experiences in connection with stuttering. In this respect, Susan represented a retraumatization. The therapist's mistake was that he did not see Susan's retraumatization in the transition from individual to group therapy. He was unable to help her with a necessary grieving process.*

In group analysis, many of the unmet mirroring needs are processed through symbolic confrontations with significant figures from the past. Through numerous such "settlements", the group members learn to assess and judge situations. They establish a code of what is right and reasonable to demand of others and oneself in different phases of life. Common remarks include "How could you put up with that?" and "If that had happened to me, I would've been furious." But often the offence is *repressed*. In such cases, the therapist must provide interpretations.

Example 33: *The previous meeting began with several members complaining that they couldn't recall their dreams and requesting more guidelines and theory from the therapist. The therapist responded with an interpretation about the loss of an idealized father. There followed a long sequence with Beate about an ambivalent relationship to her father. It was good, but also characterized by "betrayal." Kristine, conversely, discussed her strong bond with her father and the meaningful conversations they shared. Next time Kristine tells the following dream: "I walk on a path surrounded by grass aisles and meet a great man. Immediately, I think we're a good fit for each other. Then he turns and comments how stiff I'm walking." Kristine wakes up, is furious and embarrassed. In the group, she says "he would probably add that I couldn't even dance". The group starts talking about displaying oneself, like in exhibitionism. The therapist comments if the dream is related to the topic last time, about her relationship with her father, that there were aspects that Kristine left out, such as that she missed more praise from her father and that he more clearly expressed that he thought she was pretty.*

In an analytic group, situations that are potentially offensive abound. Indeed, so much so that many, like Heinz Kohut, believed that depth-psychological treatment in groups is impossible for that reason. If the therapist is blind to neglect and offences, I am inclined to agree. In most group meetings, some form of self-object failure occurs, in worst case violations. An important feature of a group analytic culture is that the group has learned to recognize and work with self-object failures and violations here and now. It does this by slowly taking the therapist's understanding and way of reacting as a model. If the therapist does not have a theoretical understanding of the significance of this and has his own blind spots with regard to sound intersubjective interaction, the group misses out on a very important tool for self-understanding and self-development. One situation that is difficult for many in this respect is the intake of new members in the group.

Example 34: *Clara is a new member of the group and "finds the tone" quite quickly with Eric and Anne. Next time, Robert starts immediately. He has been furious since the last session because of the way Clara came into the group. She found a "natural alliance" with Eric and Anne. It was as if they wanted to establish a hegemony that made no room for him. In the meantime, he's had a dream: "It was something that teased out and displaced me in space. I was cornered and could hardly breathe." Robert's associations went to his mother (besides the triggering episode in the group). She didn't make any room for him. Damn it either! She was always there with her problems. She constantly threatened suicide. Recalling it now, he could hardly breathe.*

In the next example, we see how a frustrated need for mirroring and jealousy towards mirroring (by brother) is covered up by a *compensatory helper syndrome*.

Example 35: *Irene was the group's helper. Active, supportive, and encouraging, but often at the expense of psychological understanding. She was a healthcare worker and personally suffered from fibromyalgia. She continually stretched herself. After a year and a half in group analysis, she thinks there is a mismatch between what she gives and what she gets in the group. One day, she shares the following dreams: The first is about her brother who has been out fishing and caught a big fish that he will proudly show off to his father. The second is about her brother and her. They are on a kind of balcony. The brother falls into the water. Desperately, she tries to get him back up. It's hard because he's tied to a chair under the water. She barely makes it but has mixed feelings afterwards. Happy because she made it, but at the same time annoyed with her brother. The relationship with the brother becomes the theme of the group. The therapist hardly has to say anything. A narrative unfolds highlighting a favoured younger brother, her intense but seldom-acknowledged jealousy and envy, and her role as her mother's obedient daughter and helper. The parallel to her role in the group is obvious. The death wish for her brother lingers longer, but she admits that it's her dream and that she might even have thought it best if he were gone.*

In the following example, the therapist tries to *actualize* the grandiose self.

Example 36: *Torgeir is a researcher with great ambitions. But work is slow due to his compulsive traits. At the end of an animated group session, he bravely opens up about his rage against polluters, motorists, and similar subjects. In the past, he has considered this the most natural thing in the world, but* *lately he has begun to wonder if there is something irrational about it. He has been furious about people who take what they want and don't pay attention to others. Perhaps he should also begin to claim his right? The therapist suggests that he has a current challenge through speaking out in the group.*

In the next example, understanding dreams and narcissistic rage is well integrated into the group. It sorts things out on its own.

Example 37: *Beate opens by telling a dream. "It's about two dolls dancing. One is big, but crippled. The second is small with black hair. Then an adult comes and takes the little doll and gives it to me." Beate immediately starts talking about how angry she is these days. It's terrible. She doesn't know what to make of her anger. She had an anxiety attack at church the other day. The group links this to the dream. "The little black doll is probably a part of yourself." "Yes, probably." Another group participant: 'I think it's the therapist who shows up in your dream and gives you the little doll. She's black and angry, isn't she? Maybe the therapist wants you to own more of your mind"? "Yes, but what am I going to do about it"? This topic takes the first part of the group meeting. Two meetings later, Beate sits down in the "therapist's chair" and starts up immediately: "I'm in a war mood, I want to provoke and fight." "I'm so angry, I must have someone to be angry with. I want to destroy something!" "I don't know if I believe in group therapy any more. It's just talk." Later to one of the other group members: "I've been kind all my life. I don't know how to argue. Teach me."*

Sometimes the group shares grandiose fantasies and masters a difficult exploration of fantasy and "reality". In that case, the therapist doesn't have to do much.

Example 38: *The group meeting begins by addressing the theme of being able to trust oneself. But how can one judge one's abilities and achievements? What yardstick applies? Reidar talks about his uncertainty about the future. He dreams of becoming an actor. He has joined an amateur group. Hilde has drawn and painted quite a bit. She dreams of being able to make a living from it and write a book of fiction. And what if she could remove all racism in the world? Lise dreams of being a housewife on an estate 200 or 300 years ago. No work, just indulge in idleness, interesting pursuits, and luxuries. The members exchange information about the social status of parents and grandparents. The atmosphere is characterized by both joking and seriousness. Towards the end, Terje says that he has bought a book on group psychotherapy (Yalom) and browsed it a bit. He then glances at the clock, remarking, "I suppose it's time for Sigmund Jr. (Freud) to wrap up." The therapist doesn't say much at this meeting.*

Following the grandiose self and mirroring needs, there's also the emergence of shame. Shame can often be suppressed. Even more painful when it breaks through.

Example 39: *Trude was the femme fatal of the group. Rude, active, and challenging. Slowly, she becomes "more common." After three years of group analysis, she starts one day and humbly asks if anyone else is on the leap to say something. No. Then she would like to talk about shame. About her shame. About her sexual life at the age of 15 or 16. "If you just said you liked me, I didn't need more than that, you got what you wanted. I was desperate for confirmation. But the reputation I got at school was damning. If anyone saw me now, when I'm about to finish my law degree? What will they think? Hypocrite? Oh, how I'm ashamed." Strong crying, but also strong support from the group that talks about being able to restore one's dignity.*

In connection with termination, it's common for the departing individual to receive a lot of attention. Being in a strong mirroring self-object transference can arouse intense envy.

Example 40: *Marit cries in connection with her termination and receives much comfort and understanding from the others, except Erling. Erling "doesn't trust Marit"; he senses something "hidden beneath the surface". The therapist asks what this reminds him of. Erling breaks down, crying intensely while discussing his relationship with his mother. She used to have her recurrent outbreaks of crying and reproaches about all the misfortune that had befallen her and about how troublesome Erling was for her. The reproaches were that he was so selfish and should always be the centre of attention. But the most troublesome thing is here, now in the group. His dilemma here is that he has difficulty with waiting and concentrating on others and that his intense desire to be at the centre of the group's attention (and especially the therapist's) makes him feel selfish and self-absorbed. The therapist offers an interpretation that supports "self-centredness", and other group members provide numerous examples reflecting the wish to be the "star pupil". The discussion then circles back to Marit's conclusion.*

There are myriad strategies for covering up intense mirroring needs. One such strategy is passive aggressiveness. In the following example, this strategy is softened enough to become available for reflection and change.

Example 41: *Arne has finally progressed to the point where he is about to complete a demanding course in his studies. His passive aggressive orientation has led to many delays, but now he is in the final stages of his diploma thesis. At the end of a group meeting, the therapist asks Arne how it has been that no one has asked him about the thesis lately. He begins to cry and says he feels* *overlooked. The next meeting begins with the same theme, about not being seen and not making oneself visible The group discusses a masochistic position in which one receives confirmation of one's own fears and wishes by opting for suffering rather than taking action to be seen. There is a lot of wonder from the others about how Arne could sit and ache for so long and not speak up. He talks about how he tested the group, as he is in the habit of several other contexts.*

In group analysis, one becomes, whether one wants to or not, a participant in the drama of others.

Example 42: *Espen had processed his exhibitionism through his group analysis. His starting point was panic attacks and agoraphobia. He avoided all types of social gatherings. Now he was engaged as an actor! Ole had witnessed Espen's therapeutic course and how it aroused admiration in the group. In this meeting, Ole tells the following dream: "I'm in a concert or theatre hall. There are a lot of people there and I'm sitting in the back. But then I walk forward towards the stage to get a better look. I get on the side and eventually up among the actors, but I'm afraid of being dragged onto the stage." At the previous group meeting, Espen had talked about his successful theatre performance. Based on the dream, the group discusses mirroring needs, envy, and identification.*

These examples show some of the myriad manifestations of the grandiose self, with associated mirroring needs, offences, rage, and envy that appear in group analysis. The challenge for the therapist is primarily to *see* it. Secondly, to find forms of intervention that can deal with it in constructive ways. I will elaborate on this in the chapters on self-object failure and interpretations.

An analytical group is also rich in *alter ego (twin) self-object functions.* While idealization is about admiration and leaning on others, and mirroring about being admired and acknowledged, alter ego self-object function is about being affirmed through the experience of equality. *Universality* as a therapeutic factor in groups (Yalom & Leszcz, 2020) captures something of the same: It strengthens me to experience that I am not the only one in the world who feels and thinks this way. We are several in the same boat. I am not alone and isolated in the world. I can share my experiences with others, be understood and have a conversation about this on an equal basis. An analytic group is rich in situations and statements that have alter ego features: "I can relate to what you say. I felt the same way. I've also had such thoughts. For me, it wasn't exactly like that, but it was similar, it was..." This type of statements often represents the transition from listening to a detailed story to a more in-depth dialogue about the topic of the story that is relevant to the group. A sense of equality is a prerequisite for a deeper sense of community, solidarity, and commitment – these important factors that anchors the group self. Such experience varies in terms of intensity and timing. For the individual, it is often a momentous experience: "The last time I really felt that I belonged to a community. It was strong. It's been with me for all week." In some, this occurs after a few months, in others after a few years, in some, unfortunately, never.

Alter ego means "the other like me". In Kohut (1984), the term refers to affirmative experiences in relation to like-minded people, to a mate, a best friend, a close and equal confidant, or a good sister or brother, or a pet. The need for an affirmative twin helps offset the negative experience of others as rivals. The other is for the individual both a potential rival who, in the worst case, can destroy one, *and* one who can supply the individual with positive identity through affirmation. This dynamic lies at the heart of any group. An analytic group is characterized by the fact that the fundamental polarity of confirmation versus destruction can be explored more directly and honestly than in most other contexts. But the prerequisite for this is that the self-object bond is strong. If one embarks on taming and transforming destructive forces, the positive bond must hold. To endure intense envy and lust for murder towards one's brothers requires a simultaneous sense of need for a community. If the envy is acted out through hostile attacks, this is simultaneous an attack on one's own self. This is how destructiveness and self-destructiveness are connected. The self is a self "for and with others". Attacking others can involve sawing over the branch you are sitting on.

The ambivalence between affirmation or destruction always prevails between siblings. Many group members carry with them wounds from sibling relationships that affect their ability to relate to peers. Their ability for alter ego relations (ability to close friendships) becomes processed in the group through stories of sibling relationships and actualization of sibling relationships here and now. Typical stories are being told about being pushed aside by a new and favoured sister or brother; a sibling's illness, accident, or death that enshrines a sense of guilt for their own desire to destroy; the experience of being a newcomer to the family but not allowed to because older siblings have occupied all the positions; that one or both parents fail and that the child early assumes parenthood in relation to siblings at the expense of alter ego relationships. A common theme in groups is that an only child relives an idealized longing for siblings. Other group members can become "the brother/sister that I've always wanted."

Archaic alter ego (twin) self-object transference is less common in groups. It manifests as a unique and stable alliance between two group members, characterized by closeness, familiarity, and an immediate understanding of each other. They often address each other and have a slightly different tone among themselves than towards others. The relationship does not have to be symmetrical. It may be initiated by one of the parties who has a strong twinship need and succeeds in "recruiting" another. The therapist can also experience twinship transference.

Example 43: *Rolf, a 35-year-old creative but lonely and isolated photographer, became increasingly debilitated by recurrent depressions. He grew up in an "intense family" where his two older brothers had "already occupied everything": Mom's lap, dad's interest, and the nature of the conversations at the dinner table. There was no space for him. The older brothers appeared partly as arch-rivals, partly as parent substitutes. They were never affirming like-minded peers. After three years of group analysis with much scepticism towards the other group members, he develops a marked* alter ego *transference in relation to Mette. He addresses her often and differently than to the others in the group. He often asks her how she's doing, gives her small compliments and little eyerolls and nonverbal inquiries, jokes with her. At the same time, he shows a delicate ability to understand her and pick up essential things in her stories. Mette reciprocates this in a positive way. Not so strongly, but she shows that she appreciates it. Her background is different. Having been raised by a hysteric, unstable mother and a father with pronounced paranoid traits, she sought psychological nourishment elsewhere. Luckily, she had her sister and brother. The distress bound them together and they survived by supporting each other and validating crucial experiences with their parents. Compared to this, Rolf invites a more playful twin relationship within a context that is not characterized by distress and distortion of reality. Mette accepts this and at the same time detaches herself somewhat from the close bond with her sister. The alliance between Rolf and Mette is openly acknowledged by the group and the group has never attacked it. The therapist points it out from time to time and says a little now and then about what he thinks it means for Rolf who has never experienced genuine equality and for Mette where the sibling relationship was a strained necessity to survive. Rolf's relationship with the therapist is also characterized by twinship transference. He often experiences himself as a subtle co-therapist and is convinced that he and the therapist share a deep commitment to group analysis understood as aesthetics and poetry.*

The following example illustrates the onset of twinship transference between two patients.

Example 44: *Birgit was the group's exalted, lonely, and intensely suffering narcissist. She consistently maintained a distance from the rest of the group. In this group meeting, she was more unhappy than ever. Among other defeats, she had received a script for a book in return. The book was about her attempts at self-therapy via dreams. Marius was also intellectually ambitious. He says he dreamed of Birgit last week: "The dream took place on a railway platform. We got on the same train, I in front and you behind. You were very ladylike and nicely dressed and wore a ponytail." Birgit becomes very engaged in the dream and they talk about it for a long time. Towards the end, Marius says that he thinks the dream is about him and Birgit somehow "being involved in the same project".*

Pets can also serve an important twin self-object function.

Example 45: *Trine has a severe personality disorder and hardly any satis-factory relationship with any other human being. At the first group meeting after the holidays, Trine says that she has had a much better time this summer. She has thought a lot about the group. She's wanted to bring her rat and show it off. Am so proud of it. The rat is the one closest to her. "It's weird, but it's like we understand each other."*

Other transferences

Other transferences concern rigid, distinct, and restrictive ways of experien-cing and relating to others. As we have discussed previously, group analysis aims to cultivate such transferences by emphasizing honesty, abandoning conventional forms of interaction, and diminishing defences. Other transfer-ences may present as stable and dysfunctional patterns of relating or as fleet-ing, unique reactions that emerge during the course of treatment. Sometimes other transferences are obvious from the start. Other times, it takes time to see them. These transferences might have been masked by other behaviours, or the therapist may have taken time to recognize the significance of certain personality traits. Often, understanding − for both therapist and patient − culminates in an 'aha' moment where the traits are comprehended in relation to both the past and the present, simultaneously crystallizing in a symbolic scene or dream. Once such condensation has been revealed, the further ther-apeutic process is about *working through*.

As previously discussed, self-object transferences and other transferences alternate in a figure-ground manner, and the therapeutic dialogue adapts in response. The therapist's task is to facilitate self-object transferences through the group process so that an authentic self-development can get started *at the same time as* other transferences are processed in the group. One facilitates the other. In other words, several processes take place here *at the same time.* The therapist's fundamental stance toward other transferences, which should be explicitly expressed in the group, is to welcome the problem's emergence in the present context − whether in relation to the therapist, other group mem-bers, or the group as a whole. This facilitates better exploration, under-standing, and potential transformation.

Other transferences relate to significant figures from one's upbringing. Apart from mother, father and siblings, there may be grandparents and other relatives, neighbours, playmates, health professionals, schoolmates, and tea-chers, as well as strangers if traumatic experiences are involved. It concerns multiple people for each patient and in a group, it can be a hassle for the therapist to keep track of who represents what in the past and present for seven or eight participants. This challenge underscores the importance of maintaining clear notes and revising them as new information emerges.

In previous examples of self-object transferences, we have also encountered examples of other transferences. We remember Gunnar in Example 1, who had settled in *"the back seat of his parents' car"*, a metaphor that made a lot of sense to his attitude towards the group as a whole. In Example 19, I discussed Ruth who for a long time was *critical and devaluing* towards the therapist as she had been with her father for many years. Reidar in Example 21 displayed a compensatory *submission to authority* that covered up his own need for mirroring and narcissistic rage. With Kari in Example 23, there was a *gentle surface* combined with a strong dear about revealing family secrets. With her behaviour, it was as if Kari was asking for "nice weather" in relation to her mother: "I promise to be kind and pretty and not tell anything to anyone". Underneath this adaptation, it boiled with unresolved rage that manifested itself in sadomasochistic fantasies. In the same example, Ingrid was trapped by her own sense of devaluation.

In Example 24, Terje is concerned that the idealized therapist demands *sexual recompense* from him. The fear was related to a gay relationship many years earlier in which he "paid" with sexual favours to have a relationship with an admired older man. When confusion and feelings in relation to this relationship were worked through in the group, the fear disappeared in relation to the therapist. Later, the therapist encountered a transference rooted in his relationship with his stepfather. The therapist was perceived as *cold and dismissive,* for almost two years! It was connected to his intense need for mirroring, with jealousy and envy. Stepfather and mother were more concerned about each other than about him.

In Example 26 about Ivar, the transference to the group consisted of a mother-based transference that involved *keeping distance, being indulgent and not caring too much.* When this began to crack, his anxiety increased because he had to see his mother's (and his family's) pathology more clearly in the eyes. Example 27 outlines Trude's endeavour to have the therapist recognize his guilt and offer her restitution. This was also her tragedy in relation to her father. She struggled to live up to what she perceived as the demands of a strict and demanding father. Then came her personal breakdown and in its wake, all the traumas and all the privations in relation to her father. For her to get better, dad had to acknowledge *his* share of the blame for things going so badly.

In Example 31, Frode reacts with a lot of rage to Åshild as a new member of the group. The association with the dream reveals that it is about a rage against mother that *left no place for him.* In Example 32, Irene's *helper role* in the group parallels that of being a mother's good girl and helping hand. Beate in Example 34 introduced herself from the beginning in the group as the *sweet, kind, gentle girl,* a role she had acquired in her upbringing and who covered up a seething chaos of greed, jealousy, and envy. Significantly, her plead to another group member is: "I've been kind all my life. I don't know how to argue. Teach me." Arne in Example 38 had always felt overlooked at home. He had *given up on manifesting his needs.* He met the group with the same attitude. The transference was that "there is no point in saying what I am interested in here either, as no one will understand it or take it into account". In the following, I will elaborate on the topic of other transferences with a few more examples.

Example 46: *Elisabeth quickly takes on a co-therapy role in the group. After some time, this is so clear that it is commented on by the therapist. Yes, Elisabeth feels that it is a safer position than being a "naked group member". She recounts her experiences with her psychotic mother, whom she felt compelled to protect to prevent her decline and potential forced hospitalization. Elisabeth developed sensitive antennas for the needs of others. She couldn't bring her own needs to her mother. They were misunderstood or gave birth to bizarre reactions that could leave Elizabeth confused. From this point on, this was the essence of Elisabeth's treatment: realizing that the group and the other members were not her mother, daring to lean on others and engage in mutual dialogues.*

The following example highlights the importance of not allowing oneself to be pushed into a role that is desired based on the patient's transference needs. In this case, it was a protracted power struggle in which the patient exercised a massive devaluation that could easily have provoked the therapist to act in ways that confirmed his experience of being a victim.

Example 47: *Guttorm, a 45-year-old dentist, was a test of patience in the group. He repeatedly devalued the therapist, the whole group as well as group analysis as a kind of treatment. He came up with all sorts of "tricks" to tilt the therapist out of his role. On one such occasion, he got up in the group and screamed. His associations went to the kindergarten where he was full of envy for the other children and where he did the strangest things to attract the attention of the kindergarten aunts. In the group, the therapist was accused for all that he did not do. After a year, things changed with the following dream: "I am a passenger in a large and almost lavishly decorated aircraft. Suddenly, I discover that the plane is without a pilot. What should I do? I couldn't fly and I didn't understand the lever and instrument panel. But there was no way around it. I had to take charge and eventually managed to get the plane down to the ground." Guttorm and the other group members immediately associate the dream with his main theme in the group that he wanted the therapist to steer his life. Guttorm talks about starting to take reefs in his sails. He has tried and often succeeded in forcing people earlier in his life, but with the therapist he has not succeeded. And maybe that's a good thing. Perhaps it's time to grab the levers himself.*

In the following example, the transference is condensed into the accusation that *"the therapist is only concerned with money."*

Example 48: *Merete had seven siblings to contend with, especially after the successful business-father began to live a sexually debauched life with mistresses in a way that blamed the family in public. Shame struck mother and children. In the twentieth meeting, Merete bursts into tears. She accuses the therapist of not caring about her. Yes, he doesn't care about anyone else either. All he cares about is making money. The therapist comments: "This is similar to your experience with your father, Merete. He didn't care either. Though in the early years he might have, until money and success went over his head and he started to freak out. You've probably feared the same thing with me." Merete now starts talking about what a bad big sister she had been. Several of the siblings had major problems after their father's misbehaviours. Now she experienced a terrible guilt. The therapist: "You may feel some of the same towards the members here in the group?" "Yes, I fail them too. It's only a matter of time before I'm ostracized here." The rest of the group meeting is about the relationship between Merete and the other members.*

When the transference is about devaluating the therapist, the group is good to have.

Example 49: *Reidar talks about his vulnerability and desire for recognition and care from the therapist. Geir doesn't get it. For him, the therapist is indifferent. "He's not in the group." But the group doesn't buy that. Geir is refuted by the others and the focus turns to him. Geir shakes it off, but the episode is conserved as a memory in the group that becomes reactivated later on as a perspective that challenges Geir's devaluation.*

The examples show how self-object transferences and other transferences are intertwined. They presuppose and complement each other. The therapist's challenge is to see it and then help the group to see it so that the group-analytic discourse takes on its optimal dynamics of acting and reflecting in the perspective of multiple transferences.

The therapist's self-object needs and countertransference

As with the concept of transference, there is no unambiguous definition of the term countertransference. *Historically, the perception of countertransference has shifted from viewing it as a result of a therapist's unresolved conflicts or defects, which inhibits the therapeutic process, to an intrinsic aspect of the therapeutic dialogue that should be utilized constructively.* My definition of countertransference is the following: Countertransference is the *phenomenon that the therapist's judgement is threatened or temporarily impaired due to interpersonal processes in the therapeutic field.*

This is a relatively "conservative" definition of countertransference. It is consistent with the views of Foulkes, who incidentally wrote little about

countertransference in group analysis. When I prefer a conservative definition, it's because more modern definitions include all emotional reactions of
the therapist. This, in my opinion, is overinclusive. *It is self-evident that individuals have emotional reactions to others and use these emotions to understand
the other person.* This belongs to the intersubjective basic condition of human
existence. If normal and universal human reactions are to be labelled countertransference, the term loses its meaning.

Countertransference appears as subjective experiences of fatigue, difficulties
with concentrating, irritation, impatience, etc. This interferes with the optimal
calm and distance required for the group analytic reflection that is a prerequisite for facilitating interventions. It is essential to highlight this *ideal* of a
position that is optimal for group analytic judgement. Countertransference
appears as a threat or deviation from such an ideal-typical position. We are
talking about a *normative* position, i.e., a position that our experience indicates is optimal for promoting group analytic reflection and intervention. It is
not a question of any *absolute position* from which one judges what is true or
false. This position has many co-ordinates. It is influenced by processes in the
individual group member, between the group members, in the group as a
whole, in the therapist's personality, his/her life experience, cultural identity as
well as group analytic knowledge and skills.

*Broadly speaking, in the initial stages of a therapist's practice and training,
the sources of countertransference and suboptimal judgement are as much
within the therapist as they are with the patients.* New therapists more often
feel insecure, anxious, helpless, irritated, paralyzed, and thought-blocked.
This is related to the internal confusion that arises when there is a mismatch
between the demands of the situation and the resources needed to master
these demands. To become a good group analyst, the therapist must deconstruct and reconstruct a series of theoretical, personal, and societal beliefs
that also touch his/her identity. *Gradually, as one becomes more proficient in
group analysis, the sources of countertransference shift more towards the
patients and the group.* Countertransference now becomes a signal for
reflections like: "Usually I handle similar situations better than this. What is
it that makes my judgement impaired, that I feel a little cornered with a
diminished capacity to think and express myself?" The answers vary as we
know. It may be that one is threatened by an erotic attraction to a patient,
that one feels helpless in relation to a patient, that one is furious with one,
that one feels excluded by the group, etc. The next step is to reflect on one's
own versus other's contribution to the experience. Is there a weak point in
oneself that is activated? Or is there strong role pressure from the other(s)?
What counts for one or the other? If one concludes that there is actually an
exclusion process taking place in the group, the challenge is to understand
why and how and think through possible interventions. Why was the therapist deposed? When? By whom? Who now acts as an alternative therapist?
How can the topic be brought to light so that it can be worked through and

dissolved? Similarly with helplessness. What is my contribution versus the others'? Am I the only one in the group who feels helpless with respect to patient X? Am I subtly rejected and banned? Is it a defence against retraumatization? How can this be brought to light without resorting to some reproachful "you make me helpless" intervention?

Countertransference is of course frequently discussed in group analytic supervision. An important goal of supervision is to internalize the key ingredients of the supervisory process so that the group analyst can reflect on his countertransference on his own. However, it will often be the case that group analysts participate in peer groups almost on a lifelong basis and thus acquire a permanent base from which to discuss their own countertransference problems. It should be clear from this discussion that it is *not* the case that if you become experienced and skilled enough, you don't experience countertransference!

If the therapist is in a narcissistic imbalance, they are more likely to mis-interpret group events and tolerate fewer frustrations inherent in being a group analyst. A group analyst's private life is often the primary source for satisfying their self-object needs. But his/her professional activities are by no means unimportant. Therapists, like other people, need to succeed. If the group goes badly, it devours their self-esteem. There may also be additional factors that make the therapist extra vulnerable. Some does research on groups and have invested interests in "good results". Some should have their groups approved as part of their efforts to become an approved group analyst. It is important to recognize such needs and give them full legitimacy. There are many motives that drive a group analyst. Partly it is idealism and altruism, but there is also a need to earn money, a need to do something interesting and a need to succeed in an ambitious project with other people. I once received feedback from a group member displaying that an open recognition of this can have surprising therapeutic effects.

Example 50: *It concerned Reidar, previously mentioned in Example 3, who was characterized by the model scene "sitting up in the tree, at a good distance from other people". Reidar remained in the tree also in relation to the group for a long period of time. At one point, however, he was able to tell the following, addressed to the therapist, in the group: 'It's almost a bit embarrassing to say it, but it's actually the case that what you said almost a year ago made a strong impression on me and contributed greatly to my involvement in the group and through that helped me move forward. We discussed my passivity and the fact that I didn't change. Then you said, admittedly a little jokingly, but still, that you also needed people in the group to get better. You were interested in recovery for my part, but also for yourself. You needed to feel like a successful therapist. I actually thought, okay, I'm not going to disappoint you!".*

I must admit that I sometimes think about destructive patients, pondering, "Oh my God, why did I let you into the group? You're ruining it." And in fact, there are some patients who *do*. That is, they destroy the therapist's group analytic project. They act in ways that make it almost impossible for the group to create and maintain a group-analytic culture. The group gets locked in the conflict stage. The most common mistake one makes as a group analyst is to admit people who are not really suited for group analytic psychotherapy. There are people whose level of personality functioning is too low. In addition, there may be poor matching for *this* group, poor "chemistry" between patient and therapist, too poor social structure in everyday life, covert psychotic processes, wanting treatment for opportunistic reasons (to get social security benefits or financial compensation) or being dependent on drugs or sedatives. *An important countertransference reaction is not realizing how destructive such a patient can be to the group as a whole.*

Example 51: *Ingrid (27) came to the group after previous day hospital treatment. Several years ago, she had had a couple of transient (albeit of months duration) psychotic episodes. She was now on medical rehabilitation and lived alone in her apartment. The network was flimsy. In the pre-treatment interview, she was depressed, distraught and crying. She said she spent a lot of time in bed and had no structure during the day. But she strongly believed that she could manage group analysis and appealed to start as soon as possible. The therapists knew her from the day hospital and accepted her with much doubt. On the positive side was her motivation, traces of attachment, idealization, and a possible developmental potential in her infantile appearance. The group quickly became very important to her and in the short run she improved her social functioning. But after a while, it turned out that she was unable to work through her own norming phase in the group. She got stuck in a mixture of a submissive and rebellious position. Submission involved presenting a number of practical problems to the group, wanting answers and help. When she didn't get the help she wanted for, she became angry, accusatory and punishing. The issue for both the group and the therapist lay in recognizing that she couldn't grapple with the psychological implications of her presented problems. The group was banging against a massive concretism and a very limited ability to see things in light of different perspectives. Her father was such and such and mother was such and such. Basta! She displayed unwavering psychic equivalence thinking. How she would relate to people was a matter of strategy. What strategy should she choose, she asked the group. Her concerns were discussed and problematized in different ways, but without much progress. Ingrid gradually settled in an outsider position in the group. She was unable to participate in the discourse that engaged the others. That was a way of talking about and understanding things that was quite alien to her. The therapist now and then turned to her and asked, "and how are you then, Ingrid". This eventually became frustrating for all parties. The therapists' attitude was to be patient,* *"she may gradually be able to relate in a different way". The other group members distanced themselves. One of them said, "But in the way of thinking and being, you sound like my brother, who is paranoid schizophrenic." Yes, a perfectly correct observation – she did. After a year and a half, Ingrid became acutely psychotic related to a trauma with a boyfriend. She was hospitalized and the psychosocial support around her was stepped up. However, she returned to the group. Now the distance between her and the group was even more palpable. There were different worlds. Physically, Ingrid often had to get up and walk around the other end of the room. The group showed care and concern for her, but it became more and more apparent to everyone that the care she needed was not of a group analytic kind. What people felt and thought about Ingrid in addition to the care could not be expressed. That would be too brutal. After a couple of months, the therapist took the decision and informed Ingrid that group analysis did not work for her and had to be terminated during a period of two months. Ingrid's reaction to the rejection was heartbreaking and the fear of suicide was enormous in the group. But she managed to get through without a resurgence of psychosis or need for hospitalization. The last group meeting was moving. Everyone was sad, but also relieved.*

The importance of the other(s) in group analysis

So far, I have emphasized the importance of the others (members and the therapist) in the group as affirmative self-objects and as projection figures and actors in the externalized drama that is played out in accordance with dramatized scripts in the inner world. To a lesser extent, I have underlined the importance of the other's *otherness*. I have emphasized the importance of *similarity* in the discussion of self-object functions: "I feel that way too" and "yes, I can relate to that". But equally significant are "no, that's not how I look at it", "I think completely differently" and "I can understand what you mean, *but ...*" Group analysis offers similar and recognizable stories, but also different stories, different experiences and different ways of thinking. This polarity between equality and difference, the same and the other, is a prerequisite for a fruitful dialogue. I refer to the theoretical discussions I undertook in the chapter on self-psychology and hermeneutics. Within the group analytical tradition, the Danish group analyst Bente Thygesen (1992) has highlighted diversity as a group-specific therapeutic factor.

The main issue for many individuals is that they find themselves trapped in a stagnant inner dialogue from which they cannot break free. The inner world offers only repetitions of the same limited scripts. The individual thinks and feels in unproductive circles. He/she is a prisoner of what Freud called the repetition compulsion. The conflicts seem unsolvable. The same thing happens time and time again. *Something else needs to be done.* Nothing will come out of a group of eight people where everyone has a paranoid personality disorder and where one says "I don't trust other people" whereupon the others say in unison that they feel the same way. Someone must challenge, bring in different points of view, see it all from a different perspective.

In the group analytical process, there is a movement from the need for affirmation and similarity (self-object functions) to a greater tolerance for otherness. Through affirmation and equality, a trust is built up around the others as "friendly others", which is a prerequisite for being able to open oneself to the otherness of others. The other's otherness testifies to thoughts, feelings and behaviours that the person has not dared to embark on. They may be repressed or denied, perhaps considered irrelevant or never actualized. In an analytic group, one eventually must deal with this otherness. What the individual experiences in an analytic group, but rarely reflects upon, is to be participating in a discourse that, thanks to the otherness of others, is far richer than what the individual is capable of on his own. The group-analytic discourse is often more complex, more contradictory, and more nuanced than the dialogue the individual is able to conduct with himself. This means that the group can discuss problems and work through problems in a way that the individual is unable to do because of his/her limited perspective and blind spots.

This can be regarded as a *particular self-object function of groups.* I denote this a *discursive self-object function.* The individual experiences a more thorough understanding and mastery of interpersonal processes that in the long run strengthen self-esteem. As with all other self-object functions, the individual is inclined to attribute this understanding and mastery to his own self. They may not recognize that their understanding largely depends on others' viewpoints and dialogues, representing perspectives previously inaccessible to them. An important part of the therapeutic process (and self-development) is to internalize the friendly others (and the perspectives on the world that they represent) so that the group-analytic discourse continues in the unconscious as well as in the conscious thinking of the individual. At some point during treatment, patients will often talk about this particular experience of the group as an internalized conversation partner: *"I've been so preoccupied with the group lately. It's surprising. I have long conversations with you."* Through these conversations, the self gains an expanded understanding and eye on new paths and opportunities. In short it develops itself.

In this context, the contributions of group analysis to comprehending the inner world and the dialectics of self and other become evident. Group analysis, supported by a wealth of dream material, reveals that the relationship self − other must be supplemented with self − the others (in plural). Also in the inner world, the self relates to (several) others who (already) are engaged in a discourse. *Also in the inner world, the self is a member of a group.* Yes, I would go so far as to say that the self's group membership is constitutive of the self. *The paradigm of self-understanding is therefore neither the dyadic relationship mother – child, nor the triadic relationship mother – father – child, but the multiple relationships of oneself – many others (the group).*

Empathic failure and self-object failures in group analysis

I have discussed the other as the affirmative other, the co-playing other, and the challenging different other. The possibilities are still not exhausted. Of utmost importance is *"the failing other"*. The failing other must constantly be dealt with in life, but the phenomenon acquires a special significance in group analysis (as in other psychotherapy), owing to the stimulation of archaic self-object needs with the associated hope of completing a halted self-developmental process. The failing other is a potential psychological fire. It's risky to live with. It can get out of control and consume the very process. The failure may be perceived as so extensive that the patient drops out. In smaller doses, it helps to give the process the temperature necessary for change to occur.

It was Kohut (1971) who identified empathy and empathic failures as crucial for self-development and psychotherapeutic processes. Safran and colleagues (2001) expanded on Kohut's original work and the significance of "rupture and repair" of the therapeutic relationship is in our days acknowledged by all kind of psychotherapies. Bateman, Campbell & Fonagy (2021) has recently emphasized its importance in mentalization-based group psychotherapy. By an experienced rupture, the protagonist's level of mentalizing will decline and affect the group process. It is of outmost importance that the therapist recognizes the event and mobilizes the group for repair. Rosemary Segalla (2021) has addressed the same topic from a more classical self psychology perspective. Segalla describes a quite dramatic rupture between two group members where the therapist leaves much of the repair work to the group, illustrating that appropriate interventions from the therapist to a large degree depends on the maturity of the group self.

Are empathic failure and self-object failure the same? Both yes and no. From the patient's side, it will be perceived as the same. "When you don't do this and that, or *do* exactly that, it's because you either don't understand me or don't pay attention to me, or in worst case that you hate me." From the therapist's side, it's different. The therapist may *choose* to be frustrating and thus approach a self-object failure. This does not imply that the therapist does not understand (empathically) the patient's position and experience. It is different when the therapist comes up with a wrong interpretation (or other intervention) and thus demonstrates that he/she has not understood the patient's situation and *thereby* provoke an experience of self-object failure.

Patients' responses to the boundary conditions during the conflict and norming stages might exemplify the merging of empathic failure and self-object failure in their minds. For the therapist, it manifests as an empathically comprehended frustration. For example, quite early on, patients realize that group analysts are "strict" about enforcing time boundaries. The meetings begin and end precisely. But *how* strict is he/she? In groups, this might be put to the test when a person (finally) in the closing minutes enacts a dramatic story. As the clock ticks, he/she breaks out into a (at last!) sobbing cry. Eventually, the dam bursts. The ice is melting. And time is up! Most group analysts will handle such a situation by allowing a few extra minutes and give patients a chance to recover. However, such scenes will often precipitate an experience of the therapist as cold and rigid, a rule rider (just like father!) who does not allow exceptions, one who really does not care. Similarly, when the therapist hesitates to provide individual sessions. And when the therapist problematizes one's irregular payment. "Doesn't he realize I'm terribly ill-advised at the moment? Are we going to starve for him to get his fee?". And similarly, when the therapist points out latecomers: "Should there be a psychological explanation for *everything*? Oh my God! It was impossible to find a parking space. And last time traffic was crammed". This kind of perceived self-object failure – the experience of the cold rule rider – is often contrasted with deeper self-object needs, which makes matters all the worse. "So that's what he's concerned about. Whether one is punctual or not. But how *I really feel*, he doesn't ask."

The following example demonstrates how a humorous remark, devoid of countertransference in response to the expressed devaluation, can alleviate such profound experiences of self-object failure during the conflict stage.

Example 52: *It's the tenth group meeting. Reidun has told a dream about her being on the run and eventually finding a man to help her. The therapist says something general about him wondering how this dream relates to her experiences in the group. Trine snorts: The group! Klaus says he wonders if the man in the dream might be the therapist. More people laugh. Trine objects to the group having such significance. After all, it only meets for an hour and a half weekly. Reidun agrees. Moreover, she is disappointed in the therapist. She got no response to her dream. What's the point then? What does the therapist do in the group? Jorgen gets "some dangerous thoughts": "We could do without him. He's just a wall. We're just getting the ball back." It follows a long tirade of criticism of the therapist's role and especially his passivity. Solveig wants more leadership, that the therapist directs more and makes sure that everything goes right and that no one is overrun in the group. After a while, the therapist jokingly says: "Wells, seems like I am deposed, and that Jorgen is the leader of the rebellion". Jorgen smiles and the atmosphere becomes more conciliatory. The group discusses individual therapy and after a while someone says that individual therapy is even more meaningless, there is no response whatsoever. Not in other therapies either. Jorgen then says that group therapy is actually the best he's ever encountered. Lise talks about how much happens to her, about everything that goes on between meetings, about all the thoughts and feelings that swirl up and that she ponders and processes.*

When one reads through old group records, and supervises candidates in group analysis, it is striking to see the significance this type of self-object failure has in the conflict and norming stage. That it is inherently necessary and constructive is indisputable. As we have discussed several times, the initial disappointment reaction is an essential ingredient in the creation of an analytic group self. *Once* this is established, i.e., when the group acts as a *discursive* self-object, (temporary) fragmentation of the group self will be experienced as any other self-object failure. It comes to light when the group is exposed to trauma, such as the intake of new and "wrong" group members at inopportune times. Members express the loss of the established discourse by discussing their fatigue with the group, questioning its importance, contemplating quitting, and feeling the group has become both annoying and meaningless.

Example 53: *In the second meeting after an intake of two new members, several of the old members express different kinds of frustration. Helge reports the following dream: "I'm on a train. My suitcase (left over from my mother) is open on the floor of the cabin with lots of its contents strewn about. I try to cram it back again but there is not enough space. It's like it's more than what I originally brough with me. It's very annoying and I don't get off the train where I'm supposed to." Signe immediately says, "It was a great picture of being saddled with other people's problems." The therapist: "Yes, it might be frustrating with new members in groups. It tends to be a bit of chaos and mess at first."*

In a well-established analytic group, the members align with the foundational principles, making self-object failures tied to the therapist's management of boundaries rare. The members arrive on time, end without protest, do not demand special benefits from the therapist and have come to terms with the fact that socializing outside the group is no good idea. The arena of self-object failures has changed. It now ties into everyday self-object needs here and now and to reactivated archaic self-object needs and is played out in relation to the other group members as well as the therapist. An essential part of the analytic discourse consists precisely in reflections on approach and response, affirmation, and rejection, (often subtle) disappointments and (equally subtle) offences as it unfolds here and now. *It is conversations about subtle self-object failures that are the everyday life of group analysis.* Less often it is massive self-object failures approaching what we would denote as *retraumatization.*

The following is an example of a moderate self-object failure that is corrected by an empathic interpretation by the therapist. The perception of criticism has reactivated previous experiences of not being good enough.

Example 54: *Grethe felt criticized by the therapist last time. Well into the next meeting, she tells the following dream: "We are at my house and the therapist goes through a long list, point-by-point, of all my flaws and short-comings (one point is 'stupid'). In my right hand, which I hide behind my back, I hold coins that I collect for my husband's birthday. I'm afraid the therapist will discover them." The group comments that they did not notice any criticism from the therapist. The therapist asks if there was a particular episode. "Yes!" The therapist says that it obviously triggered a strong fear that the therapist would take away from her everything good and that it was important for her to protect what's good in the relation to her husband.*

The next example shows how a (bad!) interpretation does not repair the self-object failure but reinforces the failure and only makes things worse.

Example 55: *Terje has been in the group for two and a half years. In this group meeting, he connects to another member who is wondering about quit-ting. Terje has thought of the same. He has lately been angry, critical, and dissatisfied inside and outside the group. The therapy hasn't helped anything. He gets manipulated by the therapist. It's too superficial here and he hates sharing the attention with the others. The therapist thinks: Now we have his whole infantile demanding and reproachful style that he has described in rela-tion to mother, on the table. He presents the following interpretation: "The notion that one becomes whole with lots of attention, care and love is capti-vating, but erroneous. It results in splitting off less good aspects of oneself, such as hatred, envy and jealousy." Terje replies: "I call that having your own ego-centricity thrown into your face!" The therapist shuts up, thinking that the interpretation was coined by countertransference (irritation). He leaves it to the group to soften Terje.*

Self-object function is largely linked to *the experience of being understood*. Similarly, self-object failure is often linked to the experience of *not* being understood. In the next example, the therapist comes up with an intervention that is meant to be supportive. However, the timing is bad. The intervention is perceived as *soul-fascism* (!).

Example 56: *Andreas spends a lot of time in many group meetings talking about the frustrating relationship with his girlfriend. Several of his examples from everyday life indicate that his girlfriend has been imbalanced for a long time. He himself acts like a therapist towards her. After much ado, he breaks up. In this connection, the therapist says that his girlfriend's neurosis was probably too much and that he hopes Andreas manages to get a healthier girl-friend next time. But the relationship between them was not quite over! They kept going in an intense but painful ambivalence. At a later meeting Andreas accuses the therapist of "soul-fascism" by characterizing his girlfriend as* *neurotic as opposed to a "healthy one." Two years later, Andreas engages in a satisfactory relationship with another woman. At this point, the old girlfriend has another breakdown. He can now see the therapist's point and that his relationship with his old girlfriend was too strongly influenced by what was eventually understood as his "survival syndrome" in relation to his family: a reluctance to leave, due to an enormous guilt feeling towards his mentally ill sister and brother.*

When empathic failure and countertransference get mixed, it might become complicated and confusing for the therapist, like in the following example.

Example 57: *It's the first meeting after the summer and members exchange stories about things they're proud of on their own behalf during the summer. Vera says that she went to a fashionable nightclub one evening and met a certain celebrity. The therapist comments (somewhat imprecisely) that pride seems to be an issue for the group. Vera gets annoyed. Does the therapist suggest she adores celebrities? After the group, Petter comments in passing that he saw the picture of the therapist in the newspaper during the summer. At the next meeting, Vera says she was so pissed off last time because of the therapist's comment that she barely made it today. She not only felt disparaged, but outright trampled on: "As if I was proud to have met the blah-blah-talking self-boasting idiot!" The therapist's own grandiose self is now alarmed. Should he say (self-absorbed!) that the topic last time was related to a picture of himself in the newspaper? He doesn't take the chance. Does he confuse his own theme (pride in the image) with the group's? He saves himself by apologizing to Vera (a little flatly) that it wasn't his intention to insinuate that she was celebrity-hungry. An intervention there was no reason to be proud of, he thought.*

The above self-object failure was perceived as an *offence*. The handling of violations in group analysis is of the utmost importance and deserves a separate chapter.

Offence and hatred in group analysis

By offence, I understand the experience of being treated disrespectfully and degradingly by another. *Disappointments* are experiences of failure from the (idealized) other. Offences are associated with the *grandiose self*. Disappointments arouse depressive feelings, offences arouse (narcissistic) rage. Disappointments and offences can, of course, be intertwined: "I didn't expect this from *you!*" Everybody has some bitter offences in their luggage. People with mental disorders have more than others. Violations of the past have undermined their self-respect. Attempts have subsequently been made to cover up the incidents. Psychotherapy involves opening these wounds. Working through old offences is a necessary part of all psychotherapy. It requires that the story (context) comes to light, that the patients are supported and validated in their experience and, not least, that patients are validated in their right to own their feelings. Such confirmation is necessary because offences often are buried in layers of shame and trivialization. "It was so small; there's no reason to get upset; that much you have to endure; it was really my own fault," etc.

Once one has acknowledged 1) that the event was significant; 2) that one is still bothered; 3) that one has the right to feel overrun and degraded; and 4) that the event arouses a natural rage, there follows discussions about what it takes for self-respect to be restored. What is needed varies greatly from individual to individual. It is important that this becomes a group discussion, and that the therapist does not step in with his/her own standard solutions. Some must go through a long period of hatred, intransigence, and a desire for revenge. In others, it is sufficient to be aware of the event and its associated emotions and have it discussed in the group.

Example 58: *Kristian's pivotal trauma was his father's suicide when he was twelve. Time and time again, he and the group were back in this incident. The last thing that was integrated was Kristian's sense of helplessness and humiliation as he witnessed the careless way his father's body was handled when it was driven onto the trailer of a tractor. After having told this scene with all its details in the group and expressed his immense despair, shame and rage, he could move forward.*

Should all stories of violation and abuse be believed? What about, for example, false memory syndrome? Basically, I always side with the patients. And in most cases, I think the stories can be confirmed. Partly by virtue of their own logic and consistency, partly through associated affects and partly through other things known about the person in question. For the most part, traumatic stories are initially told with a layer of trivialization and the real drama and tragedy only emerge when the person, confirmed by the group, takes more courage and tells it the way it "really" was. On rare occasions, I reject a story because it doesn't seem credible to me. Or it may be the case that the extent of the trauma does not reasonably correspond to the consequences. If so, I'll say so. The therapeutic focus then shifts, of course, from content to credibility and relationships.

It is not harmless to activate old offences with associated rage and desire for revenge:

In **Example 59**, *despite the therapist's efforts to guide the group through the norming stage, it repeatedly regressed into a profound yet poorly pronounced scepticism and distrust. The therapist thought that more work needed to be* *done on the topic of aggression and was actually quite satisfied when he went home one evening after confronting Arvid in a more honest way than before and Arvid had confessed to his own intense anger. Even more shocking to the therapist when he heard the next morning that Arvid had been admitted to the emergency department. The reason was that in the evening, after the group meeting, Arvid had driven up in front of his parents' house and fired two sharp shots through the living room window.*

In this book, I have repeated to the point of boredom that group analysis is to actualize the participant's inner drama in the group's here and now. Does this also apply to narcissistic rage, hatred, and desire for revenge? To a certain extent, yes, but there are limits. As has been shown by numerous examples, the therapist in group analysis will often be the target of aggression. He/she is trained to endure it, receives guidance in tolerating it, is to some extent protected by his/her role and, after all, receives a reward in the form of a fee for his/her services. What about fellow patients? Are they entitled to protection? Both yes and no. Not on protection from what we would consider more ordinary criticism and situational outbursts but to some extent from more malignant hatred. It is the therapist's responsibility to select patients so that the other group members *are not* exposed to runaway pathological rage.

Example 60: *Martha's (47) paranoid personality disorder became increasingly apparent in the day department. She could tell (somewhat entertaining) stories of how, everywhere and always, she had a habit of getting into cahoots with people. It became less entertaining when she threatened a fellow patient in the group. The threats were to keep certain information away from the group. When the concerned fellow patient courageously spoke about this, Martha responded with a hateful glare and snarled that she would break her nose outside the group. Repeated attempts were made to process this incident. Martha could not admit that there was something worrisome with her threats. The therapists eventually concluded that there was no alliance for this type of treatment and Martha was discharged.*

The therapist is responsible for monitoring the level of aggression in a group and, to some extent, identifying the individuals involved. A last resort is simply to stop the interaction. Therapists must assert their authority, intervene decisively, halt the disputes, and then shift the discussion towards the underlying aggression. This also entails setting limits. The therapist states bluntly that this way of talking has no purpose or that it is destructive. He/she invites the group to find other approaches. Another approach for the therapist is to redirect the aggression towards herself. Often, the therapist is the right target because the anger is displaced, owing to authority anxiety. In other cases, the therapist *gets* the anger since he/she interferes.

Aside from problematic peaks, anger, the urge to destroy, and the desire for revenge are important and frequent undercurrents in analytic groups (Gans, 1989; Nitsun, 1999; Stone, 1992). The therapeutic challenge consists of helping the group to acknowledge this, not belittle it, but also not to dramatize it. To use a Kleinian expression, the challenge is to "detoxify" the hatred. In the language of self psychology, this means that the experience of self-object functions (that someone in the group wants me well) outweigh the intensity of the hatred and desire for revenge, and instead opens for a symbolically based dialogue that can transform the narcissistic rage.

Example 61: *For a long time, there was a rivalry between Sigurd and Arne in the group. At first, it unfolded through actions in the form of "hidden" points and kicks and subtle devaluation. Gradually, the rivalry was consciously acknowledged and gradually the relationship between Sigurd and Arne improved. After all, they had many common features. One day Sigurd reported the following dream: "I'm playing basketball in a parking lot. Pretty brutally, I mow down an opponent who smashes his face to the ground and knocks out one of his front teeth. A girl blames me, and I feel guilty. Suddenly I see that the opponent is Arne". The dream makes a strong impression on Sigurd. In the discussion that follows, he speaks more worryingly about the violent and antisocial aspects of himself. The group discusses how the rivalry has been expressed in the group. Arne, for his part, talks about his violent tendencies. The therapist comments on the positive aspects of Sigurd's experience of guilt feelings.*

The therapist's interpretations and other interventions

I define interventions as all deliberate statements made by the therapist within the group, aiming to influence the therapeutic process. The therapist also influences the group in other ways. For example, by (unconscious) nonverbal communication, posture, gestures, and the way he/she dress, etc. But such influence is not considered interventions. They are not intended. The therapist has a rich arsenal of interventions at his disposal. The therapist's verbal remarks are further emphasized by glances, facial expressions, and tone of voice. It is common to divide interventions into categories such as informing, communication-promoting, interaction-promoting, exploratory, supportive, advisory, boundary-setting, reality-confronting, clarifying and interpretive.

In psychoanalysis, there is a tradition of ranking interpretive interventions as most important. I agree with such a ranking. I agree that interpretations come in a special position. That's because interpretations are carriers of theoretically grounded explanations. It is through interpretations that the group analytical theory is expressed. These interpretations convey the theoretically understood connection between intrapsychic, interpersonal and group phenomena as well as the connection between the past, the inner world and the group here and now. The understanding conveyed by the interpretations contributes decisively to shaping the group analytical discourse (culture).

But what exactly are interpretations? Since this book bases much of its analytic understanding on hermeneutics, it will be useful to distinguish between interpretations in a more general sense and psychodynamic interpretations. In a general sense, interpretation is an assertion of a supposed meaning of a cultural expression (texts, pictures, human statements, and actions, etc.): "I interpret the text as the author intention to say something about the absence of fathers in our time". "The picture shows the despair that refugees are carrying." "When my mother put it that way, I understood it as …" "The fact that he didn't show up for the funeral shows that …" This is how we incessantly interpret actions and events in daily life. The way we interpret daily life events supplies life, and ourselves and others, with meaning and coherence. In Ricoeur's words, it supplies us with "a narrative unity of life." Interpretation links understanding and explanation. In practice, we commute between these "poles". Phenomenology has an ideal of being "pure" understanding in a more descriptive sense without adding attempts at causal relations that risk being just prejudices. That is the ideal for exploratory interventions cultivated in MBT under the term "not-knowing stance". These are interventions like "can you say something more about it", "what made you believe that …", "how did you feel then?", "I wonder what is going on in the group now". The purpose is to stimulate the individual's (or group's) curiosity and own interpretive competence, like the ability to connect words to one's own feelings. For example, it is important to underline that a statement like "I feel sad" is an interpretation (of a self-state).

A lot of what the therapist does in his/her own mind and what he/she explicitly says are interpretations in this general sense. The therapist says something because he/she thinks (interprets) that there is something in what is being said that is not clearly understood by the participants and that the discourse will become more true/rich or more complex, etc, if the therapist points out connections which are yet not reflected upon.

In addition, the therapist delivers psychodynamic interpretations in a more technical sense. The therapist then tries to link the understanding to a causal explanation. Such causal explanations are based on the therapist's theoretical understanding of personality and group dynamics. This latter section of this book provides numerous examples of this. The therapist comments on what happens based on an understanding that it is about different kinds of self-object needs, especially about idealization and mirroring needs, or that it is about the experience of self-object failure or offence, about traumatic experiences, defensive strategies, fear of one's own emotions, attachment patterns, mentalization failures, etc. I also describe how the therapist preferentially interprets this based on what appears here and now in the group. In this sense, we might talk about group-relevant interpretations, but I rarely use group interpretations in the sense of "it seems that the group is now trying to avoid ...", "the group has a problem with ...", "the group is trying to get rid of ...", etc.

Do we have any knowledge of group analysts' interpretation practices? Astonishingly little. Theoretical discussions are long and in-depth, but research is rare. The same goes for psychoanalysis. In a historical retrospective study of the majority (n=43) of Freud's patients in the years 1907–39, Lynn and Vaillant (1998) found a gross mismatch between Freud's therapeutic-technical recommendations and his own practice about anonymity, neutrality, and confidentiality. Kennard and his colleagues (1990) conducted a study on interventions by group analysts. However, only 10% (n=33) of the members of GAS responded to the inquiry and the results can in no way be considered representative. Nevertheless, it was somewhat surprising that interpretations were ranked that high, and especially that it concerned interpretations aimed at the group as a whole. One should be reminded that Foulkes' did not favour interpretations, but "analyzing interventions", i.e., interventions that assisted the group in making sense of its endeavours.

Let's start with such other interventions. Especially in the initial stages, group analysts should use interaction-enhancing, exploratory and supportive interventions. Such interventions have a model-creating effect and help the group get started with their concern, which is verbal communication. Such interventions that have a common sense flavor are of the type "I have some messages to give", "can you tell more about it", "it seems that you are reacting to what Hans says, Else", "you are quiet today Erna", "I wonder what lies in the silence", "what do the rest of you think about this?", "I didn't quite understand what you meant, Sigurd", "it's nice to hear that you're doing better, Anna."

The standard finalizing intervention is "we have to quit, time is up". Group analysts also resort to limit-setting interventions when the group's boundary conditions are challenged: "I'm sorry, but I don't prescribe medication. You need to see a (different) doctor." And, as we've touched on when the level of aggression becomes destructive: "Look, now I'm stopping this argument. We don't get ahead this way. If you can keep the peace for a moment. What's going on in you that's been silent?". Limit-setting interventions may also be necessary for (new or unbalanced) patients who need help to protect themselves. In the following example, setting limits to one was perceived as an infringement of another.

Example 62: *Heidi is a new member of the group. She is anxious and franticly talkative, posting about her compulsive symptoms, including constantly pondering things she's said, whether it was right or wrong, etc. She also says that she is plagued with sadomasochistic fantasies. This captivates Tore who asks if she could elaborate on this. The therapist intervenes and reminds Heidi of her problem that she constantly ponders what she has said. Now she's about* *to say a lot. Maybe she should take it easier and find her place in the group before going into details about her fantasy life. Focus shifts. After a while, Tore comes back and talks about his experience of being offended. He felt run over and reprimanded by the therapist and was basically pissed off. Thought he could cover up and give the therapist a disguised jab at a later date. In that way he might also have concealed his vulnerability. But now he did say it. Maybe that was just as well.*

Occasionally, destructive acting out occurs. In the following example, the therapist clearly states that the described acting out is incompatible with group analysis.

Example 63: *Towards the end of a group meeting, Olav, as a kind of apropos, says that a year ago, while actually being in group analysis, he set fire to a school and a community centre. He stood in hiding and saw the police and fire squad coming. The triggering cause was a breakup with his girlfriend. He felt desperate. Gudrun, who was an outsider in the group, functioning on a borderline-psychotic level and often unable to follow the group dialogue, makes detached comments that were mainly perceived as support for Olav. A unpleasant mood arises and Anne asks the therapist to say something. The therapist then says that he understands that Olav became desperate after the breakup with his girlfriend, but that such actions are incompatible with psychotherapy. Psychotherapy presupposes that one can handle ideas and emotion on an imaginary level and not let oneself be driven into actions like this. Moreover, it is worrisome that he has not told about this in the group before. The therapist hopes that this will not be repeated, and that Olav will focus on his psychotherapy. To Gudrun, he says that he is somewhat concerned about her lack of sense of what is right and wrong. He contextualizes her behaviour considering her tumultuous upbringing with a borderline psychotic mother and a brutal Nazi father, expressing hope that her moral compass might improve during therapy. The therapist is more satisfied with his intervention towards Olav, than with Gudrun. Gudrun had already demonstrated several examples of acting out that more than indicated that she did not benefit from the group analysis. If the therapist had been consistent, he would have moved forward with this latter issue and taken Gudrun out of the group. Another year passed before the therapist did so. About Olav, it should be said that the other group members at the next group meeting followed up the therapist's limit-setting by addressing other aspects of his (self-)destructiveness, such as the fact that he often drove while drunk. The confrontation had a good effect on Olav, who eventually underwent a formidable development in the group.*

Less destructive towards others, but not towards the group is the following episode.

Example 64: *Reidar and Hans do not show up for the first time after Christmas. At the next meeting, they say that they have attended a psychodrama course together in Lanzarote and that they were aware of the coincidence before they left. The therapist gets annoyed and feels cheated. He makes an immediate and strong statement that this is unacceptable behaviour. If you are going to participate in group analysis, you must follow the ground rules, i.e., prioritize the group and avoid social interaction outside the group. If not, you can quit. In the ensuing group discussion, Hans says this was like getting a reprimand. "Yes," says the therapist, "it was."*

Normally, group analysts should avoid giving advice. But certain things must be taken into account. This includes, for example, other treatment in addition to the group analysis and the time of termination. In certain situations, you must be prepared for the fact that no matter what you do, it will be wrong.

Example 65: *Geir has been in group analysis for two years and now functions much better. During the first year, he repeatedly complained that the therapist did not give him any advice. Now he's making plans to move north. At the end of this group meeting, the therapist says that he has never given Geir any direct advice before, but now he is, suggesting that Geir should complete his therapy in the group and postpone his plans to move north. In the next group meeting, Vibeke criticizes the therapist for acting authoritarian towards Hilde. Geir agrees and says that he got angry last time because the therapist told him so clearly what he should do (!). When Geir later gets serious about moving and quitting, he asks for "leave" from the group so that he has a retreat opportunity. The therapist declines this. The last session was a moving meeting where Geir summarizes the development he has undergone. He talks about the importance of emotions and belonging, about the harrowing experience of being part of a community, being liked and accepted by others. Several in the group then launch fierce attacks on the therapist who is "cold on the border of the cynical" by not granting Geir leave.*

Interpretations can address any phenomena within the group. They presuppose a significant hermeneutic effort on the part of the therapist. First, she must constantly interpret for herself what is going on in the group. Secondly, she must choose a fruitful focus as in every situation there are multiple options. There is never one interpretation that is objectively correct. *Should the focus be on the group as a whole, the relationship between two members, the intrapsychic dynamics, emotions, thought content, defence mechanisms, or transference?* It's not accurate to say that in group analysis, group interpretations are always preferred. An exception here is in the initial stages of the group where group interpretations should be preferred over individual interpretations. But this is also relative. To pinpoint it, one can probably say that interpretations that connects different levels, several time dimensions and at the same time include transferences, would get the highest points. But star interpretations are rare! Optimal timing should also be kept in mind. Furthermore, it's a good rule to delay interpretations to see if any group members arrive at similar conclusions, or if the insight might come from the individual in question. A good interpretation often leads to an "aha" experience. It is immediately felt as something right by the patient and the group. The persons in question feel deeply understood. Good interpretations often lead to new and significant material coming to the table and they deepen the therapeutic process. But good interpretations can also be provocative. Sometimes you must elaborate on them. Especially if they are poorly worded. All group analysts occasionally come up with poor interpretations. They may depend on a poor theoretical knowledge, poor understanding of the group process, misunderstanding of the patient and/or countertransference. One of the worst things one can do is defend bad or outright wrong interpretations. When patients object to interpretations, therapists should always take this seriously and examine their own understanding. It's better to admit when you're wrong or misunderstood than to stubbornly assert your "rightness" and defend a shaky authority. Some interpretations are neither good nor bad. They are simply flat and uninteresting. They don't add anything new to what everyone already knows.

Previous examples contain many examples of interpretations. In the following, I present a number of new examples from different group situations. Here, too, several situations will contain dreams. However, the theory of dream interpretations will be reviewed in a later chapter. *Note that many of the interpretations in these examples contain educational elements about what group analysis is about.*

Example 66 *concerns the first meeting of a new group: After a short presentation round, two members exchange experiences about the same symptoms. Thereafter, Hanne says that she recognizes Tore from her hometown. He played on the football team. There follows a positive sequence between these two. Then, Per mentions feeling somewhat left out when he listened to Hanne and Tore but adds that he once worked in the same city. The therapist now intervenes and says that several members have already found significant similarities and that it is important to create some trust in the group as there is a lot of uncertainty about what such groups are and what group analysis is about.*

Example 67 highlights a notably supportive interpretation during the sixth group meeting. *Anette, 35, a medical doctor, starts crying. She's doing terribly, has gotten worse, barely manages to work, can't stand problems, gets them down her throat and can't stand patients anymore. Last week, she cried in between each patient. She had to pull herself together tremendously. Is group analysis right for her? The therapist responds that it happens that someone* *feels worse at the beginning of a therapeutic group and that it is often related to conflicts that arise when a group is new and one has to deal with many new people. It can be difficult to find one's role here, and perhaps especially for Anette, who is a doctor. One can easily feel overwhelmed by others, not quite knowing how to handle it, leading to feelings of helplessness. In addition, one is often uncertain of what to expect and demand from the therapist in the group.*

The following showcases a classic example of an actualizing interpretation. This type of interpretation is used frequently in group analysis. The essence is that the therapist says that what the conversation is about in examples from the external world also applies here and now and that it is perhaps more fruitful to embark on here and now.

Example 68: *In the sixth meeting, Jon talks about how unreasonable his previous psychiatrist was. He demanded full price, not only the patient share, but full price from Jon when he was sick and missed sessions. The group supports Jon. Jon further talks about his doubts as to whether he should raise this with the National Insurance Agency. However, it might be scary to confront the psychiatrist. The group provides additional examples of unreasonable doctors, bureaucrats, and neighbours. Several discuss their anger and the dilemma of expressing or controlling it. The therapist then says: 'I think the topic makes a lot of sense in relation to the group here. Indirectly, I think you are discussing how rigid and unreasonable I might be and whether it is possible to express one's anger here.' Grethe then says that rage is scary. In her youth, she had tantrums. She completely lost control, attacked her father and razed her room. Cautiously, the group begins to discuss their experience of the therapist. Some say that he looks nice and that maybe he is different.*

Interpretations of externalization are closely related to actualizing interpretations.

Example 69: *The group received two new members last session. Both made, in different ways, a strong impression. In this meeting, much of the time is spent discussing frustrating mothers. Randi talks about her mother's problems and especially about her troublesome dealing with the fourth birthday of Randi's son. Grethe tells about her mother, about her repeated rejections and that she could never give any love unsolicited. Trine plays the role of therapist and makes recommendations for more confrontation and boundary setting towards mothers. Then the therapist comments: 'Yes, mothers can be frustrating, but this conversation might create a notion that all that hurts is outside the group and that it's a matter of getting advice here on how to deal with the frustrating things out there. Perhaps this has to do with the two new members of the group and that it means turning a blind eye to what is frustrating inside here.' Randi now says that she was scared when she heard about the bulimia of* *one of the new ones. A thought ran through her head that here had come a troublesome competitor. (Randi had bulimia herself.) Trine records an episode from last session. Her style was commented on by the male newcomer. That she was "aunty". She had been furious since then. Others now say they didn't find it derogatory. There is a lengthy arguing. Trine is unyielding. The new man, Gunnar, apologizes and says he didn't mean to hurt her. By the way, it was tough to feel Trine's anger. It made him worry. Is that how group therapy works? The therapist concludes by saying that group analysis is not a tea party. Unpleasant things can happen here, and unpleasant things can appear from the past. But in the long run, one might gain on confronting what initially may appear as unpleasant, and which one usually used to avoid.*

While the above interpretations focus on the group, sometimes interpretations targeting an individual's intrapsychic level are pertinent.

In **Example 70**, a recurring theme in the group is Jesper's deep concern that something is "wrong" with him. *He dreams of deformed men and women. He is very anxious about having children, almost convinced that his son would be born with a defect. At a meeting, he tells about a visit to a friend who studied psychology. The friend had a job as a support contact for a mentally disabled boy. The kid was touching. Jesper thought that maybe he too should take such a job. The therapist comments on this as follows: "How about being a support contact for the undeveloped boy in yourself, Jesper?". He flinches and says, "Wow! I'm not quite sure if I know what you mean, but there's something weird inside me. Can I do something about it that way?".*

Interpretations also involve identifying redemptive words and expressions. Not least for the reciprocal nature of what goes on in the group. In the next example, the word "no-talk pact" had a good effect.

Example 71: *The group in focus had pronounced internal conflicts manifested between subgroups. Mette, a relatively new member, disappeared in these disputes. Until the therapist once says: 'Is it the case that the group has a no-talk pact with Mette?' Several now say that they are so unsure about her. They don't know how to approach because she herself participates so little spontaneously. Mette starts crying. Is it perhaps the case that she doesn't belong here? She has otherwise been rather OK during the week but gets anxious as the group meetings approach. She's afraid of what's pressing inside her. She sobs when she tells it. Well supported by the group, she eventually talks about the beast inside herself. About the fear of it coming to light. What does it look like? It's gray, four-legged, big, like a dragon. The group immediately perceives it as an expression of desire, sparking stories related to desire, demands to be sweet and kind and exhibition objects for successful parents* *versus desire to go other ways, chose one's own paths, supply oneself according to one's own needs and take the chance of being greedier and "naughty".*

Occasionally, one's interpretation is dismissed. When the constellation is as in the next example, the therapist should stick to his own understanding. The theme is rivalry. This also includes the relationship with the therapist. By reaffirming interpretations, the therapist shows resilience and emphasizes his consistent presence amid the group's challenges.

In **Example 72**, during the twenty-eighth meeting, Anette (from Example 64) remains frustrated with her challenging patients."*I would like to smash them against the wall." Geir steadfastly sticks to his theme of finding a "super girlfriend" to save him. Olav says that Geir is OK, and that it seems that he can tolerate tough responses from others in the group. But Olav attacks Reidar. He found Reidar's reaction last session childish. He reacted like a kid and took up way too much space. Reidar replies sourly. The therapist says it's as if there's a cockfight going on in the group. In the next session, Geir talks about his intense hatred and envy since last session. He had met a colleague with his beautiful wife and two successful daughters in the cafeteria at work. He was furious and sat down by himself, as far away as possible. Olav says that he has been annoyed with the therapist. He felt misunderstood and pushed into a role. Several members thought that the cockfighting metaphor was excessive. Olav states that he wasn't truly annoyed until the therapist made that comment. It was as if the therapist told him to be like this. At this point, the therapist intervenes and holds on to his previous characteristics. In his opinion, there was a clear rivalry going on in the group. Reidar: "Yes, I think so too, but maybe not in life and death." Geir says the topic bores him. He is more concerned that no one has responded to his own topic since last session. Olav is provoked and calls Geir sizzling and is supported by Bente. The therapist then asserts that the prevailing themes in the group are rivalry, anger, and envy and that it is about who gets a lot or little here. Reidar then admits that "yes, I get envious when others are praised in the group" and cites several examples. Geir follows up by deepening his immense envy and hatred of "those who stand above him", who are more successful than him, who have more money, reputation, family, about the envy of those in the group who have children, something he has not dared to acquire for fear of bonding. The next meeting, Reidar tells the following dream: "Geir and I talk, and I suggest we could come to the group two hours ahead of time." (Implied that then there will be more for everyone.) Who says that the unconscious is not solution-oriented!*

However, therapists don't always have to confront. Sometimes it is reasonable to *act* and show that special needs are considered.

Example 73: *The group starts with Bente taking a book off the bookshelf and dramatically throwing it on the therapist's desk. The book's title is* Suicidal Behavior in Norway. *She'd browsed it at work. It's a wicked book, she says! She reacted strongly to the book's "cold casuistic content". There was no humanness and empathy there. The group discusses Bente's suicidal thoughts and her unpleasant encounters with psychiatry. For the next meeting, the therapist has put the book in another bookshelf, where it cannot be seen from the group.*

Groups can be very constructive, but also astray. In the following example, this is stated bluntly.

Example 74: *At this group meeting, Peter speaks from the beginning. He talks about his studies, exams, previous studies in Austria, writing difficulties, his family, his sister who has been admitted to a mental hospital for several years. The group eventually focuses on how emotionally flat he portrays things. Several express themselves quite critically, doubt his motives and suggest other motives. Peter doesn't recognize himself and starts defending himself. The group is, in the therapist's opinion, going astray. The easiest thing is to say this bluntly. The therapist intervenes as follows: 'It seems to me that the group is going astray. It tries to say something, almost convince Peter, but he responds by defending himself. The group is characterized by one-way traffic. What if we tried to listen more to Peter's story, drawing from our own experiences, and shared these insights with the group instead of trying to 'heal' Peter?'*

In the next example, the group's self-object function is interpreted.

Example 75 could be titled "Baggage for the Summer": *It is the last meeting before summer. Some scattered talk before the group starts discussing group therapy versus individual therapy and how they thought around their first interview. Then, there's a discussion about former members of the group, how they were perceived, and how some members' views on them have changed. When the sequence is about to end, the therapist says that he thinks the group is about to "write its story" and that it does so to ensure the group's identity and existence, as a ballast against the absence during the summer.*

In the next **Example (76),** the process of change in the group is interpreted: *In the group analysis with Viktor (36), some antisocial traits were gradually revealed. Not of the worst kind, but a lot of snooping and "shortcuts". In the group, he exerted significant pressure on the therapist to get him to write a certificate as an appendix to the application for an extended rehabilitation benefit. The following dream revealed new perspectives on his anti-sociality: "I dreamed of a rather pompous event in my hometown, either a theatre or circus, with many celebrities in attendance. I went with a childhood friend. On the way* *in, we passed a great racing bike. I got a thought of stealing it but didn't. We went backstage and were unexpectedly well received. I looked through a hole in the curtain out in the hall at all the celebrities." Viktor's own associations are about feelings of inferiority while growing up, of the longing to be socially accepted, approved, and to belong, but at the same time the conviction that he would "never be one of them," i.e., the socially and intellectually successful. It was surprising that he was so well received in the dream. One group member says that it may not be just about growing up in childhood, but about the group as well, to be accepted here. The therapist adds: "Yes, and that this acceptance makes it possible to take a new look at celebrities. Perhaps also that this acceptance makes it unnecessary to steal racing bikes." The group embarks on a long discussion about needs, about supplying themselves, about stealing, about belonging, about self-esteem and justice.*

Interpretations and "interventions" from the other group members

We don't usually refer to what group members say to each other as interventions. The main difference between the "interventions" of the group analyst and the other members is that the group analyst is more thoughtful and strategic in what he/she says, while the other group members speak and act more spontaneously. The interventions of group analysts, however, might risk sounding a bit detached and theoretical. In contrast, the contributions of members often come straight from the heart, sounding more natural and vernacular, but sometimes also characterized by clichés and prejudices. In group analysis, the strength of both approaches can come into its own, the calculating and often measured contributions of the group analyst and the fresh and unadulterated directness from the peers. The group members may support each other, challenge, join, smooth out, provoke, attack, ridicule, affirm and deepen emotions, yes, adding a rich repertoire of human interactions (see also Schlapobersky, 2016, p. 108). When the group analyst watches the group in its spontaneous unfolding, he/she has Foulkes' words in mind that the group members' various initiatives can usefully be regarded as associations to some basic theme. Through these associations, a figure emerges (against a background) that can be verbalized and become an object for collective reflection.

However, group members contribute to more than associative comments to unconscious motives. They might also come up with outright interpretations, "I think you're doing this because ...". At times, what's expressed reflects current "folk psychology", partly one is influenced by the media, books, or courses, and partly that the therapist's mindset has been adopted be (some of) the members. Undoubtedly, the members pick up what is acceptable "coins" in the group. In my groups, for example, there is little talk about astrology, archetypes, Oedipus complex and good or evil breasts. But more about the self, vulnerability, self-esteem, needs, offence, shame, etc. I rarely recommend literature to group participants, but I nod in agreement when someone quotes from Alice Miller's books. When other group members come up with good interpretations, I also nod affirmatively. If I want to reinforce the interpretation, I say bluntly that I agree. When interpretations are flat or futile, I say nothing. When they're obviously off the mark, I await reactions from the others. If the understanding is not corrected, I can intervene and disagree. When members articulate key group analytical points, I will usually also affirm this nonverbally (nod, glance, smile, etc.).

Example 77: Consider when Hanne, after two years of group analysis, remarks that *"now I think I'm starting to understand where the therapist wants us to go. He keeps making comments about how things we're talking about look like here in the group and whether we can find parallels to what we're talking about here. Basically, it's a good idea. It becomes more alive that way. But also scarier in a way. I never thought that I would experience such strong feelings for you in the group. It's also strange to notice how changing they are, but at the same time so intense and meaningful."*

Self-interpretation is a type of interpretation that receives little attention in the literature. By that I mean when group members reflect on themselves, their own history, and their developmental process in the group. Such self-interpretations have an important place in group analysis because they help shape the culture of understanding in the group. When self-interpretations border on self-deception or lack depth, I consider how and when to intervene based on the context. As always, I wait and see if the group "buys" the self-deception. When self-interpretations are essentially "correct", as in the coming example, I respond in the affirmative. If the group is very involved and engaged, I can confirm non-verbally.

Example 78: *Trine, the group's counsellor, and reserve therapist, has been challenged for her style of talking. It has infuriated her, she has cried and felt unappreciated. After two years of group analysis, she visits her parents' home for three days at Christmas. She tells the group that it was the best Christmas in years. What was particularly different was that she did not engage in the role as helper or family therapist. She felt that she could involve herself less and relax. She got a lot better off with her dad. That her mother then became passive, or whether she was jealous or depressed, or what it was, she now cares less about. Trine reflects also on her development in the group. She has been in terrible opposition to the therapist. Gradually, she has noticed the underlying longing for a good father. It's been a relief really and has allowed her to approach her father. It has also implied that she has seen her mother more clearly. And it's been pretty shocking. She now sees her mother as helpless and* *manipulative. She drinks too much and eats too much tranquilizers. When the therapist hears this self-interpretation, he nods affirmatively.*

From the therapist's perspective, some questions and comments from fellow patients might come across as unempathetic. But time and again, it has struck me that "unempathetic" comments can bring something good. The person in question is given the opportunity to clarify his/her own experience or perception, or he/she might be struck by an unexpected but inspiring perspective. Sometimes it's timely to focus on the person making very unexpected comments and asking about their associations. A typical situation is a termination phase for a patient. Usually, this arouses a lot of sad feelings. When some members are completely unfazed and don't realize that terminating should be that special, it provides a good opportunity to focus on *their* problems with attachment and emotions. Some comments from fellow patients are clearly offensive. Usually, the therapist himself will react and then have his own experience confirmed by observing that the person in question becomes withdrawn, frustrated, sad or visibly irritated. *All such observable negative emotional encounters in the group must be addressed.* Both for the sake of the individuals involved and for the group as a whole.

Managing defence and resistance

Psychotherapy textbooks use to contain long chapters on the therapist's handling of defence and resistance (Greenson 1967, Sandler, Dare & Holder 1992). In the literature, self-psychology in particular has opposed the defence analysis of ego psychology (Kohut 1984). Self-psychology emphasizes more strongly than other directions the defence's protective function and claims that defences will most often be scaled down in the therapeutic process alongside with an increasing experience of being understood and contained. In the pre-treatment interviews, I explicitly use to say that the way one presents oneself in the group is entirely up to oneself and that one must find one's own pace in the therapeutic process. Self-development is something that takes time, and the therapist does not see it as his job to push on. In group analysis, addressing defence and resistance forms an intrinsic part of the group process. Essentially, it's the *group members who challenge each other.* They point out contradictions, disagree, offer counter-examples and their own experiences, and note the absence of emotions. The therapist's primary role in addressing defence and resistance is to foster a critically explorative, analytic group culture. The fact that this chapter may seem a little scarce is therefore related to the fact that the handling of defence and resistance is discussed in the earlier chapters on the therapist's handling of the dynamics of the orientation, conflict and norming stages. An important part of the group's developmental process is that the group members gain an increased

understanding of defence and resistance and incorporate this into their understanding of themselves and others.

However, even within an analytic group culture, one will of course
encounter resistance and defence phenomena. When the treatment process is
well underway, some attachment has been established, and the individual's
personality style has become evident in the group, it may sometimes be
appropriate to point out restrictive defences and resistance phenomena.
Often, the concern will be resistance to self-object transferences. In its simplest form, it will be like "you've been in the group for a year and a half,
Mette, and I still have the impression that you're keeping me pretty much at a
distance." The first step is to establish consensus *that* this is the case. Such an
intervention is often followed by a group discussion in which the group
members *compare* their experiences of closeness and distance, trust and distrust, confidentiality and any fears of the therapist. If Mette acknowledges
this, "yes, I'm keeping you at a distance," then the subsequent step is to delve
into the reasons why. There usually follows a reflection about who the therapist resembles, often with a clearly expressed fear of retraumatization. Thereafter follow *challenging* comments from the other group members, such as
"but you have to do something about it", or "you can't continue like this", or
"you have to take risks".

Example 79: *Grethe (34) has a severe personality disorder with pronounced
paranoid traits. Her relationship with her father fell apart in early childhood.
From school age, she found her father to be nasty, intrusive, sexually trans-
gressive, and very devaluing towards her. She felt like the ugly duckling in the
home. Her survival strategy was to "zero him out." She maintained a max-
imum distance and avoided him as much as possible. In the group, it gradually
became apparent that she experienced the male therapist in the same way. She
was careful to place herself in a chair at a good distance from the therapist,
preferably slightly obliquely so that she did not have to look at him all the time.
Once, Grethe and her therapist were seated next to each other, and it was on
the verge that she persevered. The similarity in her experience of the father and
the therapist was repeatedly pointed out by the therapist. Mette's problem was
an almost reality-distorting defence of a projective nature. According to her,
the father was always after her, out to torment her and denigrate her. The
group spent a lot of time listening to her stories about her father. But eventually
the others reacted: 'But Grethe, when you experience the therapist in exactly
the same way, then there must also be something about you. I don't see the
therapist at all like that, that he's out to bother you. You need to find out more.
I think you should sit closer to him and see what happens." Grethe did not, but
the perspective of the others sowed a doubt in her that struck small cracks in
her projective defences and around which it gradually became possible to build
a different understanding and experience.*

Another typical situation where the therapist might interpret defences is when a participant considers leaving earlier than the therapist deems appropriate. If I, as a therapist, do not want to get rid of the person (for counter-transference reasons), but believe that there is still a good prospect of further development, I clearly state that I consider the desire to quit an escape. One may let the group deal with the problem for a while, but at some point, I tend to give a longer interpretation that summarizes and explains my view of the course of treatment and *why* I think the person is resorting to an escape.

Example 80: *Inger (48) has been considerably troubled, with long periods of sick leave, by social phobia and avoidant personality disorder. After almost two years in the group, she is functioning significantly better. She has stabilized in full-time work and talks about difficult job situations that she now handles differently than before. Yet, outside of work, she remains limited in her activities. She isolates herself and has virtually no friends. In the group, she has processed several early traumas with strong emotions. But now she wants to quit. Everything is going so much better and her social life "she has to sort out on her own." The announcement surprises other group members, who respond with muted reactions. After a while, the therapist comes up with a longer interpretation in which he first values her progress but says that it almost becomes paradoxical that she wants to quit. There is still a lot to be done, so why not stay and work on this? The real reason she wants to leave, says the therapist, he believes stems from the fact that she has been hurt and offended by the therapist's commenting on her absence from the group and that this implicit criticism had been expressed after several new members had been admitted to the group. The therapist refers to her previous statement that she thought the therapist was unfair that focused on her absence and not the others'. The therapist goes on to say that he believes this has hurt her more deeply than she might like to admit and that it has also activated an old solution (schema) in her to manage on her own. The therapist says he understands that this concerns her pride, but still encourages her to stay and work on this vulnerability and her withdrawal and avoidance tendency. It probably will prove useful to her precisely in terms of her strong tendency to social isolation.*

This type of defence interpretation doesn't always succeed, especially when the affront felt by the person is significant enough to lead them to leave. Naturally, if the person remains firm in their decision, the therapist should respect it and utilize the standard two-month termination period to solidify the therapeutic progress made and focus on the separation process. In the above case, a lot of work was done on old violations, unhappy life circumstances and aborted grieving processes. Embarking on more extensive work on pathology linked to the grandiose self might have felt too overwhelming and threatening to Inger's sense of identity. Early in the termination process, the grandiosity was expressed through a slightly camouflaged devaluation of the group. She attributed her recovery not so much to the therapeutic process of the group, but to what she called *her struggle and thinking on her own*. The focus of the terminating process was therefore to try to "soften up" her grandiose self-understanding and make her realize that, after all, she had received *something* valuable and good from others that it was reason to mourn now when it came to an end.

Dreams in group analysis

I have previously discussed the importance of dreams in creating the special group analytic culture that I characterize as an *illusionary reality* (see also Issroff & von Adelsberg, 1997). Many of my previous examples have in fact included dreams and dream interpretations. However, it is not a given that analytic groups are rich in dreams. They *should* be, but it's not always that way. In my view, an analytic group lacking in dream content is akin to tepid champagne at best. It lacks the beady effervescence that characterizes group analysis at its best. In the following, I will discuss some dream theory, how a group might be taught about dream and how dreams should be handled in groups (see also Stone & Karterud, 2006).

Freud's main work was and always will be *The Interpretation of Dreams*, which was published in 1900. His oft-quoted statement that "dream is the royal road to the unconscious" I fully endorse. The dream is the most important testimony of an unconscious mental life. The dream testifies that we are "not masters of our own houses." We are literally populated by others. It was the work of dreams that led to Freud's distinction between *primary and secondary processes*. In the unconscious, in the dream, virtually anything could happen. The unconscious life of the mind was not driven by the same laws that characterized rational thought. Freud believed that within the unconscious, primary and secondary processes worked in tandem. The primary processes consisted of densification, displacement, and symbol formation. Freud distinguished between the *manifest narrative of the dream and its latent content*. For Freud, the manifest content of the dream was a cover-up. The defence mechanisms, or what he originally called dream sensors, had already been operating. The challenge was to get at the latent content, which he regarded as a truer expression of the person's deepest driving forces. Or to put it in more modern terms: The manifest dream had to be deconstructed in order to (re-)construct its latent meaning. The way to do this was, as we know, to ask the analysand to indulge in free associations. By virtue of the ambiguity of words and symbols, it is then possible to glimpse alternative figures that fit in with other material and thus construct a deeper and "truer" meaning.

For Freud, this deeper meaning was always linked to a wish fulfillment or need satisfaction that tangled to sexual (libidinous) or aggressive urges. In his older days, he modified this claim somewhat, acknowledging that dreams might also have their source in traumatic experiences. The general rule, however, was that the latent dream was a disguise, operated upon by the defence mechanisms.

Freud's theory of dreams has been modified and supplemented by his successors. There is reason to highlight the existential analyst Medard Boss, who as early as 1958 subdued the drive satisfactory function of dreams and pointed out its role as an existential laboratory. According to Boss, the dream tells us just as much about the person's conditions of being and *the possibilities of being*. As a person develops, new possibilities for being-in-the-world will first appear in dreams. Boss went so far as to say that "the fundamental difference between Dasein's analysis and psychoanalytic theory is nowhere more obvious than in the understanding of dreams" (Boss 1963, p. 261).

Kohut's contribution to dream theory is partly his different interpretive practice and partly his definition of so-called self-state dreams (Kohut 1977; see also Karterud 1992a pp. 115–116). Self-state dreams, according to Kohut, are dreams in which the dream essentially portrays a self-state. In these dreams, the evident narrative is the dream in its entirety. It doesn't make any more sense and no further material emerges by digging "deeper". As an example, the following dream discussed by Anna Ornstein and Kohut (in Lichtenberg and Kaplan, 1983, p. 405) can be mentioned:

"It was a ship out at sea. On the outside, the hull appeared to be in order. But in reality, it was in great danger because all the rivets and bolts that had held the parts together were gone. Besides, the ship was about to crash, or at least there was a danger of it."

The dream describes the self-perception of a person who is about to finish a longer analysis. How will it go when the rivets and bolts that hold one together (i.e., the analyst as self-object) are gone? The dream in Example 5 about Jan who after the first group meeting dreamed that he was shaken in a Tivoli machine, is an example of a self-state dream with reference to the group. He was simply shaken by the first group meeting. The metaphor shaken adequately described his self-state.

Contemporary self-psychology adopts a more radical stance on dreams than Kohut's perspective. Key authors are Fosshage (1988, 1997) and Atwood & Stolorow (1984).

"In a perspective that focuses on human subjectivity, determining the meaning of a dream involves illuminating the way in which the dream is interwoven with the dreamer's ongoing experience of the world," write Atwood & Stolorow (1984, p. 99).

From a phenomenological perspective, the aim isn't to find a causal explanation of the dream rooted in an analysis of free associations that hint at the deeper drive tensions beneath the manifest dream content. The value of free associations is that they generate contexts of subjective meaning through which dream images can be investigated and understood.

Instead of understanding the dream as choreographed by drive dynamics related to wish fulfilment, Atwood & Stolorow (1984) suggest a broader formulation: the dream consistently conveys one or multiple personal intentions of the dreamer. James Fosshage (1997) expands on this line of thought in his article *The Organizing Functions of Dream Mentation*. He provides the dream a central role in repairing, maintaining, and development of the self. He argues that "*research supports the view of dream as a complex mentational process that serves primary adaptive functions*" and paraphrases Freud by saying that "*the dream is the royal expression of unconscious mentation*" (ibid., p. 430). According to Fosshage:

> "... *Dream thinking, like waking thinking, processes information and contributes to the development of psychic structure through the representational consolidation of new psychic configurations. It contributes to development through new perceptual angles and through imaginary portrayals of new ways of being. New self and object representations (or schemas) and new relational scenarios emerge. Dream thinking can also follow up on unconscious and conscious attempts at conflict resolution by reviving a previous self-state, through defensive manoeuvres, or by creating new configurations.*"

(ibid., p. 435)

Among Fosshage's advice about managing dreams, I would particularly like to highlight the following:

1   *Not all dreams hold equal significance!* With some dreams, searching for a "deeper meaning" can be a waste of time and energy.
2   *Dreams vary in their clarity and relevance.* Like messy and incoherent "wakeful" thoughts, there are messy and incoherent dreams, which do not necessarily cover up a hidden "truth."
3   Capture the dreamer's experiences *in the dream*. In my own words, I would say that a *textual understanding* should also be sought here. *How did the individual feel throughout the various sequences of the dream, and what significance did these emotional responses hold for the dreamer?*
4   *What relevance* do the themes of the dream have to the waking life of the dreamer?

Group literature has focused on two aspects of dreams that are peculiar to group psychotherapy (Karterud, 1992a; Cividini-Stranic, 1986; Foss, 1994). One is the occurrence of *group dreams*. The second is the special interpretive practice that characterizes psychodynamic group psychotherapy (Pawlik & Pierzgalska, 1990; Rutan & Rice, 2005). The simplest definition of group dreams is that they contain, in their manifest content, either a direct reference to the group or, with slight camouflage, a very probable reference to it. Thus, the dream pertains to *both* the individual's inner world *and* the group.

It reflects the individual within the group context. Personally, I find it artificial to distinguish categorically between self-state dreams and other (classical) dreams. All dreams have an air of self-state portrayal. This may be more or less prominent. And so it is for group dreams. All group dreams contain a portrait of the group that is a highly relevant and valid perspective on the group's current dynamics or self-state. In group dreams, we get an insight into how the individual self and the group self are infiltrated into each other on an unconscious level. *Just as dreams pertaining to the "individual" are crucial for understanding one's inner and unconscious world, group dreams are essential for recognizing the underlying dynamics of the group, which can differ significantly from what's apparent on the surface.* Group dreams tell members that there are many processes going on at the same time. When I put individual (dreams) in quotation marks above, it is because all dreams, if you put it bluntly, are group dreams in the sense that they refer to experiences and events in the (outer) world. Dreams allude to experiences rooted in an interpersonal and cultural setting – essentially, a group context. When this group situation can be difficult to spot, it is related to intricate symbols and the fact that the group situation may have been ephemeral or lie many years back in time. For example, it may stem from experiences in the family group. Therefore, it can be said with some justification that it is *through group analytic psychotherapy that the innermost nature and function of dreams comes to light.*

In a review article, Pines & Hearst (1993) also place great emphasis on working with dreams in group analysis:

> *"The work with dreams in an analytic group demonstrates more clearly than anything else the application of group analytical concepts. Working with dreams is based on the understanding of group associations as equivalent to free associations in psychoanalysis. The dream, which is basically an individual product, when told in the group becomes part of the dynamic matrix, and thereby accessible to all group members while retaining its individuality. From a purely clinical point of view, this forms the basis for how the group analyst and the group members receive and handle the dream narrative. The dream becomes the property of the group. This implies that group members are free to involve themselves in the dream in their own ways. Some group analysts distinguish between group dreams and individual dreams. It perhaps does more justice to the group process to say that all dreams told in the group become carriers of both dimensions."*

(ibid., p.155)

From a technical standpoint, interpreting a dream in group analysis differs from the approach in individual psychotherapy (Neri et al., 2005). The individual mode of working with dreams would radically violate the basic principles of group analysis and involve a kind of individual therapy in group. In practice, there is no alternative but to *teach the group to work with dreams.*

The first step in this learning process contains a great deal of pedagogy. Already in the pre-treatment interviews, I inquire whether the patients typically recalls their dreams and if they can share a recent or older dream with me. If it is possible, I interpret the dream there and then. Especially if the dream has reference to the meeting with me or to the forthcoming group analysis. Furthermore, I emphasize that dreams represent a very important gateway to understanding oneself (and others), that dreams are emphasized in group analysis and that he/she is encouraged to bring his/her dreams into the group. At one of the first dreams told in a new group, depending on the context, I reinforce what has already been said in the pre-treatment interviews and add an explanation about how dreams are worked with in individual psychotherapy and why one cannot do the same in a group. I say that the dreamer's own associations are important, but that *just as important are* the *associations of the other group members*. I emphasize what I mean by associations and say that one should strive to associate with the dream, much as if it were one's own, and not try to explain it. The dreamer should aim for a detailed narration of the dream. Once completed, other group members should be given the opportunity to associate with the dream before the dreamer adds their perspective. This is partly to prevent the dream from being closed too soon by the dreamer's own attempts to explain the dream. Regarding my role, I clarify that it will vary. Often, after hearing the group's and the dreamer's associations, I will offer a more comprehensive interpretation of the dream. But it will often also be the case that the group associates and *interprets*, and that I find these interpretations good and adequate, so that I do not have much to add. I also say something brief about my own view of dreams, which is that the dream is an inner laboratory where one partly seeks to affirm oneself, partly satisfy needs, process the events of daily life, create meaning with seemingly meaningless and harrowing experiences, create a connection between past and present, but also to try out new possibilities of being. In the dream, one can experiment with oneself and others. When I explain the function of dreams to candidates in group analysis, I add Ricoeur's point about the importance of fiction in experimenting with *ipse* and *idem* identity of the self, and that fiction literature in this respect has the dream as its original source.

Can any rules be formulated for the dream-interpreting activities of the group analysts? Yes and no. Again, we are confronted with the fact of group analysis being that much of a contextual activity. Faced with analogous content, what is right in one situation will not necessarily be that in another. The most important thing, of course, is *to understand the dream*. And what are the criteria for a good dream understanding? Note that here I write "good" and not "right". Dreams, like all other meaningful and symbolic material, are ambiguous. There is no one correct interpretation. But there are good and bad interpretations. The criterion for a good interpretation is that it is possible to reconcile the dream's manifest level, with the dreamer's and the other group members' associations, with important themes in the dreamer's and group's life and what is otherwise known about the dreamer's history and current transference situation. A good interpretation can merge this knowledge into a meaningful whole. *Dream interpretation is therefore hermeneutics at its very best.* An important additional criterion is that the interpretation is *perceived* as meaningful by the dreamer and the other group members. In my interpretive practice, I also lean on dream theory that gives greater weight to the manifest dream content than Freud originally did. The metaphorical language of the manifest dream content has a value in itself, in addition to whatever camouflage may exist. *Admittedly, some dreams are challenging to decipher.* If that's the case, I'll say it bluntly: "This dream was weird. I must admit that I don't quite understand it. It will probably be clearer at a later date so we can get back to it." When one essentially believes one has achieved a good understanding of the dream, the question arises as to when and how to interpret it. As a rule, the dream should be interpreted at the same group meeting as it is told. But not necessarily immediately in the wake of the group's work on the dream. The group may well travel associatively to another topic. If so, I'll bring the dream back in at a later time. Nor is there any point, in my opinion, for the dream to be interpreted "completely". There may be elements you don't understand, or scenes you skip on purpose. Dream interpretations are subject to the same rules as other interpretations, which means that they must be interpreted in a way that considers the situation of the dreamer and the group so that the interpretation becomes a constructive contribution to the discourse of self-understanding. In the following, I will review a selection of dreams in group analysis that hopefully clarifies the above theoretical points.

Example 81. A group dream with a touch of twinship transference: *Margrete (43) tells the following dream: "I find myself in a kind of conference hall where someone is giving a lecture on a serious topic. Next to me sits Jan (another member of the group). We join our hands and rock from side to side. We have fun, smile and laugh." The dream immediately connects to an important theme in Margrete's life. She is conscientious and strongly engaged professionally and socially. But at the expense of other aspects of life. The challenge for her now is to bring more joy into life. Somehow, Jan represents a bridge for her (affirmative twinship transference). The group is involved in this topic in a longer sequence. The therapist sees no need to offer a separate interpretation as the group adeptly addresses the dream's primary theme. What the group doesn't comment on is the hint of rebellion in the dream. Does the serious speaker refer to the therapist (and father)? In the sequence that follows, Jan is unusually active and self-assertive. He is obviously stimulated (narcissistically) by being part of Margrethe's dream. This is a phenomenon that is often seen. Conversely, a group dream focusing on specific members can incite feelings of envy in those left out. Towards the end, the therapist* *comments in an appreciative manner on Jan's active involvement. He links this engagement to a dream Jan had at the last group meeting. An important element of that dream, which was interpreted as an Oedipal dream, was that Jan had a nicer (more modern) mobile phone than the therapist. The therapist says that Jan, who has previously been somewhat inhibited in the group, now seems to have come to term with a more self-assertive side of himself. Previously, being assertive in the group had implied for him a dangerous competition with the therapist. It seems like this isn't quite as scary anymore. In the previous dream, Jan used his mobile phone (more impressive than the therapist's!) to phone a woman. It's as if Margrethe has picked up on the unconscious (but interpreted) message of Jan's dream. Jan, who dares to challenge the therapist sexually, gains in her unconscious an affirmative function about her own sexuality and self-assertiveness. Through this affirmation, she gains a new and somewhat more rebellious perspective on her grave professional seriousness.*

This example shows how 1) Margrethe's oedipal conflict in relation to her father; and 2) Jan's oedipal conflict in relation to his father; 3) connects to each other; and that 4) both oedipal conflicts converge in the transference to the therapist; and 5) how they strengthen each other through twinship transference; and 6) how this is enacted in the group. Without (group) dreams, it is very difficult to spot these undercurrents in the group. And *if* the therapist spots them, what arguments would he have in trying to explain what's going on in each individual and in the group as a whole? Very few, and if so, quite theoretical. *Dreams furnish evidence to all parties – therapists and group members alike – of the underlying processes at play.*

Example 82. A latent group dream with a clear parallel between the individual's past and the group's here and now: *Morten has made sexual advances to Irene in the group. It has caused a significant commotion. Several of the women have responded strongly. The men, and especially Truls, have not wanted to get involved in the case. Overall, Truls is quite distanced. One day, he tells the following dream: "There is a man sleeping with a woman. Then it's my turn. However, I discover that she has poorly developed genitalia. I can't get it in. It all takes place on a porch. There's a knock at the door. I imagine several men are coming and will rape her and I flee down the gutter. Halfway down, I change my mind and climb back up. There on the porch, several women and men sit together and talk." Morten's associations relate to an experience when he was ten. His older brother of fifteen, along with some friends, tried to have sex with, almost raping his twelve-year-old sister. She barely managed to save herself. Truls was a passive witness. He later reproached himself for not intervening to save his sister. At the same time, there was something arousing about the whole scene. When he thinks about it now, in connection with the dream, he gets very upset. The anger is directed partly against his brother, partly against himself for cowardice. The group, and eventually Truls, have no*

*difficulty seeing the connection between the past and the here-and-now. Mor-
ten's sexual approach in the group reminded him of his brother's "approach" in
childhood. Just as he couldn't get involved then, he remains distant now due to
his own ambivalence and cowardice. So far in the group, the therapist hasn't
said much. Since no one has commented on the last part of the dream, the
therapist says that there is, after all, a significant difference between then and
now. Back then, he had no one to talk to about such things. "Several women
and men" sitting together on the porch chatting, interprets the therapist as the
group. It is the presence of the group that enables him to re-approach this part
of his past and gain a broader perspective on himself and his experiences and
(speech-)acts within the group.*

Example 83. A latent group dream that reinforces the termination process:
*This is Lene's final group meeting. She recounts the following dream since her
last meeting: "Dr X, whom I went to many years ago and who took care of me
during a difficult time, has died. I got the message too late and couldn't tell her
that now I could handle myself." The other group members make the dream
group relevant. "It's probably about the ending here." Lene's associations go to
her father's deathbed. Her last words denied the reality of death. She said, "I'm
sure it will be fine" and failed to express how much she loved him. During
heavy crying, she tells how much the group has meant to her. She comforts and
encourages the new ones and talks about her own development while she has
been in the group. Finally, the therapist comments that it may seem that this
time she can allow herself a somewhat more honest ending that can also fulfil
an important grieving process in herself. To Dr X and to Dad, and to some
extent to those new to the group, it is her consolation of others that stands in
the foreground. But what about herself? Who comforts her? Does she allow
anyone to comfort herself? And does she allow herself to comfort herself? The
therapist adds that it touched him to hear her story about how much the group
had meant to her. It is precisely through such speech-acts that it becomes
clearer and more real to her what she loses and that she has good reason to
mourn the loss of the group. He concludes by saying that he hopes she will
allow herself such a grieving process.*

Example 84. Group dream about the therapist and an individual interpretation: *Erling wonders if he should quit and has discussed this several times
in the group. When is the "right" time? The compulsive symptoms have gotten
much better, but they're not completely gone. One day, Erling tells the following two dreams: 'One is about me walking towards the therapist and scolding
him. Then I crawl up onto his lap. In the second dream, I'm with a doctor or
psychiatrist. I was going to end that treatment but had to be washed clean
first." After a brief round of associations in the group, the therapist says that
the dreams indicate that Erling still has a problem with ambivalence. While his
compulsive symptoms have greatly improved, deep down he still holds onto the*

idea that he can be "washed clean." The therapist says he doesn't think it's possible to wash away rage. He recommends Erling to stay in the group.

Example 85. Group dream about the therapist that is handled by the group: *Merete, a 30-year-old in the advertising industry, seeks therapy for her social anxiety, which she manages with tranquilizers. She is "fresh", slim, and fashion-conscious and does aerobics. She allows herself some sexual excesses. In the group, she is quite unstable. In the last group session, she voiced criticisms against both the therapist and the group. We were not worth much. Next session, she opens with two dreams: "In one dream, I meet the therapist at a party. He praises me for the way I handle my job. In the other I have been downtown, late in the evening, I think with a shabby man, but I remember little of that. I almost had a blackout. I felt miserable and was picked up by a friend. I wanted to go home and asked my friend to order a taxi to drive to the Karterud-hill 1174, Oslo 11." The group bursts into laughter when it hears "Karterud-hill 1174". At that time, the therapist's office address was Sofie's road 74. Geir remarks, "Merete, you seem so fragmented. First you scold the therapist and the group and then you have two dreams that show how much the therapist means to you. I don't get it." Nils: "I think you acts out now and then and I don't think that's good for you." Erna: "I think you're a little homeless, Merete." Merete: "Yes, I feel a little confused. This group is so different. I didn't think it mattered, but it surely does in a strange way." Through her dreams, Merete becomes more aware of conflicting forces and aspects of herself. The group discusses her tough and coping surface, that she uses sex to satisfy her great need for affirmation, and that she harbours a deep longing for attachment and a "home." The therapist doesn't say much in this sequence.*

Example 86. A group dream with twinship transference: *Espen has been in group analysis for about two years. He has held a profound fear that something is gravely wrong with him, fearing a psychotic core or the possibility of being mentally retarded. He is now in a period of strong attachment feelings with the group. He tells the following dream: 'My partner and I are visiting the therapist's house. My partner flips through the therapist's stack of records and exclaims: Hi, Espen, look here, exactly the same records that you have! You must be pretty similar." The fantasy of being like the therapist is often associated with shame. In this case, it is noteworthy that it's the partner who expresses this fantasy (displacement), not Espen himself. The therapist says: "This is a meaningful dream, Espen. You have often been bothered by the thought that deep down there is something catastrophically wrong with you. Instead, you begin to feel that the two of us have something valuable and important in common. It's a very positive development."*

Example 87. A group dream that signals the threshold to a depressive position: *Geir was caught up in a continuous and devaluing competition with* *the therapist. It never occurred to him that the devaluation could be destructive, until he dreamed the following dream: "My father and I were out jogging. I led the way, but my father was surprisingly fit and hung on well. We came to a knoll by the water and dad dove in. He obviously hurt himself and didn't move. I was afraid he was going to die. I jumped in but luckily found him alive." The group commented that this was the first time Geir had come up with a story that indicated that he cared about someone, and that life wasn't just ruthlessly pursuing his own interests. The therapist says that he believes that the father in the dream was both Geir's father, but also represented the therapist and that the dream was about the competition that unfolded between the therapist and Geir in the group. Geir: "Well, yes, possibly." The therapist: "The most important aspect of the dream is, as the group has pointed out, that you now also show a concern for the person with whom you are competing. You appreciate competing with my father and me, you like us for being able to follow you, and you won't lose us." Geir is shaken for a moment, then he says "yes, you're right".*

Example 88. A group dream that takes on an expanded meaning four years later: *Irene has been in the group three quarters of a year when she dreams the following dream: "I'm hiking in the mountains and Britt from the group is with me. She stumbles on a stream, and I struggle to save her. Later, I kind of get lost and end up on a mountain ledge. The others finally pull me up. At the top of the mountain, the therapist stands in a kind of captain's jacket and co-ordinates it all. He puts a blanket around me and comforts me. It's good. I put my head against his shoulder." When this dream was told, it was interpreted that the rugged mountain terrain was a metaphor for the scary therapeutic landscape she faced and that she needed to lean on the therapist. Four years later (!), the dream gets a more precise interpretation. Irene has repeatedly processed a trauma she experienced in her youth. She has kept coming back to this experience, with new perspectives and new details. It concerned a major fatal accident in the wilderness where she was the youngest member of the Auxiliary Corps. She was among the first to arrive at the scene of the accident. After four years in the group, she remembers returning home from the accident, shocked, exhausted, and frozen. Her parents greet her with bizarre questions and trifles, whereupon she breaks out into a hysterical laughter ("as did my mother, too") and says that it's quite okay with herself. When she relives her return through her narrative to the group, she bursts into a deep cry. The most painful thing was the loss of caring parents who could take care of her. In this moment, she recalls her group dream four years earlier: "Why couldn't they have done what you (the therapist) did in the dream, at that time, comforted me, warmed me, and hold me close?"*

This layer of meaning was present in the dream even four years ago. No one saw it at the time. The first interpretation wasn't necessarily wrong. Some might argue it lacked precision. I would say it was "correct" in terms of the context. Even then, this trauma pressed on and subconsciously she saw an opportunity to approach it in the transference. But it took a lot of intermediate therapeutic work, with many reviews of other traumatic experiences with her borderline mother and paranoid father, before she was able to realize the shock of this accident where her mother's and father's reaction almost became a model scene for long-term emotional neglect.

Example 89. A group dream as part of trauma processing: *Terje shares this dream: "I encounter the therapist at a location in my hometown. The therapist wheels a stroller. We greet each other. It was OK." While the group associates with the dream, a jolt runs through Terje. He leans forward and makes his way to his head. Stuttering, he says that the place he met the therapist was exactly the place he turned his back on his father. There comes a new sequence with the great trauma in Terje's life, which was already known in the group. It is about the divorce between father and mother when Terje was twelve years old and where he sided with his mother. After that time, he had a very difficult period where he was on the verge of joining a youth criminal gang. What now struck Terje was the following: At home, he had witnessed a violent scene between father and mother. He hears his father shout "I'll get out of here", whereupon Terje interferes to support his crying mother and screams "yes, just leave". The next day, he leaves school early. As he walks home, he sees his dad standing at the bus stop with two suitcases. It blackens for him; he turns around and runs back to school. In the group, he breaks out into a heartbreaking cry that is about the conflict between his intense desire on the one hand to run up to his father and beg him to stay and apologize for what he said the night before, and on the other hand his loyalty to his mother and his anger to his father because of his strife and insecurity at home. Towards the end of this sequence, the therapist acknowledges Terje for his courage by re-entering these painful memories. The therapist does not come up with any interpretation of the dream. His appreciative speech act is his "interpretation." This is analogous to the content of the dream. It is the therapist's presence as a caring self-object (wheeling on a stroller and greeting affirmatively) that allows Terje to approach this crucial episode of the trauma. The therapist does the same in the group as in the dream, being present as a caring self-object.*

Example 90. A typical group dream based on offence and self-object failure: *Vibeke, 39, says she has "never been so furious" as after the last group meeting. She felt labelled and run over by Arne, who had remarked that her characterization of her father was based on a "poor judgement." The group reviews what happened at the last meeting and Vibeke and Arne get a little closer. And then I've had a dream, says Vibeke: "I dreamed it was Arne, someone else, the therapist and me. The other two spoke out, but as I was about to start, the therapist said he would first run some tapes. I protested and*

stopped the therapist so I could do my own stuff." The dream needed no inter-
pretation. It became an opportunity for Vibeke to express her criticism of the
therapist. Her experience was that the therapist "used her" when he did not
relate to what she had said in the group, but responded by asking the others
what they thought, associated, thought about in relation to what Vibeke had
said. The dream led to a long discussion about the way to work in the group.
Vibeke was praised for not giving up in the dream but standing her ground.

Working through in group analysis

As previously discussed, both the group as a whole and individual participants
undergo typical stages in the therapeutic process. Working through the orientation, conflict, and norming stages paves the way for deeper self-object transferences that unfold within the group, conflicting with defensive transferences. It's
not just about clarifying these conflicts in the group through enactments but also
about working through them. "Working through" is rarely discussed in group
analytic literature. One can speculate over the reasons for this. Could the topic be
too individually oriented and not "group-analytic enough"?

The goal is to deconstruct defensive self-structures as much as possible
while building and consolidating authentic self-structures through a revised
narrative self-understanding. Deconstructing and reconstructing significant
parts of the self takes time. Once patterns are reasonably clear, individuals
often revisit the same conflicts, traumas, and character traits. During the
phase of working through, which takes several years in group analysis and
should constitute the lion's share of the therapy, the goal is to get behind the
repetition compulsion so that the seemingly "same" conflicts that are processed are not quite the same anymore. When therapy is effective, fresh
nuances, memories, and perspectives on previously discussed topics gradually
emerge. *It is important that the therapist sees this* and expresses it in the group.
Thus, the group as a whole also gains an understanding of what constitutes
genuine change, as well as a basis for providing well-founded comments to a
member who expresses a desire to leave. Often, members themselves will
describe and acknowledge changes in themselves. *"It's funny. Before, this was*
terribly difficult for me. Now it's kind of no big deal." "I notice now that I
handle the conflicts at home in a different way." "Yesterday I did something
completely new. For the first time, I offered to assume a position of trust." In
the group, the therapist can say: *'I've noticed that you're not so afraid of con-*
flicts in the group anymore, Trine. It's great because of the history that you
have and the way you were when starting with the group." "You've changed
Einar. You're not so modest anymore. You participate more and take more
chances." Sometimes I can say jokingly, *"It's nice to listen to you, Guri.*
You're soon cured. Now there's only a little bit of debris in the relationship with
authorities that remains."

Working through follows a slow but deliberate and systematic process where 1) defensive character structures are dismantled; 2) positive self-object experiences become integrated into the self; 3) emotional consciousness is enhanced; 4) attachment pattern is more secure; and 5) mentalizing capabilities are improved.

Example 91: *At the beginning of therapy, Bente (33) is extremely vulnerable, feels easily criticized and attacked by others, quickly counterattacks, and gets into conflicts and arguments with others, feels deep down worthless and homeless and often withdraws and isolates herself from others (and work) during depressive periods. Over and over again, her (denied) vulnerability is expressed in the group and her defensive handling of this (denial, displacement of emotions, suspicion and counterattack). Slowly, she develops a twinship transference to another group member, a mirroring transference to the therapist, and finally an idealizing transference to the group as a whole (and to group analysis!). These self-object transferences are accompanied by significant transference resistance, and she suffers through emotional crises by perceived self-object failures. Slowly, the self-object transferences become more stable. In line with this, her self-esteem changes. She no longer experiences herself as isolated, lonely and different from everyone else, but more like other people. Gradually, she is less ashamed of herself. She lets go of an intense desire to be liked by the therapist and be the therapist's favourite, coupled with a shameful realization of intense envy and jealousy towards supposed rivals in the group. Gradually, she finds that the therapist likes her, appreciates her, and is proud of her. In parallel with this, the depressive periods get lost and she stabilizes in a positive self-esteem. She no longer feels left over at work, in restaurants or at parties. She's more critical of boyfriends and doesn't let them sexually exploit her anymore. She increasingly appreciates the group. For a period, her idealization is very strong. The group means everything to her. What goes on in the group overshadows everything else of importance in her life. When this goes away, when (after many years of group analysis) she becomes more and more of a constructive co-therapist in the group, when she tolerates disappointments and offences without fragmenting (becoming "on tiptoe" and "crushed", self-destructively aggressive or resorting to meaningless sex), when she can tell about stable job function and a good love relationship and when she can tell a different and thoughtful story about her life that agrees with the others' (and therapist's) perception of her, the working through is finished. Repeatedly, she and the group have processed "the same thing", while gradually there has emerged something new that has slowly been consolidated: a sense of equality with others, fundamental respect for oneself and others, appreciation of fellowship with others and the ability to handle contradictions in a dialogue.*

It has been argued that group analysis is not particularly well suited to working through trauma. The rationale is often that trauma processing requires systematic focus over a certain period, and that this is technically incompatible with group analysis. As a result, many lean towards focused short-term groups. From a strictly efficiency-based perspective, there might be some validity to this argument. However, to say trauma cannot be processed in group analysis is simply incorrect. Yet, the processing follows a different, perhaps more "natural", path. Processing often takes place through therapeutic episodes spread over many years. Often, a severe trauma will be known relatively early in the course of therapy. It may concern the illness and/or death of one or both parents, the illness or death of siblings, serious accidents affecting the family, sexual abuse, suicide, divorce and the like. After the first story in the group, which often has a dramatic and condensed character, the theme can go into oblivion, only to reappear at later crossroads.

Example 92: *Already in the fifth meeting, Hans talks about the accident that befell his family when he was eleven years old. First a little hesitantly, then more precisely and in detail. His father had worked in the furniture business some distance away from home. He had been absent a lot. Mostly like a weekend dad. There are cutbacks in the workforce and the father is dismissed. Just before, he had taken out a fairly large loan and begun remodelling the little house they lived in. Of course, everyone reacted to the dismissal, but life took its course. About a month later, his father says goodbye one morning. In retrospect, strikingly winded. When Hans comes back in the afternoon from school, his mother is "hysterical" and shouts when he comes "where's father"? Hans goes out to look for him. There is still snow and he sees some tracks in the snow that he follows. There, he spots dad lying on his chest in the snow. Hans wonders if he's fallen. Then he sees blood on the snow and the rifle lying next to it. He runs home, "Dad has shot himself!" In the group, he goes on to tell of neighbours who sort things out, the funeral, the shame, that they had to move from the house and into a small shelter on a farm in the village. When he finished secondary school, he left immediately and got an apprenticeship job elsewhere in the country. He has barely been there since. It's worth noting that Hans' general demeanour in the group was marked by intellectualization and emotional detachment. Even with his detached recounting, his story profoundly impacted the group.*

The next time the group touches on such a traumatic event, it is often more digested by everyone in the group, the person in question, the therapist and the other group members. New information has often emerged. In the meantime, the patient has undergone a development process and is often able to relate to the substance in a deeper way. In this way, the trauma is digested in a spiralling motion where time and time again the group return to the same point, while moving forward. The therapist's task is to facilitate this process. He aids this by revisiting the trauma when relevant and taking steps that promote the grieving process. In the case of Hans, it was part of the defence that he avoided his home village. Everything about his home village reminded him of his father's suicide and his family's geographical and social "banishment," why it was a matter of pretending it didn't exist. He had gone all in to build a new life elsewhere. During the therapeutic process, he was urged to visit his native village, walk old paths, greet people, seek out his father's grave, attend the anniversary class party, etc. With each such event, which spread over several years, new details and new emotions were added and integrated into his history in the group. A year after Hans first shared his story, he recounted the following dream to the group: "I am at home and walk with a kind horse to the place where I found my father. There are some scary animals there that turn out to be bears. In a strange way, I manage to tame one of the bears by tying its paws to it and it lurks behind us as we move on." The group members believe that the group is the kind horse that follows him to the crime scene, and the therapist adds that the bears probably represent scary emotions associated with the incident. Despair and rage? But that his feelings are no worse than that they can be tamed when he takes the chance to seek them out. Again, we see an example of a dream where it is possible to seek out the place of a catastrophic event provided one is followed by a friendly other, i.e., a self-object.

Hans spent three years working through the trauma that upended his life during his formative years. In the final year, his defensive and compensatory tendencies were addressed. The idealization of the group is strong at this point. He contrasts the values that apply to the group with his own tendencies to bend off, avoid and "take shortcuts". Previously, he had no experience that he owed anyone anything. On the contrary, he saw society as a jungle where "only the strongest survive." After a period of much shame, many confessions, and a lot of guilt, he experiences a different and communal ground with others. By the end of four and a half years, this understanding was firmly established.

Termination in group analysis

The terminating process in group analysis is discussed by many authors: for example, Wardi (1989), Maar (1989), Schermer & Klein (1996), and Schlapobersky (2016). Schematically, we can distinguish between premature and mature endings. Regardless of the reason for termination, the therapist should recommend a termination period of at least two months. Sometimes this will fail as some finishes abruptly. Such endings are traumatic for all parties. Everyone has suffered a defeat. If dropouts do not agree to attend the group for at least one session (and one is better than no session whatsoever), the therapist should propose a finalizing individual session. The purpose is to process some of the disappointments and offences underlying the withdrawal, allay the patient's fantasies about the therapist's reaction to his withdrawal, summarize the treatment for as long as it lasted, give reasoned advice about any other kind of treatment and try to achieve a mutually respectful termination for both parties. For the group as a whole, it is important to provide some kind of report if such an individual final conversation has taken place. The group must also be given the opportunity to process their feelings concerning people who drop out. Here, there isn't a rule such as "do not talk about those who are not present". To the contrary. Someone who has dropped out might be very much present in the dynamics of the group. In particular, the members must be given the opportunity to vent their feelings of betrayal and abuse. This should not be interpreted in any intricate way by the therapist. Often, members feel the group has been betrayed and mistreated. Rather, it should be interpreted if *none* of this is expressed. It should also be part of the process that the group (and the therapist) reflect on *their* contribution to a possible process of expulsion. Did that person come in at an unfavourable time? Didn't the group have the energy to receive the person in a good way? Was there something that went wrong pretty early? Were there particular events that became traumatic?

At some rare occasions, it is the therapist who asks a member to quit ("throwouts"). As always, one should stick to a termination period. In such cases, the termination is extra painful, and many will want to shorten it. However, the therapist should be a role model for the ethos of the group. Here, too, everyone faces a defeat. Not to mention the therapist. He/she must openly acknowledge that he/she has failed to accomplish the project he/she presented to the patient and him/herself in the first place. Something went wrong along the way. It became a negative therapeutic experience rather than a positive one. As far as possible, efforts should be made to arrive at a common understanding of why things turned out the way they did and on what issues there might be a disagreement between the therapist and the person in question. In my opinion, when someone is removed from the group, the therapist has an extra responsibility to facilitate alternative treatment. The two times I have 'dismissed' patients in group analysis, I have contacted a psychologist and a mental health centre an agreed on alternative therapies that have started in the patient's final phase. In such a final phase, one must endure a great deal of despair and reproach and make sure to keep one's own countertransference at bay. One can partly feel mean and brutal by throwing out a desperate and help-seeking fellow human being, and partly want to defend oneself against unreasonable accusations. Don't let it become a problem between the therapist and the person who is about to quit. Let this also become a group problem. Not that the therapist should run from his share of responsibility, but those questions such as "is the therapist brutal and ruthless?" is an excellent topic for the group as a whole.

In practice, not all terminations can be categorized as either premature or mature. Sometimes people quit for practical reasons. Some move and some change jobs that cannot be reconciled with therapy. And not infrequently, patients quit before the therapist thinks they have properly worked through their deficits and conflicts. It is important that the therapist decides early on how to handle the termination process. Is the case settled and is there a "clean" termination process to go through, or is there an ambivalence and doubt that must be worked on with an openness to the person in question of changing his or her mind? One should remember that therapy takes place "to the bell rings". Sometimes patients change their minds in what is supposed to be the last meeting. Terminations characterized by doubt and ambivalence are challenging because they involve at least two parallel processes. On the one hand, grief processing and preparations for parting and, on the other hand, hope and doubt for a "new beginning". As for people who want to quit before the work is done, my position is clear. I provide clear advice to continue but respect the desire to quit. The advice to continue remains open until the last minute. I have experienced several times that patients have changed their minds at the twelfth hour, but, oddly enough, that no one has approached me again shortly after a termination and asked to start again.

Terminations that occur after mutual agreement that the goals have largely been achieved are usually unproblematic. The first time this happens in an analytic group, it's a milestone. The therapist should take the opportunity for an educational explanation of what constitutes a termination process. At later endings, he/she should repeat parts of this, depending on how long it has been since the last ending and what is special to the ending one is facing. In the termination phase, there should be a grieving process, a separation process, a reflection on the overall therapeutic process and a completion of "unfinished businesses" in relation to individual members or the therapist. The termination phase is an excellent opportunity for a renewed processing of past losses, of previous ways of dealing with grief and of ways of saying goodbye. This applies to everyone, not just the one who leaves. The final meeting itself differs from other group analytical meetings in the sense that it *has* a specific theme and a specific protagonist. This applies regardless of the reason for ending! The therapist should intervene if the topic and the protagonist tend to be pushed aside by the group. Often, the final meeting will have a dramatic climax towards the end, when pent-up emotions break loose. Often in connection with a discussion about *how* to say goodbye in concrete terms. Members of an analytic group rarely touch each other. Should one end with a handshake? Should one hug each other? Can you hug the therapist? The therapist should await the reaction of the patient and the group. My personal view is this: I do not consider it "unanalytic" for a group analyst to hug whoever quits after the meeting is over!

At the last meeting, of course, one does not interpret phenomena that one considers to be poorly worked through. The therapist's main task is to promote grieving processes and direct the ending itself.

Example 93: *In the closing process for Grethe, her ambivalence to the therapist flared up again and he had to endure a series of reproaches. In particular they concerned his failure to acknowledge her. She claimed that he had often been critical of her contributions to the group. At the last meeting, she* *talks about her feelings of grief at quitting. She is surprised at how strong it is and admits that she actually considered dropping this last session. She is grateful for what she has received in the group, especially from Pernille and Kristoffer, their understanding and unconditional care. The therapist has been OK to have as someone she could be angry with. She functions much better in her studies and at work. She is not depressed anymore and not as isolated. She uses her friends more. Above all, she has gained a fundamental and different insight into her role in her family. She previously took on a Sisyphean task trying to bring her mother and father together, hoping to belong to a family. The group increasingly became a different family for her, which allowed her to have a greater distance and another perspective on her upbringing. And now she's created her own "red wine group" that meets regularly. The therapist thinks that there is still some unprocessed grandiosity, some unresolved offences and rivalry with the therapist, but says nothing about it and wishes her luck.*

Modern group analysis. A summary

My starting point for this book was the pioneering work of the founder of group analysis, S. H. Foulkes. He was far ahead of his time when he pinpointed the essence of group analysis as "ego-training in action". However, the ego psychology of his time was a deficient theoretical framework for exploring the complex group dynamics that is created by a sensitive group analyst. The generation of group analysts after Foulkes spread in different directions. There were those who claimed that Foulkes "idealized" the group and had neglected destructive forces and attempts were made to integrate group analysis with Wilfred Bion's theories of basic assumption phenomena and Kleinian explanatory principles. Other argued that group analysis should develop along other object-relational lines, above all by Donald Winnicott's casting.

My own contribution has been to deconstruct Bion through empirical research and theoretical analysis and provide group analysis with alternative self-psychological perspectives, in particular through dialogues with Malcolm Pines in England and Walter Stone in the United States. Later by developing mentalization-based group therapy for people with severe personality problems and more recently by highlighting the importance of modern personality theory for group analytical practice.

During the 2000s, group analysis lost some of its vitality and relevance. Competing therapies, and above all cognitive behavioural therapy (individually and in groups), made themselves felt. Applications for group analytical training declined in several countries at the same time as demand also fell. This was particularly true in public mental health services. For more severe personality disorders, specialized treatment programmes such as dialectical behaviour therapy, schema therapy, and MBT appeared. All of these had a group component.

In this book, I have discussed how group analysis can be revitalized. Theoretically and therapeutically, I have argued why a return to Bion is a dead end. I have also expressed doubts as to what more can be squeezed out of object relations theory. In contrast, I've advocated a return to Foulkes' condensed formula "ego-training in action". However, the concept of ego has no relevance in our time. How can it be deconstructed and invested with new meaning? In our time, it's all about the self.

At this point I refer to theoretical and therapeutic resources from self-psychology, intersubjectivity theory, emotion theory, attachment theory, theory of mentalization, and hermeneutics of the self. I further and expand upon the group analytical tradition that Pines and Dennis Brown initiated but never fully realized. I also argue that group analysis has got stuck in conceiving the group as object. I turn it around, to the group as subject, to the we and the group self. Through the individuals' active involvement in creating the group self, the full range of their emotions, attachment systems and mentalizing capacities are activated ("the group as a training ground for mentalization").

With these resources as a new starting point, I return to the clinical group and its need to evolve through different stages until it masters a group analytic discourse. I illustrate the text with 93 clinical vignettes. I place great emphasis on the understanding and handling of the self's needs for both recognition and otherness and a capacity for dealing with self-object failures. Through these processes, prosocial forces are activated in the individual and in the group, which are care, love and empathy, recognition of separation anxiety and release of capacity for pleasure and ability to play. I draw here on modern emotion theory (Panksepp & Biven, 2012; Karterud, 2017) and the individual's inherent desire to live in harmony with "his flock", or "in the company of others in just institutions" as Ricoeur puts it. These forces, directed by increased individual and collective self-reflective abilities, enable the group to deal with destructive forces such as hatred, the urge to destroy, vindictiveness, self-sufficiency, arrogance, excessive jealousy, envy, etc. An essential prerequisite is the therapist's theoretical understanding of these processes, which enables him/her to interpret what is going on in a meaningful way and thus build a group analytic culture. Mentalization is a key concept in this process and the group analyst must be familiar with how different levels of mentalization manifest themselves here and now. If the level of mentalization is generally low, the group analyst should consider structural measures such as being more educational, taking a firmer lead or allow turn-taking, as in MBT-G. "The art of group analytic psychotherapy" implies that the therapist is attuned to the needs of the group self. Therapists must actively relate to how much frustration the group tolerates and reconcile their interventions accordingly. In this way, group analytical psychotherapy can be a flexible approach that encompasses both classic group analysis and group psychotherapy with more serious personality problems (Karterud, 2018).

References

Agazarian, Y. M. (1994). The phases of group development and the systems-centered group. In V. L. Schermer & M. Pines (Eds), *Ring of Fire. Primitive Affects and Object Relations in Group Psychotherapy*. London: Routledge.

American Psychiatric Association. (2013). *Diagnostic and statistical manual of mental disorders: DSM-5*. Arlington: American Psychiatric Association.

Arensberg, F. (1998). A consideration of Kohut's views on group psychotherapy. In I. H. Harwood & M. Pines (Eds), *Self Experiences in Group*. London: Jessica Kingsley Publishers.

Atwood, G. & Stolorow, R. D. (1984). *Structures of Subjectivity: Explorations in Psychoanalytic Phenomenology*. Hillsdale: The Analytic Press.

Austin, J. (1962). *How to do things with words*. Oxford: Oxford University Press.

Bacal, H. A. (1998). Notes on Optimal Responsiveness in the Group Process. In I. H. Harwood & M. Pines (Eds), *Self Experiences in Group*. London: Jessica Kingsley Publishers.

Bakali, J. V., Wilberg, T., Hagtvedt, K., & Lorentzen, S. (2010). Sources accounting for alliance and cohesion at three stages in group psychotherapy: Variance and component analyses. *Group Dynamics: Theory, Research, and Practice*, 14 (4): 368–383.

Bales, R. F. & Cohen, S.P. (1979). *Symlog: A System of Multiple Observation of Groups*. New York: The Free Press.

Baron, C. (1987). *Asylum to Anarchy*. London: Free Association Books.

Barwick, N. & Weegmann, M. (2018). *Group therapy. A group-analytic approach*. London: Routledge.

Bateman, A. & Fonagy, P. (1999). Effectiveness of partial hospitalization in the treatment of borderline personality disorder: a randomized controlled trial. *American Journal of Psychiatry*, 156 (10): 1563–1569.

Bateman, A. & Fonagy, P. (2001). Treatment of borderline personality disorder with psychoanalytically oriented partial hospitalization: an 18-month follow-up. *American Journal of Psychiatry*, 158 (1): 36–42.

Bateman, A., Campbell, C., & Fonagy, P. (2021). Rupture and repair in mentalization-based group psychotherapy. *International Journal of Group Psychotherapy*, 71: 371–392.

Battegay, R. (1976). The Concept of Narcissistic Group-Self. *Group Analysis*, 9: 217–220.

Behr, H. & Hearst, L. (2005). *Group-analytic psychotherapy. A meeting of minds.* London: Whurr Publishers.

Bennis, W. G. & Shepard, H. A. (1956). A theory of group development. *Human Relations*, 9: 415–437.

Bion, W. R. (1961). *Experiences in Groups.* London: Tavistock Publications.

Blackmore, C., Tantam, D., Parry, G., & Chambers, E. (2012). Report on a Systematic Review of the Efficacy and Clinical Effectiveness of Group Analysis and Analytic/ Dynamic Group Psychotherapy, *Group Analysis*, 45 (1): 46–69.

Bloom, H. (1994). *The Western Canon.* New York: Harcourt Brace & Company.

Bogdan, R. (2013). *Mindvaults: The sociocultural grounds for pretending and imagining.* Cambridge: MIT Press.

Boss, M. (1963). *Psychoanalysis and Daseinsanalysis.* New York: Basic Books.

Bowlby, J. (1988). *A secure base. Clinical applications of attachment theory.* London: Tavistock/Routledge.

Brown, D. G. (1994). Self development through subjective interaction. A fresh look at "ego training in action". In D. G. Brown & L. Zinkin (Eds), *The psyche and the social world.* London: Routledge.

Brown, D. G. & Zinkin, L. (1994). *The psyche and the social world.* London: Routledge.

Braaten, L. J. (1991). Group cohesion: A new multi-dimensional model. *Group*, 15: 39–55.

Carruthers, P. (2015). *The centered mind. What the science of working memory shows us about the nature of human thoughts.* Oxford: Oxford University Press.

Christensen, T. B. et al. (2020). Level of personality functioning as a predictor of psychosocial functioning – concurrent validity of criterion A. *Personality Disorders*, 11 (2): 79–90.

Cividini-Stranic, E. (1986). The Group Dream in Group Psychotherapy. *Group Analysis*, 19: 147–152.

Cohn, H.W. (1993). Matrix and Intersubjectivity: Phenomenological Aspects of Group Analysis. *Group Analysis*, 26: 481–486.

Cohn, H. W. (1996). The Philosophy of S. H. Foulkes: Existential-phenomenological aspects of Group analysis. *Group Analysis*, 29: 287–302.

Cohn, H. W. (1997). *Existential Thought and Therapeutic Practice.* London: Sage Publications.

Coop, G., Bullaughey, K., Lucaa, E., & Przeworski, M. (2008). The timing of selection at the human FOXP2 gene. *Molecular biology and evolution*, 25 (7): 1257–1259.

Dalal, F. (1998). *Taking the group seriously. Towards a Post-Foulkesian group analytic theory.* London: Jessica Kingsley Publishers.

Damasio, A. (2000). *The feeling of what happens. Body and emotions in the making of consciousness.* London: Vintage, Random House.

Esposito, G., Formentin, S., Passeggia, R., Marogna, C., & Karterud, S. (2021). Pseudomentalization as a challenge for therapists of group psychotherapy with drug addicted patients. *Frontiers in Psychology*, 12: 684723.

Finlayson, C. (2009). *The humans who went extinct. Why Neanderthals died out and we survived.* Oxford: Oxford University Press.

Folmo, E. J., Karterud, S. W., Bremer, K., Walther, K., Kvarstein, E., & Pedersen, G. (2017). The design of the MBT-G adherence and quality scale. *Scandinavian Journal of Psychology*, 58: 341–349.

Fonagy, P., Gergely, G., Jurist, E. L., & Target, M. (2002). *Affect Regulation, Mentalization, and the Development of the Self.* New York: Other Press.

Fonagy, P., Target, M., & Gergely, G. (2000). Attachment and borderline personality disorder. A theory and some evidence. *Psychiatric Clinics of North America*, 23: 103–122.

Forsyth, D. R. (1990). *Group Dynamics.* Pacific Grove: Brooks/Cole Publishing Company.

Foss, T. (1994). From Phobic Inhibitions to Dreams. *Group Analysis*, 27: 305–318.

Fosshage, J. L. (1988). Dream interpretation revisited. In A. Goldberg (Ed.), *Frontiers in Self Psychology. Progress in Self Psychology, Vol. 3.* Hillsdale: The Analytic Press.

Fosshage, J. L. (1997). The Organizing Function of Dream Mentation. *Contemporary Psychoanalysis*, 33: 429–458.

Foulkes, E. (1990). S. H. Foulkes: a brief memoir. In E. Foulkes (Ed.), *Selected papers of S. H. Foulkes. Psychoanalysis and Group Analysis.* London: Karnac Books.

Foulkes, S. H. & Lewis, E. (1944). Group analysis: studies in the treatment of groups on psycho-analytical lines. *British Journal of Medical Psychology*, 20: 175–184.

Foulkes, S. H. (1946a). Group analysis in a military neurosis centre. *Lancet*: 303–313.

Foulkes, S. H. (1946b). On group analysis. *International Journal of Psycho-Analysis*, 27: 46–51.

Foulkes, S. H. (1946c). Principles and practice of group therapy. *Bulletin of the Menninger Clinic*, 10: 85–89.

Foulkes, S. H. (1948). *Introduction to Group-Analytic Psychotherapy.* London: Wm. Heinemann Medical Books.

Foulkes, S. H. (1968). Some autobiographical notes. *Group Analysis*, 202–205.

Foulkes, S. H. (1973). The group as matrix of the individual's mental life. In L. R. Wolberg & E. K. Schwartz (Eds), *Group Therapy 1973.* New York: Intercontinental Medical Book Corporation.

Foulkes, S. H. & Anthony, E. J. (1957). *Group Psychotherapy: The Psychoanalytic Approach.* Harmondsworth: Penguin Books.

Freud, S. (1900). *The Interpretation of Dreams. The Standard Edition, Vol. 4–5.* London: The Hogarth Press.

Freud, S. (1921). *Group psychology and the analysis of the ego. The Standard Edition, vol 18.* London: The Hogarth Press.

Fukuyama, F. (1992). *The end of history and the last man.* New York: Free Press.

Fukuyama, F. (2012). *The origins of political order: From prehuman times to the French revolution.* London: Profile Books.

Gadamer, H. G. (1960/1989). *Truth and Method.* London: Sheed & Ward.

Gans, J. S. (1989). Hostility in Group Psychotherapy. *International Journal of Group Psychotherapy*, 39: 499–516.

Gibbard, G. S., Hartman, J. J., & Mann, R. D. (1974). Group Process and Development. In G. S. Gibbard, J. J. Hartman, & R. D. Mann (Eds), *Analysis of Groups.* London: Jossey-Bass Ltd.

Greenson, R. R. (1967). *The Technique and Practice of Psychoanalysis.* New York: International Universities Press.

Gustavson, J. P. & Cooper, L. (1979). Unconscious planning in small groups. *Human Relations*, 32: 689–703.

Habermas, J. (1968/1971). *Knowledge and Human Interests*. Boston: Beacon Press.

Harwood, I. H. (1986). The need for optimal, available selfobject caretakers: Moving toward extended selfobject experiences. *Group Analysis*, 19: 291–302.

Harwood, I. H. (1992). Group Psychotherapy and Disorders of the Self. *Group Analysis*, 25: 19–26.

Harwood, I. H. (1998a). Can Group Analysis/Psychotherapy Provide a Wide Angle Lens for Self Psychology? In I. H. Harwood & M. Pines (Eds), *Self Experiences in Group*. London: Jessica Kingsley Publishers.

Harwood, I. H. (1998b). Advances in Group Psychotherapy and Self Psychology. An Intersubjective Approach. In I. H. Harwood & M. Pines (Eds), *Self Experiences in Group*. London: Jessica Kingsley Publishers.

Hegel, G. W. F. (1807/2019). *The phenomenology of the spirit*. Cambridge: Cambridge University Press.

Heidegger, M. (1927/1962). *Being and Time*. New York: Harper & Row.

Hill, W. F. & Gruner, L. (1973). A study of development in open and closed groups. *Small Group Behavior*, 4: 355–381.

Honneth, A. (2012). *The I in We. Studies in the theory of recognition*. Malden, MA: Polity Press.

Honneth, A. (2021). *Recognition. A chapter in the history of European ideas*. Cambridge: Cambridge University Press.

Hopper, E. (1972). Report and Comments on "Basic Principles, Changes and Trends". *Group Analysis*, 5, 91–94.

Hopper, E. (1998). Introduction. In M. Pines (Ed.), *Circular Reflections*. London: Jessica Kingsley Publishers.

Hopper, E. (2003). *The social unconscious: Selected papers*. London: Jessica Kingsley.

Hopper, W. & Weinberg, H. (2011). *The social unconscious in persons, groups, and societies: Volume 1: Mainly theory*. London: Karnac Books.

Hopper, W. & Weinberg, H. (2016). *The social unconscious in persons, groups, and societies: Volume 2: Mainly foundation matrices*. London: Karnac Books.

Hopper, E. & Weinberg, H. (2017). *The social unconscious in persons, groups, and societies. Volume 3: The foundation matrix extended and re-configured*. London: Karnac Books.

Hughes, K., Bellis, M. A., Hardcastle, K. A., Sethi, D., Butchart, A., Mikton, C., Jones, L., & Dunne, M. P. (2017). The effect of multiple adverse childhood experiences on health: a systematic review and meta-analysis, *Lancet Public Health*, 2 (8): 356–366.

Indrehaug, T. & Karterud, S. (2015) Authority and not knowing stance in mentalization-based group therapy. *Group Analysis*, 48 (2): 150–163.

Issroff, J. & von Adelsberg, E. S. (1997). Dreams in an Analytic Cotherapy Group. *Group Analysis*, 30: 187–202.

Johansen, M., Karterud, S., Pedersen, G., Gude, T., & Falkum, E. (2004). An investigation of the prototype validity of the borderline DSM-IV criteria. *Acta Psychiatrica Scandinavica*, 109: 289–298.

Kalleklev, J. & Karterud, S. (2018). A comparative study of a mentalization-based versus a psychodynamic group therapy session. *Group Analysis*, 51 (1): 44–60.

Karterud, S. (1988a). The valence theory of Bion and the significance of (DSM-III) diagnosis for inpatient group behavior. *Acta Psychiatrica Scandinavica*, 78: 462–470.

Karterud, S. (1988b). Group focal conflict analysis: A reliability study of a hermeneutic method. *Group analysis*, 21: 325–338.

Karterud, S. (1988c). The influence of task definition, leadership, and therapeutic style on inpatient group cultures. *International Journal of Therapeutic Communities*, 9: 231–247.

Karterud, S. (1989a). *Group processes in therapeutic communities*. Oslo: University of Oslo.

Karterud, S. (1989b). A study of Bion's basic assumption groups. *Human Relations*, 42: 315–335.

Karterud, S. (1989c). A comparative study of six different inpatient groups with respect to their basic assumption functioning. *International Journal of Group Psychotherapy*, 49: 355–376.

Karterud, S. (1989d). Bion or Kohut: Two paradigms of group dynamics. In B. E. Roth, W. N. Stone, & H. D. Kibel (Eds), *The difficult patient in group: Group psychotherapy with borderline and narcissistic disorders*. New York, International Universities Press.

Karterud, S. (1992a). Group dreams revisited. Group analysis, 25: 207–221.

Karterud, S. (1992b). Reflections on group analytic research. *Group analysis*, 25: 353–364.

Karterud, S. (1998). The group self, empathy, intersubjectivity and hermeneutics. A group analytic perspective. In I. Harwood & M. Pines (Eds), *Self Experiences in Group. Intersubjective and Self Psychological Pathways to Human Understanding*. London: Jessica Kingsley Publishers.

Karterud, S. (2000). On the scientific foundation of group analysis. *Group analysis*, 33 (4): 514–518.

Karterud, S. (2010). On narcissism, evolution, and group dynamics. *Group Analysis*, 43 (3): 1–10.

Karterud, S. (2011). Constructing and Mentalizing the Matrix. *Group Analysis*, 44 (4): 1–17.

Karterud, S. (2015a) On structure and leadership in MBT-G and group analysis. *Group Analysis*, 48 (2): 137–149.

Karterud, S. (2015b). *Mentalization-Based Group Therapy (MBT-G). A theoretical, clinical and research manual*. London: Oxford University Press.

Karterud, S. (2017). *Personlighet*. Oslo: Gyldendal Akademisk.

Karterud, S. (2018). A high-quality mentalization-based group therapy session. *Group Analysis*, 51 (1): 18–43.

Karterud, S. (2022). *Personlighetsfokusert terapi*. Oslo: Gyldendal.

Karterud, S. (2023). *Gruppeanalyse og psykodynamisk gruppepsykoterapi*. Oslo: Pax forlag.

Karterud, S. & Bateman, A. (2010). *Manual for mentaliseringsbasert terapi (MBT) og MBT vurderingsskala. Versjon individualterapi*. Oslo: Gyldendal Akademisk.

Karterud, S. & Bateman, A. (2011). *Manual for mentaliseringsbasert psykoedukativ gruppeterapi*. Oslo: Gyldendal Akademisk.

Karterud, S., Folmo, E., & Kongerslev, M. T. (2019). Personality and the group matrix. *Group Analysis*. doi:10.1177/0533316418824210.

Karterud, S., Folmo, E., & Kongerslev, M. (2020). *Mentaliseringsbasert terapi (MBT)*. Oslo: Gyldendal Akademisk.

Karterud, S. & Foss, T. (1989). The group emotionality rating system. A modification of Thelen's method of assessing emotionality in groups. *Small group behavior*, 20: 131–150.

Karterud, S. & Kongerslev, M. T. (2019). A Temperament, Attachment and Mentalization-based (TAM) theory of personality and its disorders. *Frontiers in Psychology*, 10: 518.

Karterud, S. & Kongerslev, M. T. (2021). Psychotherapy of personality disorders needs an integrative theory of personality. *Journal of Psychotherapy Integration*, 31 (1): 34–53.

Karterud, S., Pedersen, G., Johansen, M., Wilberg, T., Davis, K., & Panksepp, J. (2016). Primary emotional traits in patients with personality disorders. *Personality and Mental Health*, 1–13. doi:10.1002/pmh.1345.

Karterud, S. & Stone W. N. (2003). The group self: A neglected aspect of group psychotherapy. *Group Analysis*, 36 (1): 7–22.

Karterud, S., Wilberg, T., & Urnes, Ø. (2010/2017). *Personlighetspsykiatri*. Oslo: Gyldendal akademisk.

Kennard, D., Roberts, J., & Winter, D.A. (1990). What do Group Analysts Say in Their Groups? *Group Analysis*, 23: 173–183.

Kibel, H. D. (1981). A conceptual model for short-term inpatient group psychotherapy. *American Journal of Psychiatry*, 138: 74–80.

Kohut, H. (1959). Introspection, Empathy and Psychoanalysis. An Examination of the Relationship Between Mode of Observation and Theory. *Journal of the American Psychoanalytic Association*, 14: 459–483.

Kohut, H. (1971). *The Analysis of the Self*. New York: International Universities Press.

Kohut, H. (1976). Creativeness, Charisma, Group Psychology. In J. E. Gedo & G. H. Pollock (Eds), *Freud: The Fusion of Science and Humanism*. New York: International Universities Press.

Kohut, H. (1977). *The Restoration of the Self*. New York: International Universities Press.

Kohut, H. (1984). *How Does Analysis Cure?*Chicago: The University of Chicago Press.

Kohut, H. (1985). *Self Psychology and the Humanities*. New York: W.W. Norton & Company.

Kvarstein, E., Pedersen, G., Urnes, Ø., Hummelen, B., Wilberg, T., & Karterud, S., (2015) Changing from a traditional psychodynamic treatment program to mentalization-based treatment for patients with borderline personality disorder. Does it make a difference? *Psychology and Psychotherapy: Theory, Research and Practice*, 88 (1): 71–86.

Lacoursiere, R. B. (1980). *The life cycle of groups*. New York: Human Sciences Press.

Lewin, K., Lippit, R., & White, R. (1939). Patterns of aggressive behavior in experimentally created "social climates". *Journal of Social Psychology*, 10: 271–299.

Lewis, P. (1987). Laughter and Humour. Does it Have a Place in Group analysis? *Group Analysis*, 20: 367–378.

Lichtenberg, J. D. & Kaplan, S. (1983). *Reflections on Self Psychology*. Hillsdale: The Analytic Press.

Lichtenberg, J. D., Lachmann, F. M., & Fosshage, J. L. (1992). *Self and Motivational Systems.* Hillsdale: The Analytic Press.

Livingston, M. S. (2005). Self psychology, dreams and group psychotherapy. Working in the playspace. In C. Neri, M. Pines, & R. Friedman (Eds), *Dreams in group psychotherapy. Theory and technique.* London: Jessica Kingsley Publishers.

Lorentzen, S. (2014). *Group analytic psychotherapy.* London: Routledge.

Lorentzen, S., Ruud, T., Fjeldstad, A., & Høglend, P. (2014). Personality disorder moderates outcome in short- and long-term group analytic psychotherapy: A randomized clinical trial. *British Journal of Clinical Psychology*, 54 (2): 129–146.

Lynn, D. J. & Vaillant, G. E. (1998). Anonymity, Neutrality, and Confidentiality in the Actual Methods of Sigmund Freud: A Review of 43 Cases, 1907–1939. *American Journal of Psychiatry*, 155: 163–171.

Maar, V. (1989). Attempts at Grasping the Self during the Termination Phase of Group-analytic Psychotherapy. *Group Analysis*, 22: 99–104.

MacIntyre, A. (1981). *After virtue: a study in moral theory.* New York: Gerald Duckworth & Co.

MacKenzie, K. R. (1990). *Introduction to Time-Limited Group Psychotherapy.* Washington, DC: American Psychiatric Press.

Mahler, M.S., Pine, F., & Bergman, A. (1975). *The Psychological Birth of the Human Infant.* London: Hutchinson & Co.

Main, T. (1946). The hospital as a therapeutic institution. *Bulletin of the Menninger Clinic*, 10: 66–90.

Main, T. (1977). The concept of the therapeutic community. Variations and vicissitudes. *Group Analysis*, 10: 2–16.

Malan, D. R., Balfour, F. H. G., Hood, V. G., & Shooter, A. M. N. (1976). Group psychotherapy: a long-term follow-up study. *Archives of General Psychiatry*, 33: 1303–1314.

Maratos, J. (1986). Bowlby and Kohut: where science and humanism meet. *Group Analysis*, 19: 303–309.

Maratos, J. (1996). The Emergence of Self Through the Group. *Group Analysis*, 29: 161–168.

Marrone, M. (1994). Attachment theory and group analysis. In D. G. Brown & L. Zinkin (Eds), *The psyche and the social world.* London: Routledge.

McCullough, L., Kuhn, N., Andrews, S., Kaplan, A., Wolf, J., & Hurley, C. (2008). *Treating affect phobia.* New York: The Guilford Press.

Montag, C., Hahn, E., Reuter, M., Spinath, F. M., Davis, K., & Panksepp, J. (2016). The role of nature and nurture for individual differences in primary emotional systems: Evidence from a twin study. *PlosOne.* doi:10.1371/journal-pone.0151405.

Mullan, H. (1987). The Ethical Foundations of Group Psychotherapy. *International Journal of Group Psychotherapy*, 37: 403–416.

Mullan, H. (1991). Inherent Moral Practice in Group Psychotherapy. *International Journal of Group Psychotherapy*, 41: 185–197.

Neri, C., Pines, M., & Friedman, R. (2005). *Dreams in group psychotherapy. Theory and technique.* London: Jessica Kingsley Publishers.

Nitsun, M. (1996). *The anti-group. Destructive forces in the group and their creative potential.* London: Routledge.

Northoff, G. & Panksepp, J. (2008). The trans-species concept of the self and the subcortical-cortical midline system. *Trends in Cognitive Sciences*, 12: 259–264.

Ornstein, P. H. (1991). Why self psychology is not an object relations theory: Clinical and theoretical considerations. In A. Goldberg (Ed.), *The evolution of self psychology. Progress in self psychology, vol. 7.* Hillsdale: The Analytic Press.

Panksepp, J. (1998). *Affective neuroscience: The foundations of humans and animal emotions.* Oxford: Oxford University Press.

Panksepp, J. & Biven, L. (2012). *The archeology of mind: Neuroevolutionary origins of human emotions.* New York: W.W. Norton & Company.

Paparo, F. (1981). Self Psychology and Group Analysis. *Group Analysis,* 14: 117–121.

Paparo, F. (1984). Self Psychology and the Group Process. *Group Analysis,* 17: 108–117.

Paparo, F. & Nebbioso, G. (1998). How does group psychotherapy cure? A reconceptualization of the group process: from self psychology to the intersubjective perspective. In I. H. Harwood & M. Pines (Eds), *Self Experiences in Group.* London: Jessica Kingsley Publishers.

Pawlik, J. & Pierszgalska, E. (1990). The Use of Dreams in a Small Analytic Group. *Group Analysis,* 23: 163–171.

Pedersen, G., Wilberg, T., Hummelen, B., & Kvarstein, E. (2022): The Norwegian network for personality disorders – development, contributions and challenges through 30 years, *Nordic Journal of Psychiatry.* doi:10.1080/08039488.2022.2147995.

Pines, M. (1972). Basic principles, changes and trends. *Group Analysis,* 5: 85–91.

Pines, M. (1978). Psycho-analysis and Group Analysis. *Group Analysis,* 11: 8–20.

Pines, M. (1979). Group psychotherapy: Frame of reference for training. *Group Analysis,* 12: 210–219.

Pines, M. (1990). Group Analytic Psychotherapy and the Borderline Patient. In B. E. Roth, W. N. Stone, & H. D. Kibel (Eds), *The Difficult Patient in Group.* Madison: International Universities Press.

Pines, M. (1990). Group Analysis and the corrective emotional experience: Is it relevant? *Psychoanalytic Inquiry,* 10: 389–408.

Pines, M. (1991). The matrix of group analysis: An historical perspective. *Group Analysis,* 24: 99–109.

Pines, M. (1996a). Dialogue and Selfhood: Discovering Connections. *Group Analysis,* 29: 327–341.

Pines, M. (1996b). The Self as a Group: The Group as a Self. *Group Analysis,* 29: 183–190.

Pines, M. (1998). *Circular Reflections. Selected Papers on Group Analysis and Psychoanalysis.* London: Jessica Kingsley Publishers.

Pines, M. & Hearst, L. (1993). *Group Analysis. I H. I. Kaplan & B. I. Sadock (Eds) Comprehensive Group Psychotherapy.* Baltimore: Williams & Wilkins.

Piper, W. E., McCallum, M., & Azim, H. F. A. (1992). *Adaptation to Loss Through Short-Term Group Psychotherapy.* New York: The Guilford Press.

Posner, M. I. & Rothbart, M. K. (2000). Developing mechanisms of self-regulation. *Development and Psychopathology,* 12: 427–441.

Rawls, J. (1971). *A Theory of Justice.* Cambridge: Harvard University Press.

Ricoeur, P. (1981a). *Hermeneutics and the human sciences.* Cambridge: Cambridge University Press.

Ricoeur, P. (1981b). What is a text? Explanation and understanding. In P. Ricoeur, *Hermeneutics & the Human Sciences.* Cambridge: Cambridge University Press.

Ricoeur, P. (1981c). The model of the text: meaningful action considered as a text. In P. Ricoeur, *Hermeneutics & the Human Sciences*. Cambridge: Cambridge University Press.

Ricoeur, P. (1992). *Oneself as Another*. Chicago: The University of Chicago Press.

Rutan, J. S. & Rice, C. S. (2005). Dreams in psychodynamic group psychotherapy. In C. Neri, M. Pines, & R. Friedman (Eds), *Dreams in group psychotherapy. Theory and technique*. London: Jessica Kingsley Publishers.

Rutan, S. J., Stone, W. N., & Shay, J. J. (2014). *Psychodynamic Group Psychotherapy; 5th edition*. New York: Guilford Press.

Safran, J. D., Muran, J. C., Wallner Samstag, L., & Stevens, C. (2001). Repairing therapeutic alliance ruptures. *Psychotherapy*, 38: 406–412.

Sandler, J., Dare, C., & Holder, A. (1992). *The Patient and the Analyst*. London: Karnac Books.

Schermer, V. L. & Klein, R. H. (1996). Termination in Group Psychotherapy from the Perspectives of Contemporary Object Relations Theory and Self Psychology. *International Journal of Group Psychotherapy*, 46: 99–115.

Schlapobersky, J. (2016). *From the couch to the circle: Group-analytic psychotherapy in practice*. London: Routledge.

Schultz-Venrath, U. & Felsberger, H. (2016). *Mentalisieren in Gruppen*. Berlin: Klett-Cotta Verlag.

Searle, J. (1969). *Speech acts: An essay in the philosophy of language*. Cambridge: Cambridge University Press.

Segalla, R. (2021). Self psychological approaches to ruptures and repairs in group psychotherapy. *International Journal of Group Psychotherapy*, 71: 253–274.

Slater, P. E. (1966). *Microcosm: Structural, Psychological and Religious Evolution in Groups*. New York: Wiley.

Solms, M. & Turnbull, O. (2002). *The brain and the inner world*. London: Karnac Books.

Stern, D. N. (1985). *The interpersonal world of the infant*. New York: Basic Books.

Stern, D. N. (2004). *The present moment in psychotherapy and everyday life*. New York: W.W. Norton & Company.

Stock, D. & Thelen, H. (1957). *Emotional dynamics and group culture*. Washington, DC: National Training Laboratory.

Stolorow, R. D. & Atwood, G. (1992). *Contexts of being*. Hillsdale: The Analytic Press.

Stolorow, R. D., Brandchaft, B., & Atwood, G. (1987). *Psychoanalytic treatment. An intersubjective approach*. Hillsdale: The Analytic Press.

Stone, W. N. (1992). A Self Psychological Perspective on Envy in Group Psychotherapy. *Group Analysis*, 25: 413–428.

Stone, W. N. (1996). Self Psychology and the Higher Mental Functioning Hypothesis: Complementary Theories. *Group Analysis*, 29: 169–181.

Stone, W. N. (2009a). *Contributions of self psychology to group psychotherapy*. London: Karnac Books.

Stone, W. N. (2009b). Group-as-a-whole: A self psychological perspective. In W. N. Stone, *Contributions of self psychology to group psychotherapy*. London: Karnac Books.

Stone, W. N. & Karterud, S. (2006). Dreams as portraits of self and group interaction. *International Journal of Group Psychotherapy*, 56 (1): 47–62.

Talia, A., Miller-Bottome, M., & Daniel, S. I. (2017). Assessing attachment in psychotherapy: Validation of the Patient Attachment Coding System (PACS). *Clinical Psychology and Psychotherapy*, 24 (1): 149–161.

Talia, A. et al. (2022). An exploratory study on how attachment classifications manifests in group psychotherapy. *Research in psychotherapy: Psychopathology, process, and outcome*. doi:10.4081/rippo.2022.653.

Taylor, C. (1989). *Sources of the Self. The Making of the Modern Identity*. Cambridge: Cambridge University Press.

Thygesen, B. (1992). "Diversity" as a Group-specific Therapeutic Factor. *Group Analysis*, 25: 75–86.

Tomasello, M. (2014). *A natural history of human thinking*. Cambridge: Harvard University Press.

Tomasello, M. (2019). *Becoming human: A theory of ontogeny*. Cambridge: Belknap Press.

Tronick, E. Z. & Weinberg, M. K. (1997). Depressed mothers and infants: Failure to form dyadic states of consciousness. In L. Murray & P. J. Cooper (Eds), *Postpartum depression and child development* (pp. 54–81). Guilford Press.

Tuckman, B. W. (1965). Developmental sequences in small groups. *Psychological Bulletin*,

Wampole, B. & Imel, Z. (2015). *The great psychotherapy debate. The evidence for what makes psychotherapy work*. London: Routledge.

Wardi, D. (1989). The Termination Phase in the Group Process. *Group Analysis*, 22: 87–98.

Whitaker, D. S. & Lieberman, M. (1964). *Psychotherapy through the group process*. Chicago: Atherton Press.

Yalom, I. D. & Leszcz, M. (2020). *The theory and practice of group psychotherapy*. New York: Basic Books.

Index

Note: Page numbers in bold refer to tables